The Last Word On Running

The Last Word On Running

Richard Karlgaard

Photography by David Madison

Caroline House Publishers, Inc.
Ottawa, Illinois & Thornwood, New York

Contents

7.95

Acknowledgements

For your help and concern, I say thank you—

— To you who endorsed my book:

Senator Alan Cranston
Joel Ferrell
Tom Jordan
Dr. Ronald Lawrence

Marty Liquori
Bill Rodgers
Dr. Steven Subotnick
Dr. Joan Ullyot

— To those who have done a superb job of working with me:

Murrell Boyd, who convinced my publisher to do it.
Jameson Campaigne, Jr., my publisher, who indeed did it.
Susan Fox, my female model.
Dave Madison, my photographer.

— And especially to my friends and teachers, who are totally absorbed into my thinking, writing, running and being:

Darrell (Henderson) Anderson, runner, friend, and maybe the funniest bwilo on God's planet.
Dr. Joe Cleary, who infected me with a love for running.
John Goepp, a Z boy.
Joe Henderson, who convinced me that running was my identity.
John L'Heureux and L. Scott Momaday, two Stanford profs who
ˑthought I could write.
Jim Lilliefors, who knows how it feels.
Bruce Perry, world class friend and retired Highland Acres sprinting champ.
Jeff Prater, another Z boy.
Jim Ward, who did nothing less than reshape my thinking when it badly needed it.

and *Bob Latta,* Z boy, best friend, and the type who would write a blank check if you needed a dime.

Dedication

This book is nothing if not for —
  — Dick and Patricia
  — Mr. Rasmus Karlgaard
  — and the lovely Mrs. Charles Hook

CHAPTER ONE

Don't Call It Jogging

Q **Why is everyone jogging these days?**

A Wait a minute. If this book is going to be a serious discussion of running, we must forever do away with that ugly, aggravating and jarring imposter word which calls to mind and rhymes with flogging.

That boring, dog-eared, and soggy synonym you always hear mentioned with gestalt therapy and frozen yogurt.

That bounceless, bogged down, and baggy idiom which Webster defines as trudge.

That dreadful word jogging.

Q **Haven't you just insulted the millions who jog?**

A Listen, we're all brethren of sorts — we all perambulate over the country roads and city streets wearing little more than shoes and short shorts. It's vital we hang together.

What's insulting to all of us is that name which too many have chosen to call our wonderful activity. Running is such a clean, elemental, and aesthetic sport — why call it jogging?

Perhaps troglodytes jog, but humans run. Calling our graceful sport jogging is like calling a sunset a sundump. Or the god Mercury The Big Jogger.

So, if we can't kick jogging out of department store ads and prime time television, we will at the very least, and unceremoniously, do so in this book.

1

In droves, pairs, or alone, millions discovered running in the late 1970s.

CHAPTER TWO

The History And Future Of Running

Q **Okay, why has running become so popular in the last few years?**

A Up until the middle 1960s the motivations to run seemed few and definable. Runners were either purists or competitors, or else mutants of the above. We fancied ourselves as future Glenn Cunninghams and Roger Bannisters, and even raced on occasion, but in the end we ran mostly for sheer enjoyment.

Together, our numbers were small. Running in the early 1960s was a downhill slide to social ostracism — a pastime then among fellow outcasts was drinking coke (we hadn't yet discovered the congruity of beer and running) and sharing tales of dog attacks, of being run off the road by hoods in '57 Chevies, or of some poor accountant in Kansas City being fired when the boss discovered the accountant trying to balance his training mileage during work hours.

Then in the mid-sixties a gangly Oklahoman who had finished last in the 1962 Boston Marathon began to change the country's attitude about running and fitness. He was Kenneth Cooper, an Air Force doctor assigned to study astronauts and the unusual stresses they would encounter during weightless orbit.

To help the astronauts cope, Cooper was further assigned to develop a fitness training program. A runner himself who had won an Oklahoma schoolboy mile championship in addition to that last place Boston finish, Cooper prescribed running for the astronauts.

When he tested them at the end of the training program, Cooper found the astronauts had all significantly lowered five of the 10 known risk factors for heart attacks — blood pressure, body fat, cholesterol, triglycerides and glucose.

Feeling that others might want to share in that discovery, in 1966 Cooper wrote an article describing his findings for *Family Circle* magazine.

Response to the article overwhelmed even Cooper, and so a year later he began writing a book on the same subject. It was called *Aerobics*, and when it was published in 1968, it had the immediate effect of getting 10 million people to run. The book has since sold eight million copies in 20 languages.

Q   **Why did *Aerobics* make such a big impact?**

A   As Hal Higdon writes in his book, *Fitness After Forty*, Cooper's book was not successful just because it told people that exercise would reduce coronary risk. Dr. Paul Dudley White and others had been saying that long before Cooper ever heard of aerobics.

As Higdon says: "Perhaps the single contribution Ken Cooper made in improving the fitness of millions throughout the world was that he was the man who uncovered an easily understood method of *quantifying* exercise."

Q   **In other words, Dr. Cooper took the guesswork out of exercise.**

A   Exactly. Cooper outlines four points in his book. First, he explains the principle of aerobic exercise and why it pertains to health and lowered coronary risk. Secondly, he invents a point system to quantify aerobic activity. Thirdly, he assigns point values to different exercises and their durations. And fourthly, Cooper tells you the minimum point total you must accumulate each week to have good health and cardiovascular protection.

Q   **What is the principle of aerobic exercise?**

A   The principle of aerobic exercise is founded in the knowledge that organisms function and reproduce best in the presence of oxygen. Push an increase of oxygen through the body, as you do in running, and the body will flourish.

Q   **What effect does this have on health and longevity?**

A   As for your health, it is standard medical opinion that sustained aerobic exercise, like running, does the following:

     ○ *Improves Cardiovascular Health*, and hence protection from the two big killers, heart attack and stroke. Critics may disagree with the protection part, but how does one argue against the fact that aerobic exercise lowers, as mentioned before, five of the 10 cardiovascular risk factors?

     ○ *Improves Endurance* by greatly increasing your utilization of oxygen. This measurement is called your oxygen uptake, and is as good as any definition of fitness. A world class distance runner has *twice* the oxygen uptake of the average scrabble player.

     ○ *Burns Calories*, and thus carves excess pounds if you otherwise keep your diet constant. Running is the most efficient calorie-burning exercise at 100 a mile, regardless of pace.

     ○ *Reduces Tension*, which is now the major reason Americans run, according to a recent poll of *Runner's World* readers.

As well, many psychotherapists are now using aerobic exercise to treat mild anxiety and depression.

And as for longevity, no study has yet proved that aerobic exercise stretches a lifetime. But since aerobic exercise is a still young phenomenon, I suspect the jury will be out on the matter for a few more years. I would also suspect, though, that a 70-year-old man with clean lungs, a strong heart, and low cholesterol and body fat is less likely to drop dead of a fatal heart attack than his overweight and inactive twin brother.

Q   **How does Kenneth Cooper quantify aerobic exercise?**

A   What Cooper sought to measure was the increase of oxygen that circulates through the body during aerobic exercise. Cooper found that oxygen consumption, for practical purposes, is synonymous with pulse rate — a normal pulse rate means normal oxygen consumption; an elevated pulse rate means an increase in oxygen consumption. Since the pulse rate is easy to measure, but the oxygen intake isn't, Cooper bases his aerobic exercise points on one, the rate of your pulse, and two, the length of time the pulse is raised above normal.

Roughly, Cooper bases his point system on the total number of additional heartbeats produced by exercise.

Thus Cooper gives you one aerobic point approximately each time exercise makes your heart tick 80-100 additional beats. That is, if your resting pulse is 70, but exercise raises it to 110-120, you will score one aerobic point every two minutes.

Q   **How many points do we need to accumulate for good health and cardiovascular protection?**

A   Dr. Cooper thinks 30 points a week will give any person a reasonably good level of cardiovascular health and protection.

Q   **How much running per week is this?**

A   It really isn't much. Running, at almost any pace, scores four to six aerobic points a mile. A five-minute mile will elevate your pulse 80-100 beats each minute, while a leisurely 10-minute mile will raise your pulse only 40-50 each minute.

One way to score the 30 points is to run two miles a day, three days a week. This is what Dr. Cooper himself does, and recommends for others.

Q   **How does running compare with other aerobic exercise?**

A   Without question, running is the most efficient exercise. Cooper says you can score more aerobic points in less time by running, than by doing any other activity.

As Hal Higdon quotes Cooper in *Fitness After Forty*: "You definitely get more benefit — and quicker — from running than from any other form of exercise. Look at the examples: five points in eight minutes! You get more benefit from this than you do from seven hours of golf!"

But rather than stealing any more of the doctor's well-deserved thunder, I suggest you buy a copy of *Aerobics*, if you haven't done so already.

Q   **How many people began running after *Aerobics* was published?**

A   The President's Council on Fitness reported 10 million people started running in the late 1960s, after *Aerobics* was published.

Q   **What happened to all of these runners? I don't recall seeing very many people running in 1970.**

A   That's because there weren't many runners in 1970 — more than half of the 10 million who started in 1968 quit shortly afterward. When Dr. Cooper told us how good running was *for* us, we all did it. But as is almost axiomatic with anything like that, be it the daily drinking of prune juice or going to bed early, we Americans quickly tire of doing anything simply because it might be good for us. (And that's not meant as a blanket criticism — as a result, America is relatively free of much oppressive thinking, from puritanism to prohibition.)

What Kenneth Cooper forgot to tell us, either because he didn't himself believe it, or else didn't know how to express it, was that running is fun. Quiet exhilaration. A chance to be alone with your body and mind. Adult playtime, as Dr. Sheehan puts it.

You see, running is not quick fun, as sliding down the Big Slide at an amusement park is quick fun. You must cultivate a taste for running, as you must also cultivate a taste for the ballet or mountain stream fishing.

As we will learn in later chapters, you can't cultivate a taste for running by going only two miles a day, as Cooper recommends. Running for the first 20-30 minutes is, for anyone, a painful bore, matched only by the boredom of television game shows. But at 20-30 minutes, your running is magically transformed. The painful trudge becomes a merry and lightfooted romp. The boring miles become one incredible sensory journey.

Stick to Cooper's minimal plan, and you'll never find running much joy and fun.

Q   **Are Cooper and his ideas obsolete?**

A   Quite the contrary. The ideas of Dr. Cooper are as medically sound today as they were 10 years ago. His Institute of Aerobics Research in Dallas remains the country's best equipped and staffed center for research physiology and the study of human performance. And Cooper is still the man most directly or indirectly responsible for the 23 million runners today. It's just that most readers of *Aerobics* in 1968 needed more than the clinical advice Cooper gave them.

Q **Then what has caused the renaissance of running today?**

A Running's revival, and now boom, is the result of a curious, but volatile mixture of grass roots zeal, media influence, and sociological phenomena.

Its resurgence in the early 1970s was grounded in the belief that more than just a healthful activity, running could also be fun, as well as accessible for nearly everyone who wanted to do it. This was the message preached by the four or five million runners who were left in 1970 after the other Cooper converts had quit.

This ground-swell movement was in turn roused, inspired and encouraged to multiply by its own collection of gurus and heroes.

One of the gurus (and I'm not sure who first tagged him as such, but it fits) is Joe Henderson, the editor of *Runner's World* magazine from 1970 to 1977, and a man far ahead of his time. Before it was proved in a laboratory, Henderson argued that the slow running of long distances was the quickest road to fitness. And before it was used as treatment by psychiatrists and psychotherapists, Henderson told us that a pleasant hour of running would surely chase away anxiety and the blues.

Another guru, or more precisely, a cardiologist turned philosopher, is George Sheehan, the medical editor of *Runner's World* and author of the best-seller, *Running and Being*. A zesty and uninhibited man who wears a paper 'clip to pin his tie, and who once claimed he drank six beers during the Boston Marathon, Sheehan has not only given us answers to our special medical problems, but also, as runners, to our very identity. This he did in *Dr. Sheehan On Running*:

> "We distance runners are meditative men. If we have a religious tradition, it is one of non-conformity and withdrawal, the hermit, the anchorite. At best, we hope for a secluded meadow where we won't be disturbed."

Running invades the mass media and department stores.

The Runner's World *influence:*
Left, *publisher Bob Anderson; Right, long-time editor Joe Henderson*

We also had within our sport, heroes. We had élan and charisma with Marty Liquori, spirit and sass with the late Steve Prefontaine, and sentimentality with Jim Ryun.

But the man who became our biggest hero, and the one who came to symbolize running in the late 1960s, and now the 1970s is Frank Shorter. Here was a man who braided his hair, drank beer, and spent a good deal of his energy during 1969-71 evading the War in Vietnam. Here was a Yale graduate who said you shouldn't think too deeply about running. Here was a skinny waif who didn't look like a Liquori or Ryun, but who ran twice the mileage they did, and then became the best in the world.

In 1972, Roone Arledge of ABC Sports decided to take an expensive gamble and devote almost two hours of Olympic television coverage to the marathon. It was a gamble because Frank Shorter was America's only hope — and a slim one at that — of winning the marathon. Arledge rightly figured that a race fought between Mamo Wolde of Ethiopia and Karl Lismont of Belgium would be no gold in the Nielsen's.

But Frank Shorter came through with a win, and the nation saw. Hey, this guy isn't a nut. He's a Yale graduate, and he's going to law school. He's a rational man. He says running is not only fun, but quite compatible with drinking beer and sleeping in late in the morning. You don't have to look like an athlete, or even give a damn about the National Football League to be good at running, was the message Shorter conveyed. The nation approved.

Another wind of media influence was *Sports Illustrated*. With a couple of runners on their editorial staff, the nation's premier sports and leisure magazine took an early interest in running. As well, *SI* knows talent when they see it, and so they hired running's most eloquent and brilliant writer, Kenny Moore, who as an almost equally brilliant runner, finished a surprising fourth behind Shorter in the 1972 Olympic marathon.

To the millions of *SI* readers, Moore described alluringly the joys and beauty of running. To an eager runner, a Moore article was exhortation to head for the mountains, the woods, the beaches, or any place where running could be enjoyed with splendor equal to Moore's writing.

Q **What about the different sociological phenomena?**

A My bias as a runner tends to downplay the notion that sociological changes have had much to do with, or as some say, even have precipitated a running boom. We runners like to think our sport is above the unending tides of popular taste and emotion, and that we created the boom ourselves from within — a real grass roots movement!

Yet, such is not the case. For one, many of us who began running in the late sixties would never have started, *Aerobics* notwithstanding, had the late sixties not been a period when you were free, in society's eye, to do your own thing. Running was only one of many social question marks that became acceptable, if not yet popular, in the late 1960s. It is difficult to imagine a similar response to *Aerobics* in 1958, when scantily clad runners were usually thought of as sexual perverts, or as evidence America would lose the space race.

About the same time, another grass roots movement which would have a profound effect upon running in the seventies, was itself building. This was women's liberation, and as it affected running, the acceptance of women as athletes.

Of the 10 million who began running after *Aerobics* was published, less than one million — less than 10 percent — were women. Of the nearly thousand people who ran the 1967 Boston Marathon, only *one* was a woman, Katherine Switzer, and she had to *sneak* into the race, since women were banned at Boston. During the race, Switzer got into a shoving match with Boston officials trying to remove her, and photographs of the confrontation made the wire services. Switzer thereafter became the Alamo around which the growing number of women runners rallied.

In the first half of the seventies, the number of women runners soared while, interestingly, the do-your-own-thing philosophy evolved into a much broader movement — the "me" generation. Now everyone, from overbooked executives to overworked mothers, was learning of the need to make time for one's self if one was to enjoy mental health in this frenzied and tension-filled decade.

And, as the devotees had been preaching all along, what better way to call time out from ringing telephones and crying babies than by slipping away for an hour's run on a country road? Escapism became the new feature attraction of running in the mid 1970s.

By 1975-76, the country again had 10 million runners, including two million women. But this group, aware of both the physical and mental benefits, and aware that running could be quite fun, was vastly more eager and devoted than the runners of 1968. As an indication, *Runner's World* magazine (then as *Distance Running News*) sold less than 5000 copies every two months in 1968. But in 1976, with the same sized market, *Runner's World* had grown to a monthly with a circulation of more than 100,000.

Q   **Still, 1976 was only the beginning of the real boom. What has caused the huge gain in runners during the last two years?**

A   Until 1976 the growth of running was mostly internal — runners persuading non-runners to join, someone picking up a stray copy of *Runner's World* or an issue of *Sports Illustrated* with a Kenny Moore article, or even rediscovering a copy of *Aerobics* that had been sitting idly on a bookshelf in the attic.

In 1976 two events pushed the number of runners to a level high enough for business to take notice, and hence change running from a cult sport to an advertising-hyped fad.

One event was the 1976 Olympics, in which Roone Arledge billed the marathon as the showcase event of track and field, already the showcase sport of the Olympics.

Again, Arledge's hunch paid off. In the marathon race, the country saw a dramatic confrontation among the two best-known runners in the world, Frank Shorter and Finland's Lasse Viren, and a darkhorse from East Germany, Waldemar Cierpinski, who eventually won the race. (Shorter finished second; Viren faded at the end to fifth.)

The other event of 1976 was the full blossoming of women's equality in the running world. Money from Title IX began to flow, and from it sprung women's track and cross country teams in high schools and universities all around the country. Nearly every road race was fully integrated by 1976, and even the stuffy United States Olympic Committee allowed coed Olympic Trials in track and field.

These two influences increased the number of runners from 10 million at the start of 1976 to 15 million by the end of the year.

Q   **And then running was discovered by business?**

A   Yes, to the extent that shoe companies and clothing manufacturers now found it profitable to expand their distribution and advertising from sporting goods stores and running magazines to department stores and the mass media.

The result has been an unprecedented exposure of running. Where once you found ads for running clothes only in *Runner's World*, you now see them daily in other magazines, newspapers, radio and television. And where once you found running shoes only in a few sporting good stores, you now can buy them in almost any sports and leisure shop, hardware store, department store (in both the shoe and sports section), discount center, and fashion boutique.

This, more than anything, has caused the number of runners to double in the last two years.

Q   **And so how many people are running today?**

A   According to the latest Gallup poll, taken in early 1978, 11 percent of Americans — 16 percent of men and seven percent of women — run at least one mile a day, two days a week.

In raw numbers, this means 23 million Americans think of themselves as runners.

However, if we applied a stricter minimum definition of running — say Kenneth Cooper's recommendation of two miles a day, three times a week — the number of those who call themselves runners would probably fall below 20 million.

Q   **What is the future of the running movement?**

A   Because the pinnacle of the running boom is mostly the result of advertising hype, the number of runners will peak, then fall when the money spent for advertising is no longer justified by business revenues.

At that time, when the fad crowd leaves as national exposure dwindles, the number of runners will probably recede to the pre-boom levels of 1975-76.

As yet, this hasn't happened, and probably won't for another year or two. But rest assured, the first indication that the boom is deflating will not be a drop in *Runner's World* subscriptions or people who finish marathons. Instead, it will be signaled by a drop in department store ads or reduced availability of Adidas in fashion boutiques.

And what could be better? With a loss of the disco and musk oil crowd, the streets will be a little less congested. We won't have to continue watching Macy's models destroy the act of running. We won't have to hopelessly explain the joys of running to our barber, who tried it briefly, but said it didn't do anything for him. We won't have to be called fashion moths just because we've always worn Nike shoes and Frank Shorter shorts.

Running isn't for everyone, or even for 23 million. The number of people who will truly enjoy, and thus truly benefit from running seems closer to 15-20 million, and even that could be high if *maximum* enjoyment is the prime consideration.

And for you who don't find running your thing, I say bravo and good luck to you! What's important is that you keep trying to find a healthful, calorie eating, and tension relieving activity that suits your tastes, and most of all, your idea of fun. After sampling tennis, running, swimming and racquetball, you may suddenly fall in love with backpacking. Great! Pursue the outer edges of backpacking, and wring every drop of enjoyment you can from it. It's your inalienable right, no, your *duty* to do so.

Or you might find the most gusto in mixing several sports — that's fine, too. Run for a couple of days, swim for a couple more, and then go cross country skiing on the weekend. People who choose this way to health, fitness and fun undoubtedly show the greatest imagination and daring.

Myself, I'm quite ecstatic living in my tight world of running!

Triumph, joy, and peace are only three of the runner's rewards.

CHAPTER THREE

The Ecstasy of Running

Q   **Why are you ecstatic about running?**

A   My love of running has little to do, really, with scoring a lot of aerobic points in a short period of time.

Nor does it have much to do with the fact my blood pressure has remained at 110/65 since puberty, or that I have a resting pulse of 42, or that my blood cholesterol, triglycerides, and glucose levels are all extremely low.

My contentment has scarcely anything to do with being slender, healthy, and having a year round suntan. Or having women in discos stare at my tight you know what. The fact is, most runners like myself become quite bored with the disco scene. The bars never appear to serve Gatorade.

Not that runners can't or won't drink. Such is not the case! Because of high calorie demands, runners like Frank Shorter, John Walker, and even myself when training hard, can drink beer all evening and still wake up the next morning fresh and ready to run. But that, of course, adds nothing to the bliss of running.

Nor does the fact I can pile three scoops of rich vanilla ice cream on my double helping of German chocolate cake, and not worry about gaining weight.

My joy of running is in no way affected by the fact I can see the inside of my navel at a glance. I find my navel quite uninteresting.

That running is an uncostly sport — all you need is a pair of $30 shoes, $5 shorts, and a $4 tee shirt — adds nothing to my ecstasy. For the pleasure I derive I would gladly pay hundreds more.

The fact running is so ecologically pure that the only thing wasted is calories contributes zilch to my fulfillment. Actually, I hope to buy a 12

17

cylinder, gas guzzling Jaguar XKE from the profits of this book.

The enjoyment I get from running rarely has anything to do with the fact I can run anywhere, at any time, and with or without anyone. I find a Saturday afternoon group run up and down the hills of San Francisco no more delightful than a solitary run on Pismo Beach at three in the morning.

Especially irrelevant to my ecstasy is the recent finding that running relieves anxiety and tension. Of what use is that for a bum who hasn't had his alarm clock fixed for six months?

My serenity has hardly anything to do with always getting a restful night of sleep. I sleep too much as it is.

Nor does it have much to do with regularity, since running never allows Nature to forget.

The good spirits running gives me is quite apart from being able to thrash tennis players of greater skill in a long three-set match. Always winning that last set 6-0 makes the whole game boring.

It is absurd to think my merriment from running is somehow related to the fact I'm not helpless without an elevator or taxicab. To smirk at the chain smoker who is forced to climb three flights of stairs is sadistic and cruel.

In the same way, not any part of my satisfaction comes from knowing that I hardly ever catch colds and have better health and cardiovascular fitness than 90 percent of Americans. How disgusting and elitist to compare myself with others.

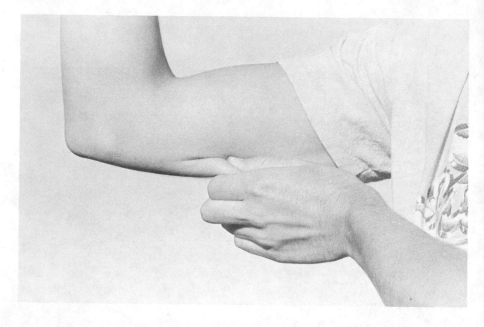

A complete physical exam includes tests for fat, oxygen uptake, and cardiac efficiency.

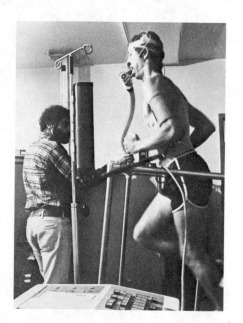

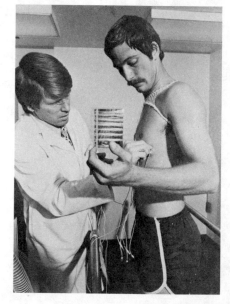

CHAPTER FOUR

Is It Safe For You To Begin?

Q   **Is it safe for me to begin a program of running if I've been inactive up until now?**

A   Before you start running, an accurate assessment of your health and fitness is important, and vital if you tend to be older, heavier, inactive, type A, and male.

I don't say this to scare people away from running — then there would be no point in writing this book — but nonetheless it is a bald fact that a sizeable number of Americans are at such a low level of health and cardiovascular fitness that a sudden and overenthusiastic burst of running might have calamitous results for some.

Q   **In other words, you're going to tell me I should get a doctor's approval before I start running?**

A   As Hal Higdon wryly notes in *Fitness After Forty*, no fitness or running book is complete without the "semi-obligatory physical examination disclaimer."

But more than just a disclaimer, an appeal for a physical examination is sound advice *if* you are starting from inactivity, and *if* you can find a doctor who knows how to administer and has the right equipment for a cardiovascular stress test.

The trouble is, such doctors are as rare as original copies of *Distance Running News*.

A standard physical examination, without a stress test, won't tell an older and heavier person all there is to know regarding whether or not it is safe to begin running. Aside from possibly uncovering a disease, the only two important facts you learn from a standard exam are blood pressure and blood analysis — levels of cholesterol, trigylcerides and glucose. And if these facts don't deviate much from the fat and sedentary norm, you'll be issued a "clean bill of health," with perhaps fatherly advice to "lose weight and get some exercise."

Q **What other information is needed?**

A What is needed is a thorough monitoring and analysis of all your cardiovascular functions, and at four different stages: 1) at rest; 2) at regular intervals during sub-maximal, but increasing exercise stress; 3) at the point of maximum exertion; and 4) at regular intervals during recovery. This is a complete stress test. In detail, it works like this:

The first part of the examination is much the same as any other — the doctor inquires about your health; measurements are taken for resting pulse and blood pressure; and a sample of blood is drawn from your arm.

Next, the doctor measures your percentage of body fat, either by pinching various parts of your body with a skin caliper, or by submerging you in a tank of water to measure your density — the more dense your body weight, the less fat you carry. When Olympic steeplechaser Mike Manley found he was the most dense person ever tested at the Institute of Aerobics Research, Manley replied: "My wife has always said the same thing."

That finished, you are dried off and hooked up to an electrocardiograph machine by way of leads taped to your chest. You are allowed to slump in your chair and relax for a few moments as the ECG monitors and records your cardiac functions at rest.

Don't get too complacent, though, for soon the doctor will direct you out of your chair and to a treadmill, which you will step onto and begin walking or trotting at a comfortable pace until your pulse stabilizes and the doctor is satisfied you are warmed up and ready for the actual stress testing to begin. At this time the doctor hands you a mouthpiece attached to a tube which will collect your exhaled breath. This is how oxygen uptake — the amount of oxygen supplied to your heart — is computed. To make sure that all breathing is done through the mouth, the doctor also hands you a nose clip.

Now the race against the treadmill begins. The doctor slowly increases the treadmill speed, as he carefully watches your body's response on the ECG. Seeing no dangerous abnormalities, the doctor speeds the treadmill more.

This he keeps doing until your pulse reaches its maximum and you signal to him that you've reached your limit and can't go on. Is the test over now? No, to make sure you aren't sandbagging, the doctor makes you sprint for another 15-30 seconds!

At the moment you are finally allowed to quit, two important readings are taken. One is your maximum pulse, which records somewhere between 160-200 beats per minute.

The other reading is your maximum oxygen uptake, which is the most accurate indication of cardiovascular fitness. This tells the doctor how much oxygen is being fed to the heart every second. Champion distance runners and cross country skiers consistently have the highest oxygen uptake readings of anyone tested. While the average horseshoe pitcher has a reading of 45, a world class distance runner is closer to 75. The late Steve Prefontaine, once the American record-holder at every racing distance between 2000 and 10,000 meters, is still the Aerobics Institute record-holder in oxygen uptake. Pre's reading was 84.4.

The last stage of the test is your recovery period. The oxygen uptake mouthpiece is removed, but the ECG leads are left taped to your chest. The monitoring of your heart during recovery from stress is vital to the whole analytical picture. A strong and fit heart quickly returns to a near resting pulse level. A heart not accustomed to physical stress takes much longer to recover, and sometimes beats irregularly.

From all the information gathered, a competent doctor can tell you not only your current level of cardiovascular fitness, but also at what level of intensity and duration you can safely begin an aerobic exercise program, like running.

Q   **Are complete stress tests easily accessible?**

A   Not really. Finding a cardiologist or physiologist with the knowledge and equipment to properly administer a stress test is a big obstacle. And so is paying them to do so.

Aside from the Aerobics Institute in Dallas and the Human Performance Laboratory at Ball State University in Muncie, Indiana, the only places where you will consistently find doctors who give complete cardiovascular stress tests are in university medical centers or other medical research centers like the Mayo Clinic in Rochester, Minnesota.

Of course, now and then you might find an enlightened and equipped doctor in smaller clinics.

But wherever you find such a doctor, his cost for administering a stress exam is likely to exceed a hundred dollars.

Q   **Well that raises the question, is it all worth the time and expense? I mean, all disclaimers aside, do I really need a cardiovascular stress test?**

A   The importance, and even validity of having a stress test before beginning running has been a long-standing argument among running experts.

Two notables, Joe Henderson and Dr. George Sheehan, think the whole thing is a waste of time and money. Sheehan writes in his book, *Dr. Sheehan On Running*, "We don't need all this electronic wizardry to tell us how hard and how long and how often to exercise. We simply set our (perceived exertion) at 'very light' to 'fairly light' and start in."

Henderson criticizes stress tests for a different reason. As he writes in *Jog, Run, Race*: "I don't include it (the medical disclaimer) for several reasons — the least of which is that most of you would pay no attention even if I told you to see your doctor first. I don't want you starting with the idea that you're likely to do yourself damage or even die from running. And this is the message the medical warning implies: 'Caution: Exercise may be hazardous to your health.' "

Taking the opposite viewpoint is Dr. Cooper and the Aerobics Institute. There, a preliminary stress test is not only deemed important, but necessary, since the length and duration of each person's exercise program is based upon results of the test.

I don't believe the discrepancy in viewpoints is as wide as the two camps maintain. Henderson and Sheehan are both associated with *Runner's World* magazine, where they see a rather gilded sample of humanity — young, robust health, low cardiovascular risk.

The Aerobics Institute sees an entirely different sample. Many who set foot on the Institute grounds have been ordered there by family physicians who discovered in their patient a heart murmur or extreme hypertension. Others, and Cooper's Kingdom fairly swarms with them, are actual heart attack victims, now recovering and practicing preventative medicine.

The point is, both viewpoints are correct under their own circumstances. Young, thin, and active people probably don't need to take a stress test before they begin a program of running. Older, heavier and inactive people probably do.

What about yourself? On the next page is a personal inventory which can help you determine whether you need to take a cardiovascular stress test before you start running.

Should You Take A Stress Test?
(add your points to see)

Age	- 20	21-30	31-40	41-50	51-60	60 +
Points	0	1	2	3	4	5

Systolic Blood Pressure	- 110	110-130	131-150	151-170	171-190	190 +
Points	0	1	2	3	4	5

Skinfold Thickness*	- ¼"	¼-½"	½-1"	1-1½"	1½-2"	2 +
Points	0	1	2	3	4	5

Cigarette Smoking	Never	Quit	Light	Moderate	Heavy
Points	0	1	2	3	4

Family Deaths from Cardiovascular Disease	Grandparents	Parents	Siblings
Points	1 for each	2 for each	3 for each

Sex	Male	Female
Points	2	0

Personality Profile**	Type A	Type B
Points	3	0

Diabetes	Yes	No
Points	5	0

* Measures Body fat. Pinch the skin on the bottom of your upper arm.
** As first defined by Dr. Meyer Friedman.

Should You Take A Stress Test?
(Results)

If your point total is:

O *20 or above* or if you scored a 5 in any one category, your life pattern thus far points to high cardiovascular risk. You almost certainly should have a stress test before starting running.   *A risk factor*

O *16 to 19* or if you scored a 4 in any one category, your cardiovascular risk factor is still more than average. A preliminary stress test is strongly advised.   *B risk factor*

O *12 to 15* you are probably the typical American adult — underexercised and overfed, but in otherwise good health. A stress test is advised, but not vital if you begin your running program carefully.   *C risk factor*

O *11 and under* You are a low cardiovascular risk — at this time anyway — and so you can safely begin a running program without a stress test.
                                                                   D risk factor

* Your present cardiovascular risk factor. In the next chapter your risk factor is used to show you at what level you can safely begin your running program.

Q   **If the chart indicates I should have a preliminary stress test, but I don't have the time or money to travel to a university med center, who should I see?**

A   It's important to see a cardiologist or research physiologist who knows what he's doing, regardless of whether he has the latest testing equipment — treadmill, oxygen uptake measuring apparatus, etc.

Dr. Sheehan says any cardiologist who knows what to look for can conduct an adequate stress test with just an ECG machine (which every clinic has) and a soapbox for the patient to step up and down on.

Again, what's needed is a thorough monitoring and analysis of your cardiovascular functions at four different stages: 1) at rest; 2) at regular intervals during increasing stress; 3) at maximum stress; and 4) at regular intervals during recovery.

The trouble with most doctors who give stress tests is that they don't let you sustain your treadmill running or step test for a long enough period.

They don't let you warm up and let your functions stabilize; they don't apply graduated doses of stress; and they rarely let you go to your maximum.

Instead they have you run until "breathing becomes hard," at which point the test is stopped.

Here many doctors feel they are caught between a rock and a hard place. They are understandably hesitant to make an obese smoker with high blood pressure go all-out on the treadmill or step test. Yet, testing a patient at maximum exertion is important, since a great number of cardiovascular abnormalities and potential dangers occur at or near maximum stress.

A doctor who knows how to give a proper stress test will try to learn all that he can from a patient undergoing physical stress, without putting the patient in a high cardiovascular risk situation.

Q **How do I find such a doctor?**

A As mentioned before, if you live close to a university medical center, finding a doctor who knows how to administer a stress test should be no problem. Just call the cardiology department and explain what you want — a complete cardiovascular stress test.

If you live elsewhere, your search to find the right doctor is going to take diligence. First, call the cardiology department at your local clinic and ask if there is anyone on the staff who runs. If there is, your problems are over — the runner is the person you want to see.

If you can't be tested by a runner, then try to find someone who has read *Aerobics* or is at least familiar with its principles. One perhaps insults the medical profession to compare it with auto repair, but don't be afraid to grill the cardiologist with questions much as you would grill an auto mechanic before letting him touch your car.

Ask the cardiologist to explain his testing procedure in detail. If it doesn't meet your satisfaction, tell him why. If he can't fill the holes in his arguments, then call the next doctor, and keep calling them until you've found what you want. As I say elsewhere in this book, your money and body deserve the right medical advice and treatment.

Most need to begin with timed intervals of walking and running.

CHAPTER FIVE

Getting Started—
Beginning Training

Q   **I'm ready to start running now — where do I begin?**

A   We start by setting a goal of what we want to accomplish in running. I use the word goal hesitantly, because it seems antithetical to a leisure activity, but I think our objective justifies its use. *The goal of this chapter is to raise your fitness to a point where you can comfortably run for 20 minutes.*

Q   **Why 20 minutes?**

A   Twenty minutes is an arbitrary figure, but it is chosen for two good reasons. The first is that when you are finally able to run for 20 minutes, no matter how slowly, you will be covering at least two miles. Do this three times a week, and you'll satisfy the aerobic point total needed for maintaining good cardiovascular fitness.

The second reason is that I want you to fall in love with running. This is possible only when the sport is fun, and running is fun only when you can comfortably sustain it for more than 20 minutes.

As you'll find from reading Chapter 17, or better yet, from your own experience, the first 20-30 minutes of running is a chore. Then, all at once it seems, the muscles loosen and the body becomes filled with oxygen. The adrenal glands reward your effort with a rush of energy. The brain suddenly closes the side of logic and reason, and opens the side of creativity and emotion. You are magically transformed, and giddy with newfound power. In short you are high, and the rest of your run is going to be an emotion-filled trip through your soul. It is then you fall in love with running.

Q   **Twenty minutes seems like a lot of running at this time. I don't know if I'll ever be able to go for that long.**

A   The majority of beginners *won't* be able to run for 20 minutes at the start. But don't despair. The purpose of this chapter is to show you, step by step, how you can achieve that goal.

The easiest, safest and surest way to do it is with a graduated schedule of 20-minute training programs, progressing from walking to running. I like to call this The Seven Steps to Running.

The Seven Steps to Running

○ *Step 1* Continuous walking for 20 minutes. The pace should be brisk, but comfortable — if brisk isn't comfortable, slow down.

○ *Step 2* Walk for nine minutes, and run slowly for one. Repeat the cycle for a total of 20 minutes. If running for one minute isn't comfortable — if you breathe too hard — then devise your own intermediate step. One suggestion is to walk for 4½ minutes and run for 30 seconds, a cycle you can repeat three times for 20 minutes.

○ *Step 3* Walk for three minutes, and run for one. Repeat cycle four times.

○ *Step 4* Walk for two minutes, and run for two. Repeat cycle four times.

○ *Step 5* Run for three minutes, and walk for one. Repeat four times.

○ *Step 6* Run for eight minutes, and walk for two. Repeat.

○ *Step 7* Run continuously for 20 minutes. Our definition of continuous is purposely loose — a brief pause or two along the way is allowable. Never let any schedule or training program, or even your stubborn pride prohibit you from stopping during a run. If you feel so fatigued that you need to stop, then do it. Your will-power isn't being questioned here, but your health could be.

Q   **At which step should I begin my running program?**

A   If you are starting from complete inactivity, turn back to page 26 in the preceding chapter and find your cardiovascular risk factor. Then match your CRF to one of the steps in the following way:

CRF	Step
A	1
B	2
C	3
D	4

In other words, if you are a high cardiovascular risk, you should start your running program with a complete walk.

Of course, this is only a suggested guideline to help you find your proper and safe starting level. Many Cs and Ds can already run comfortably for 20 minutes. Then again, some Cs and Ds might have to start with step one, a complete walk. The important thing is find the level just right for you.

Q **And that is?**

A The highest level which you can do comfortably.

Q **You keep using the word "comfortably" to describe an activity that, frankly, I don't think of as comfortable.**

A Well, if you're thinking of the comfort of lying under a Tahitian palm tree, or of sunning yourself on a beach in southern France, I can understand your confusion. We don't mean *that* comfortable!

Throughout this book the word comfortable will define any running or walking which is done without strain or breathing difficulty. And to that definition, Bill Bowerman, the former US Olympic track and field coach and consultant to Kenneth Cooper, would add that comfortable is any pace at which you can maintain a normal conversation. That is, if you can't talk in full sentences, you are running too fast for comfort.

This is what the concept of aerobic exercise is all about — doing something in the presence of oxygen; running slowly and comfortably to always have enough air. Running with discomfort is not only a hardship, but counterproductive to aerobic fitness.

Q **So getting back to my first question, if I score a C in cardiovascular risk, should I begin with step three?**

A Go ahead and try a step three workout. And then either move up or down until you find the highest step you can do comfortably.

Q **How many workouts a week should I do?**

A Three is plenty for now.

What most weekend athletes and do-it-every-day enthusiasts fail to understand is that training is a two-step process. In order for an organism to improve its physical condition, it must 1) be given regular doses of physical stress, and 2) be given regular rest periods of rest and adaptation.

What has been learned in the laboratory and been proved on the running tracks, in weightrooms, swimming pools, or anyplace where athletes are trying to improve their physical condition, is that a full cycle of stress and recovery takes 48 hours, and not one day or one week.

The first track coach to grasp this concept was Bill Bowerman when he was turning out all those sub-four-minute milers at the University of Oregon. Bowerman constantly amazed the visitors who came to Eugene looking for the secret of his success. For three days each week Bowerman's runners trained quite similarly to runners all around the world. But on the other days, when no races were scheduled, Bowerman ordered his troops not to the track or roads, but to the saunas, sundecks and swimming pools!

So, both weekend athletes and everyday runners are making a mistake in their training. The weekender is not getting enough physical stress, and the everydayer is getting too much, with not enough recovery and adaptation time.

Q **How quickly should I be able to progress from one step to the next?**

A I think you should try to move up a step every two weeks. This isn't to say you will always be ready for a new step every two weeks, but only that you should try. If your health is good and you are following the program, you will, in most instances, be able to jump a step every two weeks.

The most difficult jump for most is from step one to step two, since there is a wider range of ability in step one than in any other. The elderly, the grossly overweight, the lifelong smokers and many others who fill step one are going to have great difficulty running for an entire minute, as is called for in step two. This is why a basic understanding of a graduated exercise program is more important than blindly memorizing and obeying each step. If the jump between steps is too much, simply devise your own intermediate step.

Once you've made it past the first step, you should find it quite easy to move every two weeks. If improvement takes longer than a month, something is wrong. For women, it could be anemia. But for most, slow improvement probably means you are running too fast.

Q **How fast should we run?**

A Here is where I would like to use the word jog, except that I find the very pronunciation of the word revolting. So instead we'll use trot or shuffle or anything to indicate slowness and comfort. Use Bowerman's talk test to see if your running is comfortable. If you're running as slowly as you can, but still are having trouble breathing toward the end of each one-minute run, then divide that minute into two 30-second, or even four 15-second intervals.

Q **But if I run too slowly, I might as well be walking!**

A Now you sound like my old high school track coach. It might be true that your running and walking are nearly indistinguishable in the beginning, but nevertheless, you must get used to the motion of running. You must learn, or relearn, to move in that way. If you run so slowly that tricycles are a threat, think nothing of it. As your fitness level improves, so will the speed and comfort of your running.

Q **Might not I also improve faster than a step every two weeks?**

A   You might indeed have remarkable adaptive powers, but usually fast improvement indicates that you had started well below your ability.

The right step for you at all times is one which makes you work to the limit of your comfort and aerobic capacity. This is a training maxim that will be repeated throughout this book, since it applies equally to Olympic marathoners and beginners. The yogis call this playing the edge — working to the edge of your comfort. You don't improve by heroically bashing through the edge, but instead by gradually pushing the edge back.

If you improve too fast, be suspicious. You probably don't have a realistic concept of your edge. Once you discover where it is and how to move it, improvement becomes steady and gradual.

When you've found your right level, don't get overly anxious for improvement, and don't skip steps. Be patient. Moving a step every two weeks is actually quite fast. It means you can start from scratch and be running more than two miles inside of three months. And from there, you have it made. It will probably take you less time to move from 20 minutes to one hour of running than it took you to get to the first 20 minutes. But more of that in a later chapter.

Q   **Should I carry a stopwatch with me to time the running and walking intervals?**

A   Most runners haven't carried stopwatches since the days of Paavo Nurmi. Stopwatches are expensive, fragile, and awkward to carry. Besides, you don't need one. Everything you need to know can be learned from a wristwatch with a second hand.

Even the value of a wristwatch is arguable. I recommend you wear one during these initial stages only so that you can define the seven steps clearly, and thereby monitor your progress. Once you have reached the seventh step — running continuously for 20 minutes — leave your watch at home. As a runner, you have now outgrown it.

Q   **What else should I wear?**

A   Wear a pair of comfortable athletic shoes for starters. If you have an old pair of tennis or basketball shoes, go ahead and use them for now. If you don't have any shoes, then buy a pair of top brand running shoes as described in Chapter Seven. Once you are able to run for 20 minutes, you will want a good pair anyway.

Other than that, dress comfortably and dress to meet the weather. The standard warm weather uniform of runners is a tee shirt and shorts. Add a warmup suit, stocking hat and mittens in cold weather. When you are finally able to run for 20 minutes, there is waiting for you an entire chapter devoted to the necessities and frills of running apparel.

Q **Where should I do my running and walking?**

A Any place that is safe, convenient and enjoyable is a good place to do your running and walking.

By safe, we generally mean free from heavy traffic. Crowded roads are safe only if they have adequately wide shoulders or boulevards. Residential streets and country roads are generally safer.

A less frequent safety consideration is the protection your routes give you from weather extremes. While free from traffic, a barren country road is no place to be during a blizzard or oppressive summer heat.

By convenient we mean within five minutes of your home, office, YMCA or wherever you dress and shower. Occasionally it is fun to drive to the country just for a run, but as a general practice this wipes out one of running's prime attractions — its efficiency.

By enjoyable, we mean, well, that's up to you. My most enjoyable runs follow no distinct geographical pattern. I like parks, golf courses, residential areas, lakes, beaches, game reserves, mountains, woods, athletic fields, and even downtown city streets when they aren't crowded.

Unlike most experienced runners who love to exhibit themselves publicly, beginners often don't like to be seen. This is understandable, but don't fall into a paranoiac trap. You don't need society's approval — in fact, ignore them all! A harmless anti-social gesture like running does wonders for your health.

The only other locational consideration is hills — in the beginning you should avoid them. Wait until you can run for 20 minutes.

Q   **Is it permissible to run on pavement?**

A   Despite its hardness, pavement is not a bad running surface if it is level, and if you wear a good pair of running shoes, which are designed to absorb shock.

On the other hand, a lush looking grass field can be deceptively bad, since thousands of tiny ruts, holes and undulations are often hidden underneath.

The best running surfaces are smooth dirt trails and gravel road shoulders. But even those should be level.

Q   **When is the best time of the day to run?**

A   The best time to run is whenever you can most easily and regularly set aside 30 minutes to an hour, since you must also include the time it takes you to dress and shower.

There are advantages and disadvantages to whatever time you choose. Early morning running gives you the most privacy, and is an invigorating way in which to start the day. If you are the type who naturally rises early, I suggest you try early morning running. The disadvantage here is that your muscles are coldest and stiffest upon waking. An additional warmup walk of five minutes is recommended if you run in the early morning.

If your job permits it, midday running is fun and refreshing. It invokes the same response and feelings as recess did when you were in grade school. Many large companies today are installing locker room facilities for the growing number of noontime athletes — if you have such an opportunity, take advantage. Trading your lunch for a workout is an easy way to drop a lot of calories.

Running after a day's work is another convenient time for many, especially for the single person who doesn't have family and dinner waiting. My own favorite time to run is in the early evening of a summer day, when the air is balmy and the sun casts shadows longer than the length of my body. I find this time most uplifting.

Night running is exciting for beginners and younger runners. The muscles are loose, the inhibitions disappear, and the impression of speed is greatly exaggerated. It is not uncommon to hear that someone ran the fastest mile time of their life along a dark road at midnight. In the track world, a "midnight time" is synonomous with suspicious. Yet, there is value in upward misperception of one's abilities, especially in the beginning when you need all of the positive reinforcement you can get.

Q   **How long should I wait between eating and running?**

A   Give yourself two to three hours after a light meal, and three to five after a heavy meal.

Q   **Should I run alone, or with people?**

A   Until you can run for 20 minutes, you are better off doing it alone. You will improve fastest when you run/walk at your own rate. In the delicate beginning, the last thing you need is the strain of trying to keep pace with a more experienced runner. And even if you run with someone of your own ability, the temptations of competition and one-upmanship can ruin what you are trying to accomplish.

But more than that, I think you should use running to cultivate the immense but subtle joys of being alone. And it does take cultivation, because society teaches us that loneliness and being alone are equally undesirable states. Nothing could be more erroneous. When you are lonely, you feel incomplete without the presence of others. By that definition you can never make loneliness attractive.

But to learn the joys of being alone is to learn how to be complete and whole with or without others. Do this and you'll never be without your best friend. If running can teach you anything, it is that.

Q   **How should I run? Is there a correct running style?**

A   There is, and it is discussed in the next chapter.

It all starts with good style.

CHAPTER SIX

Running Style—Putting Your Best Foot Forward

Q **What do we mean by good running style?**

A Good style is that which is most free, uninhibited, expressive and dynamic. Good style is running in the way the body was meant to perform.

Q **Is running a natural activity for humans?**

A It can be. It certainly is for children between four years old and puberty. Visit a playground one day and watch the children at their play. If you watch them closely you will see, in most cases, free and uninhibited movements — no tensions, no poses, no attempt to run correctly. Children have no concern for kneelift; they don't care if their heels or toes strike the ground first. Whether their strides are long or short, it doesn't make much difference to them.

Q **Many are returning to running after a long period of physical inactivity. If running is so natural, why do most of us feel awkward just putting one foot in front of the other?**

A Several factors work against us to make running seem an awkward chore. Age has something to do with it. As children we had an almost unlimited range of muscle and tendon flexibility, but at puberty we lose much of this. Not only does age make us more injury prone, it also reduces our range of motion and makes free flowing running more difficult. This is especially true if, like most of us, we stopped running after our youth.

Clothes, shoes and man-made surfaces also hinder natural running. Ideally we should all be running naked on a smooth fairway, or on the soft wet sand of a beach. Runners so bold as to try this have found the sensation most pleasurable, an instinctive craving to function as one is meant to function. The foot itself is actually made for surfaces soft enough to conform to the foot, with the ball and heel striking the surface, and then sinking to the level of the arch. With shoes and pavement, the arch must flatten to absorb the shock. This flattening, or pronation as it is called, is the root of most running ills.

Lastly, our running style is corrupted by the role models we see. Because a man pitches for the New York Yankees we mistakenly assume he is a perfect running specimen as he slunkers to and from the mound. Or worse, we think the Six Million Dollar Man demonstrates good form with his grossly exaggerated kneelift and tightly held arms. After all, he is doing sixty!

Q   **Shoes, pavement, getting older — all these are inevitable. Can we ever run naturally?**

A   Surely. These factors are obstacles, but nothing insurmountable. What we must do is try to recapture the natural way of running, and adapt it to modern living.

Q   **That sounds complicated. I got into running because I thought it was such a simple activity.**

A   Learning to run naturally, correctly, is not complicated. All it involves is understanding a few principles of human movement. We can learn all there is to learn about good running style in 10 minutes. From there it is a matter of practicing it until it becomes habit.

Q   **But do we have to do even that much? Why is good style so important?**

A   Good running style allows us to run with much greater ease and efficiency, all of our muscles performing in synchronization, each muscle doing precisely what is called for at any speed.

Good running style allows us to fill our lungs more fully and freely.

Good running style allows us to strike the ground with less shock. This reduces both fatigue and injuries, since most injuries relate to the way we strike the ground.

Lastly, good running style looks good. It looks good on others, and feels good on us. It is a proclamation of our physical potential. It gives us the confidence we need to invade the public roads wearing nothing but shoes and nylon briefs.

Q   **Putting those hundreds of muscles, tendons and ligaments into synchronization still sounds awfully complicated. Where do we begin?**

A   We begin with correct posture. Since this can't be said strongly enough, we'll say it again. *Good running form starts with correct posture.*

If a runner has correct posture, that is, if he holds himself correctly from the waist up, then every other motion — of the arms, the legs, the feet, the hands and the head — will fall into place.

Olympic champions and world record holders at every distance observe this principle. Emil Zatopek, the great Czech distance runner, was called "the beast of Prague" for his apparently horrible running style. Zatopek ran with hands clawing his chest and wore a facial expression suggesting bare feet on hot asphalt. But Zatopek ran with correct posture, and for that reason was able to win Olympic gold medals in the 5000 meters, 10,000 meters and marathon in the 1952 Olympics.

Bob Hayes, the great sprinting champion and hero of the 1964 Olympics, was so pigeon-toed that he often cut the inside of his calves while running with spiked shoes. But Hayes knew the importance of good posture.

Good posture is universal. It is the same whether you are a sprinter, a marathoner or a before-breakfast jogger. What we call style is the end result of posture, speed and individual characteristics. The style of Bob Hayes was radically different from Emil Zatopek. But both styles were perfectly suited to their practitioners, because both started with correct posture.

Q   **What exactly do you mean by correct posture?**

A   Correct posture is the way in which you hold your body from the waist up. You can achieve good posture in this way: First take off your shoes or wear any flat-soled shoe, such as your running flats. If you can, find a full length mirror so you can view yourself in profile.

Now, stand as tall as you can without straining, and shift your weight toward the front part of your foot. Make your torso rise upward from the hips. But don't strain. Don't hunch your shoulders or pull them back. Hold the torso high with abdominal muscles. Let the arms hang loosely at the sides.

Q   **As if at military attention?**

A   No, not at all. A military pose is rigid. In a military pose we thrust our chest, draw the shoulders back, and arch the spine. This is a terrible posture, fatiguing and unnatural.

There should be no tension with correct posture. Your back does not arch, but rises straight upward from level hips. You will find your stomach is flat, and held in without conscious attempt to do so.

The hands should be resting comfortably by the front pockets. The shoulders must be loose and under no tension. The same is true for the muscle and tendon above your collarbone.

Even the neck and head must be held properly to achieve good posture. The neck must rise straight upward from the shoulders, just as the torso rises from the pelvis. The neck must not be held rigid, nor so loosely that it sags. The head rests comfortably on the neck, and is level. You are free to turn your head in any direction, although the neutral position is straight ahead.

Q   **So, the idea here is to stand erectly and loosely?**

A   Well, you don't want to stand too erectly. If you do that, your back will arch, and your whole body will tense. The shifting of your weight to the front part of your feet will lean you forward very slightly. If you let your head drop and look straight at the ground, you should see a point three or four inches in front of your feet. If you see a point twelve inches in front of your feet, you are leaning forward too much. You'll find tension in the legs, especially the calves. If you find yourself looking at your feet, you are too erect and probably feel tension in the lower back.

Q **If nothing else, this posture makes me feel alert.**

A The effects of good posture are immediate. You feel relaxed but alert, responsive and powerful. Your senses are alive. This is how you want to feel when running.

Q **What should my posture be when I begin to run?**

A The posture you have now is the correct posture for all runners at every speed. Posture is never adjusted to speed or fatigue. It remains constant.

Q **I'm ready to start running. What next?**

A Your posture looks good, but you will have to know how to carry your arms. Try this: Loosely cup your hands and bring them up to waist level, right above the top of your pant pockets. There is now approximately a 90° bend at the elbow, but this is held loosely, since the elbows must be free to bend. What you have now is the correct arm carriage in a neutral position.

Notice the arm carriage is lower than you might have expected. Notice, too, how natural and balanced it feels. Arms held too high disrupt that balance, and unwanted tension results. Arms held too low will inhibit the stride, forcing you to run like a caterpillar.

Q **So how should I run?**

A What's important now is to get the feel of running with good posture.

Starting with the correct posture and arm carriage, begin to shuffle forward, very slowly. Don't think about what your legs are doing. Concentrate on your posture. Imagine yourself being pushed from behind by a giant hand or a breeze. Your arms are free to swing from the shoulders and bend at the elbows, but they don't do much of either at this slow speed. Let your arms find their own rhythm and range of motion.

Q **You said we shouldn't think about our legs. Don't we run with the legs?**

A Not exactly. We run *with* our whole body. We run *on* our legs. As you shuffle, relaxed and with good posture, your legs, like your arms, will find their own rhythm and range of motion to suit the speed. Just as the arms are free to swing from the shoulder, the legs must be free to swing from the hips. And just as the arms are free to bend at the elbow, the legs must be free to bend at the knee.

At a shuffling speed, of course, the movements of the arms and legs are minimal. With correct posture, the body exerts no more effort than is necessary.

Q **As I shuffle this way my feet touch the ground much more softly than before.**

A Good. With correct posture you should feel uplifted and light. Your feet should touch, not strike the ground. More on footfall later.

Let's increase the pace a bit. Imagine the wind at your back has become stronger, and your back is a sail.

You'll notice increased movement of every muscle. As the pace increases the arms swing more from the shoulders and bend more at the elbow. You feel more lift and swing at the hips. The knees come up further. You push more strongly with thighs, calves and ankles. Your trail leg extends out longer and folds up higher. Every limb, ligament, tendon and muscle works harder as you run faster. And everything works in synchronization, and no more than necessary, if the posture is held right.

Q **How hard should I push off of my legs?**

A Just hard enough. Now that sounds glib, but if your posture is good, then you'll push off of your legs just hard enough to meet the speed you have chosen.

Let's increase the pace a bit more, say to eight minutes a mile. Notice any changes?

Q **I notice the rhythm of my strides remains pretty much constant, but the length of my stride increases.**

A That's a good sign. Each runner, like each cyclist, has a fairly small range of rhythms, which is used for every speed. The rhythm is like the rpm of a car. The stride lengths are like gears. The idea is to hold the rpm, or rhythm, constant. If you struggle with a faster pace, shorten the stride and try to hold the rhythm. If you wish to speed up, hold the rhythm, and let that imaginary wind at your back push you to greater strides.

The rhythm, or stride frequency, you have while shuffling is the same rhythm you'll use at much faster paces. The optimal stride frequency is something in the order of three to four strides per second, depending on the individual. Taller people have lower frequencies than shorter runners.

Let yourself find your own rhythm. It's yours to keep.

Q **As I let that "wind" push me to faster speeds, I find myself becoming detached from the whole running process, almost as if my body were doing the thinking instead of me.**

A Then you've got it! Let that imaginary wind or giant hand or cow catcher do the work. You just hold your posture and go along for the ride.

To paraphrase Ray Bradbury in his marvelous book, *Zen and the Art of Writing*: This detachment from your activity, letting the body do the thinking, gives you the same kind of dynamic relaxation as in sculpting, where the sculptor does not consciously have to tell his fingers what to do.

Neither does the surgeon tell his scalpel what to do.

Nor does the runner advise his body. Suddenly a natural rhythm is achieved. The body thinks for itself.

Good running style is the same for men and women.

Q **Can you be more specific on a few matters? For instance, how should my feet touch the ground? My high school coach told me to stay off of the heels and land on the toes. He said all of the good runners land on their toes. Is this true?**

A Remember that all parts of our running style, including our footfall, are a function of four things. One is posture, which is learned. The second is speed, which is chosen. The third is terrain, which we adjust to. And the fourth is the way in which our body is put together, over which we have no control and to which we should never adjust.

The peculiar way in which each of us is built — the length of our limbs, the ratio of our slow/fast muscle fibers, etc. — affects our running style in hundreds of ways we should leave alone.

For several years Frank Shorter and the late Steve Prefontaine had classic duels in the three mile and 5000 meters. Both ran with great posture typical of all world class runners. Both were running the same speed and on the same track. Yet Prefontaine and Shorter differed radically in style. Pre hit the ground heavily on his heels; Shorter lightly on his toes. Pre's arms stirred like eggbeaters; Shorter's swung in tight rhythm. Pre grimaced and snarled; Shorter looked detached. For everything Pre did, Shorter did differently. These differences resulted not from posture, speed or terrain, but from individual characteristics. Pre was built differently than Shorter.

So, to address the question of whether you should land on your heels or toes or anywhere in between is meaningless. Most runners land on their heels at slower speeds and on their toes or ball of foot at higher speeds. But you, like Shorter, might very well land on your toes all of the time. Never attempt to place your foot to the ground in either manner. Just let it fall where it may as a function of those four things: good posture, speed, terrain, and your own characteristics.

Q **Does the same hold true for the motion of the legs and arms?**

A Yes, exactly. Hold your good posture, choose your speed, adjust to the terrain, and see what happens. All of the correct motions should find themselves. They may be somewhat different for you than for other runners, but then you are built somewhat differently than other people.

Q   **Is that all there is to say about running style?**

A   Well, actually I'd like to mention briefly three other points. A few words must be said on how to breathe correctly, a few more on the importance of trunk strength, and, finally, on fatigue and relaxation.

Q   **I have two questions about breathing. Should I breathe through my nose or mouth, and should I time my breathing to my stride cadence?**

A   The idea is to get all the air you can, so breathe through both orifices. Hold your mouth and throat open for easy breathing. Exhale through both nose and mouth, too.

The East Germans once tested the effects of breathing in cadence versus breathing randomly. The results were inconclusive. Some runners like to breathe in cadence, such as during every other stride, but I like to breathe whenever I feel like it. Who knows, I may be breathing in cadence — I don't really care. All I want to do is get all the oxygen I can.

There is only one important bit of advice to remember in breathing, and that is *fill your lungs from the bottom to the top*, not from the top to the bottom. You get much more oxygen this way. Picture this idea in your mind. Starting in the deepest part of your lungs, fill with air. Feel your midsection expand, then your chest and on up to your neck. Now, exhale in reverse manner, from the top to the bottom. Teach yourself to breathe correctly, and it will become habit quickly. Your body likes oxygen.

Q   **You also mentioned trunk strength . . .**

A   Yes. The muscles that must be strongest in a runner are not those of the legs, but those of the trunk. Correct posture, as we've mentioned, is the proper way you hold your upper body. Your upper body is held up by the abdominal muscles, and to a lesser extent, by the lower back. Both must be strong.

Only a strong trunk can maintain a level pelvis. Percy Cerutty, the late genius coach of Australian distance runners, said the hips should be thought of as a bowl containing precious fluid. If the hips are allowed to tilt forward, which happens when the abdominals are not sufficiently strong, the result is a swayback posture which tightens the legs and constricts their range of motion.

Constant swaybacked running can lead to one of the hardest to cure running ailments — irritation of the sciatic nerve. The symptom of sciatica is a chronically painful tightness from the heels to the buttocks. Severe sciatica can lead to numbness in the legs.

Abdominal strength is doubly important in runners with inherently swayed backs, or lordosis, since these people already have poor posture.

Leg raisers and bent-knee situps, preferably on an inclined board, will strengthen the abdominal muscles.

The lower back can be strengthened by dead lifts. Begin by lifting a light object, such as a dictionary. Do dead lifts slowly and carefully.

Further discussion of these exercises are found in chapter 13.

Q **How can I maintain good running style when fatigued?**

A The greatest temptation you'll face when fatigued is giving up your posture. All such temptations must be resisted.

Marathoners have a term to describe the running style one often sees in the last six miles of the race, after the runners have "hit the wall" of fatigue. It's called the survival shuffle, and its practitioners are those who have lost good posture.

During aerobic fatigue, you'll feel heavy; your legs will hit the ground harder and harder. You will be tempted to drop your posture and leg it out in a caterpillar-like slither. Don't do it. This is the survival shuffle.

During anaerobic fatigue — the fatigue of interval training — the tendency is to lean backward. Fight it. The strength of your limbs is lost if you lose good posture. This is like moving your weapons from a battleship to a canoe.

As a football team is exhorted to hold that line, you must tell yourself to hold your posture.

Q   **Isn't relaxation an effective way of fighting fatigue?**

A   Yes it is, but proper relaxation is misunderstood, even by most coaches.
       When the body tightens with fatigue, the way to fight it, say the coaches,
       is to relax, letting the jaw slack and the wrists dangle.

       Slacking the jaw and dangling the wrists may work for some, but the
       overwhelming tendency of these practices is to let the entire body,
       including the posture, fall into a heap. Do that, and you'll soon be
       survival shuffling.

       Proper relaxation is dynamic. Proper relaxation is possible only when
       the posture is good and the other moving parts follow in synchroniza-
       tion.

       If you always remember to hold your posture correctly, then you can
       occasionally slack your jaw or dangle your wrists. You can even shake
       the arms if they are tight, or roll your head if the neck is tight. You may
       even, if your legs are tired, lengthen or shorten the stride for a few steps.
       Just be sure to maintain good posture.

Tee shirt, shorts, and shoes are the staple clothing of all runners.

CHAPTER SEVEN

What You Wear Does Matter

Q   **What is the first item of running apparel I should buy?**

A   Whatever else you decide to wear, first buy a pair of quality running shoes. As we will learn in a later chapter, a good majority of all running injuries originate from the foot. It is vital, then, to equip our feet with the best available shoes.

Q   **Is it important to buy shoes that are made just for running? I just spent thirty dollars for a pair of tennis shoes. Can't I run in them?**

A   Tennis shoes (or basketball shoes) are not bad shoes for someone experimenting with running. It's better to first see if you like running before plunking down money for running shoes.

The basic difference between running shoes and tennis shoes is that the former are constructed for linear motion and the latter for lateral motion.

Q   **So?**

A   The thing you want most in a running shoe — support — is purposely absent in a tennis shoe. In a tennis shoe, you must have freedom of movement within the shoe for maximum lateral mobility. In a running shoe, we don't need that kind of freedom; in fact, it is just that kind of side-to-side motion within the shoe that is the primary cause of running injuries.

What we want is a shoe that actually inhibits lateral motion. We can find this kind of support and stability only in a good running shoe.

Q   **Why is there a wide price range among running shoes? I see shoes in the grocery store selling for eight dollars a pair, and to me they look the same as the forty dollar shoes I see in the sporting goods stores.**

A   As the cliché goes, you get what you pay for. The range in quality is as wide as the range in prices. The eight dollar shoes are designed specifically to look like the quality brand shoes, but there the similarity ends.

Examine closely a pair of cheaper shoes. The soles of these counterfeits are attached to the uppers not with glue, as they should be, but with big horse stitches of cotton thread. As soon as you wear out the cotton thread, you've lost your sole.

Notice, too, how the arch supports in these cheaper shoes are tossed in haphazardly. Sometimes the arch cookie is found floating somewhere in the toe of the shoe; other times it is sighted hiding in back near the heel. Instead of a support for the longitudinal arch, you have a randomly placed lump of foam.

The good shoes always have a precise balance between a stiff shank and a flexible forefoot. That is to say, a good shoe bends easily in the front half of the sole, and with great difficulty in the rear. The grocery store shoes I've examined are either all stiff or all flexible.

If we look carefully, we can find dozens of faults in the cheap shoes. Don't waste your money on them.

Q   **What about the department store brands? I believe they cost from fifteen to twenty dollars.**

A   Department store shoes are considerably better than grocery store shoes. They do make a more thorough attempt to copy the quality brand shoes, but they still are copies, and guesswork copies at that. The soles and uppers on department store brands are adequate, but again, it's the hidden aspects of a shoe, such as balancing, sole flex, shank support, and orthopedic heel counters, which are not up to par with the quality brand shoes.

Q   **Is there really that much of a difference between the top brand shoes and all others?**

A   Yes. The top shoe companies have all invested thousands of dollars in research and development. They have on their staffs orthopedists and podiatrists who work closely with design engineers to ensure the right combination of lightness and orthopedic safety.

The finished shoes are then tested meticulously for quality control — sole durability, upper durability, and so on. The quality brand shoes sold in the store have all passed rigid quality control standards.

More importantly, the quality brand shoes, exclusively, have met the standards of world class runners.

Q   **I thought world class runners wore the shoe of whatever company paid them the most money.**

A   To an extent, that's true. Some major shoe companies are known to pay top athletes large sums for the implicit advertising. Lasse Viren, the great Finnish distance runner, held his brand of shoes aloft for the world to see as he jogged his victory laps at the Montreal Olympics.

But these payoffs occur among the top brands, where the quality difference is, in the end, slight. I've never heard of an athlete taking a payoff to wear an inferior shoe. In my years of observing international track and road racing, I've yet to see a top athlete wear an inferior shoe. The kind of money worth jeopardizing an Olympic athlete's feet or career doesn't yet exist.

Q   **What should I look for in a running shoe?**

A   For starters, look for the following material features, which you'll find only in the top brands:

○ *Sole* A good running shoe typically has a durable outer sole and one or two layers of softer midsole. The outer sole is made from a tough rubber compound and should be ⅛″ to ¼″ thick. There are commonly three types of tread design on the outer sole — standard or flat, ripple, and waffle or studded.

A standard sole, which includes crepe, shallow suction cup and herringbone, is the best for all-purpose running. It is also the longest wearing, especially on pavement. The Adidas Runner, Tiger Montreal II, New Balance 320, and Brooks Villanova are examples of shoes with standard tread.

A ripple sole offers better traction on grass and dirt, but tends to wear more quickly and has a bad reputation for collecting mud and dirt between the ripples. The Adidas SL series and Osaga Moscow are ripple soled shoes.

A waffle or studded sole gives the best traction on grass, but wears quickly on pavement, and is quite difficult to repair. The Brooks Vantage, Adidas TRX and Nike LD-1000s are among the popular waffle shoes.

The layers of midsole should be softer than the outer sole. Ideally, the midsole should capture the fine area between softness for shock absorption and firmness for stability. You don't want a shoe too mushy or too hard. Experienced runners, who have learned to run with a minimum of shock, generally opt for firmer shoes. Beginning runners might try a middle ranged or soft shoe.

In my experience, Adidas are the hardest shoes. Tiger, Nike and Brooks are in the middle, and New Balance, the newer Pumas and Etonic make the softest shoes. This can change from year to year, though, so you determine for yourself.

○ *Flexibility and Shank Support* A good shoe has to be flexible in the forefoot. It must bend easily where the foot bends during the toe-off phase of the stride. Any shoe with a sole more than ⅜″ thick in the forefoot is not going to bend easily. A shoe that does not bend where the foot bends will inhibit true running motion and cause undue strain. Injury is a likely result.

At the same time, a shoe must be fairly rigid in the rear sole, from the front part of the arch to the heel. This portion of the shoe is called the shank, and rigid support here is important. If you can bend the shank more than a few degrees, the shoe doesn't have proper shank support.

○ *Heel Lift* The sole of the heel should be ½″ to ¾″ thick, or about twice that of the forefoot. This double thickness softens heel strike and prevents straining of the highly vulnerable achilles tendon. Additionally, the heel sole should curl in the back to let the runner roll into his stride after initial heel-first contact.

○ *Upper Material* Since the early 1970s nylon has all but replaced leather and suede as the primary material in uppers. The reasons for this are several. Nylon costs less, it chafes the foot less, it doesn't harden and crack from constant wetting, it dries faster, it is cooler (especially the new nylon mesh), and it requires little or no break-in period.

Leather is still available in a few shoes, like the Adidas Country and Tiger Munich. It retains a certain charm among runners who fondly remember the days when it was the only material. Leather is often preferred by winter runners in the Midwest; leather is warmer and easier to winter-proof than nylon. Perhaps leather's best feature is its snug fit after the break-in period.

Suede, my own favorite for its lightness and glove-like fit, has curiously vanished as a primary upper material. However, suede is still used for reinforcing nylon uppers.

Nylon shoes should be reinforced with suede around the toe, heel and laces. The suede here must be thick and tough, since these are the prime stress points in the wear of a shoe. Make sure the suede is attached to the nylon with durable stitching. Double stitching is best.

○ *Lacing* Two types of lacing patterns are available in running shoes. One is the standard pattern of eyelet holes punched in the suede. The second is called speed lacing, with plastic rings substituting for eyelets. I recommend the speed lacing for two reasons. One, the slippage in speed lacing gives the wearer a uniform tightness. Two, the plastic rings last longer than eyelets. I tie my shoes tightly, and always seem to break through the eyelets in a matter of weeks.

○ *Arch Support* Most running shoes are equipped with a simple foam cookie. Only two shoe companies, Brooks and Etonic, at this time offer anything more substantial.

The Brooks Vantage, Victor, Vanguard and Delta have insoles made of Iron Texon which will, after a few miles of running, conform to the shape of the wearer's foot. This unique system was designed by Dr. Steven Subotnick, a leading "running podiatrist" who has similarly worked with ski boots. The idea behind Iron Texon is to achieve the same cushioning you might get while running barefoot on soft beach sand.

Etonic shoes, designed by podiatrist Rob Roy McGregor, has implanted in their shoes a one piece heel and arch support which is sized according to the size of the shoe. It does not conform, but offers semirigid support.

Much documented research has shown that 50-80 percent of adult Americans have less than fully adequate feet. If runners are a random sample of Americans, then this same percentage needs additional support in their shoes. We'll discuss how you can determine what you need, and where you can get outside support in Chapter 13.

○ *Heel and Achilles Support* All good shoes have padded heel counters. A heel counter is a semi-plastic inner liner which wraps around the heel, and extends high enough to cup the heel even if you put inserts in your shoes. On the inside of the shoe's heel should be plastic vinyl covering the foam wrapped heel counter. This padding is to reduce chafing and ensure a snug fit.

Be careful to first unlace your shoes before removing them. Otherwise you may pull the heel counter from its attachment at the base of the heel.

Q   **You keep referring to the top quality brands, and I believe you've already mentioned some. Can you be more specific?**

A   To mention top brands is to insult all the rest. But, indolence ascending, the shoes I refer to are (in alphabetical order):

○ *Adidas* Adidas has led the world in running shoes since it began making track spikes 25 years ago. Adidas are the easiest to obtain, slightly more expensive, and of high quality and workmanship.

○ *Brooks* Brooks has grown the fastest of all companies since 1976. The least expensive quality shoe available today (1978) is the Brooks Villanova at $19.95. Brooks also makes, for ten dollars more, those shoes with the Iron Texon insole. Brooks are available in three sizes: narrow, medium and wide.

○ *Converse* Well known as a basketball shoe manufacturer, Converse has only recently entered the running shoe market. Their sales have been remarkably good in the first year. Converse shoes are available in three sizes: narrow, medium and wide.

○ *E. B. Sport Shoes* These shoes are handmade and quite expensive ($35-$50). They are designed by Arthur Lydiard, the world's foremost distance running coach. They are more popular among European track runners.

○ *Etonic* Etonic running shoes are manufactured by the Eaton Company, whose biggest success thus far has been in golf shoes. As mentioned previously Etonic shoes feature the unique Rob Roy McGregor heel and arch piece. Etonic shoes are available in three sizes: narrow, medium and wide.

○ *New Balance* Long a favorite of the old New England road running crowd, this Boston company exploded in popularity in 1976, when the New Balance 320 was ranked first in the *Runner's World* shoe survey. New Balance is the only major shoe company that makes shoes in more than three widths, from AA to EEEE.

○ *Nike* As New Balance is the shoe of New Englanders, Nike is the favorite of Northwesterners. The shoe from Oregon has been the pioneer in distance running shoes: the first to go nylon, first waffle soles, first ultra-wide heels.

○ *Puma* Ten years ago Puma was selling nearly as well as Adidas, but somehow this German company missed the recent growth of running. They have now reentered the market with a shoe called the Easy Rider.

○ *Tiger* When this Japanese company appeared in the United States a dozen years ago, theirs became a cult shoe for what was then a cult sport. Recently, though, Tiger's primary emphasis has been in racing flats and spikes.

Other top quality brands which don't yet have the sales of the above shoes, and hence are more difficult to get, are:

Braun
Mitre
Osaga
Patrick
Pony
Reebok
Saucony
Tred 2
Uniroyal

Q **Where can I find the quality brand shoes?**

A   You can find them in almost any sporting goods store. In recent years running specialty shops have opened throughout the country, but mostly on the coasts and in metropolitan areas. The Athlete's Foot and Athletic Attic are two national chain stores almost certain to carry most brands.

With the recent boom in running, many department stores now stock top brand shoes. The risk here, though, is that department store salespeople often don't have the shoe knowledge sporting goods store people have.

Q   **How much do these top shoes cost?**

A   The least amount of money you can pay for a good shoe is twenty dollars, as in the case of the Brooks Villanova or Saucony Hornet. The common price range is 25 to 35 dollars. Shoes with special features, like nylon mesh, ultra flared heels and studded soles, are the most expensive. The Nike LD-1000V, which has all those features, is the single most expensive training flat at forty dollars.

There are two ways of beating the prices, if you are willing to look hard and are persistent. One way is to search the market for sales. Sale priced shoes are usually closeout models, but if they have the features you want, and if they feel good on your feet, buy them. There is nothing wrong with a model one or two years old.

The second way is to find colorflawed models which, say, are murky orange shoes that are supposed to be red. Last year I bought a pair of colorflawed Nikes for fifteen dollars.

Q   **What about extra features like nylon mesh and ultra wide heels. Are they worth the added price?**

A   Nylon mesh is a good product. It is lighter, stronger, and cooler than nylon tricot. If the increased price discourages you, wait a year or two. Like the transistor radio and ball-point pen, its price is coming down with increased competition. Brooks already sells a nylon mesh shoe for 28 dollars. The original mesh shoes, the Adidas Runner and the Nike LD-1000, are still ten dollars more.

Flared heels were introduced in the Adidas Country in 1974, and Nike took the idea to extremes in 1976 with the original LD-1000, which sported a heel four inches wide. A flared heel adds stability. However, ultra-wide flares add so much stability that natural footplant, which is *supposed* to have a few degrees of internal roll, is restricted. Nike has since cut the flare on the LD-1000 to reasonable width. Any top shoe you buy today has adequate heel flair.

Q **Is there any real difference among the top shoe brands?**

A Sure, there are differences, but usually in features, fit, and, of course, the identifying mark. In terms of quality control the differences are slight, and vary among the shoes from model to model and year to year.

Q ***Runner's World* magazine annually ranks the top twenty shoes. Is it possible to name one shoe the best?**

A If you invent a grading system, it is possible to assign one shoe more points than the others. It's important here to understand how the *Runner's World* survey works.

To begin with, the *Runner's World* survey considers only top quality shoes. For every shoe appearing in their survey, a dozen more have been rejected.

Secondly, the shoes are sent to a laboratory where they are comparatively ranked in sole durability, flexibility, heel impact, forefoot impact, and lateral strength.

Thirdly, the shoes are subjected to the opinions of ten people well versed in running shoe knowledge. Each panel member ranks the shoes in order of preference, after first looking at them, bending them, trying them on, and wearing them around the testing room.

For the sake of argument, say there is a panel member who wears size 10 C. This member may choose an Adidas shoe simply because Adidas shoes are built on a narrower last than Tiger or Brooks. On the other hand, a panel member with a triple E width may choose New Balance because it is the only shoe that fits.

Q **In other words, a panel member is largely influenced by what feels best.**

A   That's right. And the opinions of these ten people are weighed equally
       with the laboratory results. The result is the *Runner's World* shoe
       survey.

Q   **Well, that's not very scientific.**

A   No, but *you* don't want to be too scientific, either, when you buy your
       shoes. Like each panel member on the *Runner's World* survey, you'll be
       influenced by what feels best as you wear each shoe around the store.
       That's perfectly good. You should be influenced by what feels best on
       your feet. (Note: For 1978 *Runner's World* plans to rank shoes in five
       general categories, rather than in numerical order.)

Q   **I was almost ready to buy my first pair of shoes. Now I'm more
       confused than ever.**

A   Don't be. Any of the top quality shoes could be the right pair for you
       provided 1) they have the features you want, 2) the cost is right, and 3)
       they feel "just right" as you wear them around the store.

       So, here is how to buy your first pair of shoes: Go to your nearest
       sporting goods store. Try on as many top brand shoes as you can. Wear
       them around the store. Ask the salesperson if you can jog (ugh!) around
       the block in the new shoes. If the salesperson says no, ask the store
       manager. Always go to the top in these matters. Promise the store
       manager you won't get the new shoes dirty. After you've personally
       tested several pairs, make your choice based on what felt the best. Not
       very scientific, but that is still the best way to buy shoes.

                            *   *   *

Q   **How long does a pair of running shoes last?**

A   The soles of your running shoes are normally the first area to wear out. If
       you wear your shoes only when you run, as you should, the soles should
       last up to a thousand miles on pavement, more if you run on dirt, and
       much longer if you run on grass.

       The uppers should outwear the soles. People who run on their toes, such
       as sprinters, are much harder on uppers than distance runners, who

usually land on their heels. Also, people who lace their shoes tightly run the risk of breaking through the eyelets.

Q   **When the soles wear out, should I try to repair them, or should I buy new shoes?**

A   If you've kept the uppers in good shape, and you are otherwise satisfied with the shoe, then by all means have the soles repaired.

If the entire sole is shot, you can take the shoes to an athletic shoe retreading center, and get the original soles replaced for 12 to 15 dollars, or about half the price of a new pair. There aren't very many retreading centers in the country, but they will do work by mail order. The addresses of such places are included in the last chapter.

If only a part of the sole is worn, such as the heel, you can have it repaired at any shoe repair shop for about five or six dollars. Make sure the cobbler uses material the same consistency as the original sole. This is important. Material harder or softer than the original sole will upset the shoe's balance.

Shoe glue, a glue and latex concoction available at most sporting goods stores, is okay for very minor repairs. Use shoe glue only when less than ⅛" of the sole needs repairing. Shoe glue never dries the consistency of the original sole, and major shoe glue repairs will only upset the balance of the shoe. The best way to use shoe glue is to apply a razor thin layer to the worn part every fifty miles.

Q   **Should I wear socks with my running shoes?**

A   That's a matter of choice. Try both ways, and choose what is most comfortable. Socks were almost a necessity back in the days of leather shoes, because leather chafed all but the toughest feet. With nylon shoes, many prefer to run sockless, especially in warmer weather.

Q   **What are the advantages of running sockless?**

A   Running sockless gives the runner better contact with the shoe, which is a feeling many find preferable. Also, running sockless is cooler.

There are disadvantages to running without. This practice can cause blisters in runners whose feet haven't been toughened sufficiently. Running sockless is also bad for the shoe, since the shoe directly absorbs the sweat. In time, this can cause problems for anyone within fifty feet of the old shoes.

One way to preserve your shoes (and friends) is to buy a washable insole for the shoe. Spenco makes a green blister repellent insole (for three dollars) that's quite popular among sockless runners. Simply handwash the insole once a week.

If you like to wear socks, but find them too warm or bulky, then try a pair of ankleless socks, or footies. Companies make them especially for runners, for men and women. These are available at most sporting goods stores.

Q   **Do the top running shoes come in widths?**

A   Only about half of the top brands at this time come in more than one width. The one-width shoes, like Tiger and Nike, are lasted on a men's D width. Adidas is slightly more narrow — between a C and D. Brooks, Converse and Etonic are now available in three widths: narrow (B-C), medium (D) and wide (E-EE). If you do not fall within these boundaries, you should seek a shoe with unusual widths.

Q   **Who makes such widths?**

A   New Balance built its reputation on its unusual widths, from AA to EEEE. They claim to offer 168 sizes, all of which are readily available.

Maybe now that this country has more than 23 million runners, the other shoe companies will find it profitable to start meeting the demands of those with unusually narrow or wide feet.

Q   **Does any company make women's shoes?**

A   Most of the major companies make women's shoes, if they don't already make variable widths. Adidas, Tiger and Nike make women's shoes, which are lasted on a women's B width. Brooks, Converse and Etonic make shoes in narrow widths which many women might find fitting. Of course, New Balance has always made shoes to fit women.

*   *   *

Q   **What can you tell me about running clothes? What kind of running shorts should I wear?**

A   You should consider two things when buying running shorts. First, decide how you want them cut. You can buy running shorts cut in the traditional boxer style or in the new and briefer style cut at crotch level. The briefer shorts are more comfortable, but only if you feel comfortable wearing them in public. Don't buy a pair of running shorts without first unfolding them and observing how they are cut.

The second thing to consider is material. Traditional material is cotton. This is the cheapest; you can find cotton gym trunks for two, three or four dollars. The disadvantage of cotton is that it gets heavy and droopy when damp with sweat. Another disadvantage is chafing in the groin area.

Another material is a half cotton, half polyester stretch fabric, commonly found in tennis shorts. These running shorts cost from four to six dollars. When wet, this material stays light and holds its form better than cotton. However, it chafes as badly as cotton.

A third material, and very popular among runners, is nylon shell, the same kind of nylon used in windbreaker jackets. This material is light, non-chafing, and quick to dry. The price range is three to six dollars.

The newest and most expensive material used in running shorts is nylon tricot, a limp, silky nylon. Nylon tricot is extremely light, non-chafing, and dries as quickly as it becomes damp. Nylon tricot shorts cost from eight to ten dollars and are cut in the briefest style. They are available at most running stores. Among the manufacturers of these shorts are Dolphin and Adidas. Frank Shorter Sports, Starting Line Sports, Phidippides, Sub 4, Athlete's Foot stores and Athletic Attic stores all sell their own versions of this fashionable pair of shorts.

Q   **Should men runners wear athletic supporters?**

Training shoes vary little among top brands.

Fashion in racing clothes.

Brief or Boxer: you choose.

A   I did once in high school, and never will again. Jocks are the worst chafers known. The best support for men is a simple pair of cotton or nylon briefs. Some of the newer running shorts come with in-lined supporters. These are fine, but washing machines have a way of ruining in-lined supporters.

Q   **Should women wear a bra?**

A   As Dr. Joan Ullyot has informed me, most women who normally wear a B-cup or larger need to wear a bra while running. Since chafing can be a problem, Dr. Ullyot recommends a one-piece nylon or cotton-polyester model which are commonly worn under leotards. Danskin currently makes such a bra.

For women who want support, but don't like bras, a one piece swimsuit or ballet suit is suggested. Simply wear a pair of shorts over the bottom. This may be the women's competition uniform of the future, by the way.

Q   **What material and cut should the shirt be?**

A   For your everyday runs, a simple cotton tee shirt is the best, and is what most everyone, from beginning jogger to Olympic runner, wears. Unlike the shorts, you want the shirt to get damp, for this is how the body cools itself. A nylon tee shirt would have a greenhouse effect.

In hot weather, men don't need to wear any shirt, unless you embarrass or sunburn easily.

For competition, a loosely fitting nylon tricot tank top is good. You can buy them cheapest, for three or four dollars, in a men's underwear department.

Better, but more expensive, is a two piece affair with nylon tricot shoulder straps and a mesh body. This combines the best qualities of lightness and ventilation. These shirts cost from ten to fifteen dollars, and are available from Athletic Attic (Marty Liquori Sportswear), Frank Shorter Sports, and Starting Line Sports.

Q   **Why is there such a wide price range among warmup suits?**

A   Like shoes, it depends on quality. Unlike shoes, the price of warmup suits also depends on fashion. You can buy a fully functional grey cotton sweatsuit for as little as ten dollars. Or you can spend 70 dollars for Adidas glossies, the suit worn by the 1976 United States Olympic team.

Even fashion designer Oleg Cassini plans to design a warmup suit. So, there is really no limit on what you can spend. A good nylon and polyester warmup suit can still be had for thirty dollars. Check your local sporting goods store. Warmup suits frequently go on sale.

Q   **Do I need a warmup suit?**

A   We will discuss that in a later chapter.

Just like home – a balanced meal is still the best.

CHAPTER EIGHT

What You Eat Matters, Too

Q **Do I need to follow a special diet for running?**

A There is no "special" diet you need to follow, but for optimum health, which will undoubtedly help your running, you should pay heed to a few guidelines established over the years by nutritionists, mothers and a few top athletes.

○ *Eat A Balanced Diet* To satisfy the body's needs, a diet must provide all of the essential nutrients, which include proteins, fats, carbohydrates, vitamins, minerals and water.

To satisfy the nutrient requirement you must eat a balanced diet, since no one food, not milk, eggs, meats, grains, or any fruits and vegetables provides everything you need. Nutritionists say the easiest and surest way to satisfy the nutrient requirement is to eat daily from the four basic food groups.

1. *Milk Group* Milk and milk products are the chief source of calcium. In addition, the milk group is a rich source of protein, vitamin A, vitamin D, most of the B vitamins, and fat.

   It must be noted here, though, that most adults with a Middle Eastern, Asian or African heritage cannot tolerate milk or its products. More on this later.

2. *Meat Group* This is the main source of protein, and includes red meat, poultry, fish, eggs, vegetable proteins like beans, and nuts.

   It is also the main source of the entire vitamin B complex, which includes iron, and is essential for cell growth and maintenance.

   On the bad side, the meat group is the biggest source of cholesterol, the blood fat which slowly clogs the arteries and veins. The biggest offenders are cooked egg yolks and red meat, and for that

71

reason both of those foods should be eaten no more than twice a week. Poultry and fish are less expensive than beef, pork or lamb anyway. Give both your blood vessels and checkbook relief.

3. *Cereals and Grains* This group is a well-known source of carbohydrates and a surprisingly good source of proteins and B vitamins.

White bread and processed cereals are not the villains they are made out to be, because most of them, by law, are enriched with the same B vitamins and proteins taken out during the processing. However, untampered whole grain products are still better because they also provide a rich source of fiber. I stopped eating white bread the day a friend balled up a slice in his hand and told me that is how white bread looks in the intestines.

4. *Fruits and Vegetables* This is a primary source of vitamin C, and a good source of vitamin A, minerals, bulk and roughage, and carbohydrates.

Unfortunately, when a typical American pocketbook tightens, vegetables and especially fruits are the first to be discarded from the diet. This is nutritional stupidity. Red meats cost far more and do much less for you than a plentiful supply of fruits and vegetables.

Here are two things to remember about fruits and vegetables: All are good, but fresh is better than canned or frozen, and undercooked is better than overcooked. In fact, the cooking juice of vegetables contains the most vitamins and minerals and was once thought to be an elixir. Maybe it is.

○ *Eat Plenty of Bran and Roughage* A hundred years ago this didn't have to be said. Even if people had an inadequate supply of fruit and vegetable roughage, they still had lots of whole grain, which is high in bran fiber.

Simply put, if you eat a typical American diet of bacon and eggs, white bread, gooey desserts and lots of meat, you are going to be constipated a great deal of your life. And chronic constipation causes far greater damage than headaches, stuffiness and orneriness. Unmoved bowels are a breeding ground for viral infection, intestinal ulcers, and even intestinal cancers.

Eat plenty of fruits and vegetables and buy only those breads and cereals with high fiber contents. Cure constipation with a proper diet, not with chemical laxatives.

○ *Don't Stuff Yourself* Worse than the American diet is the American tendency to chow down and pig out at the dinner table. Babe Ruth is one of our biggest heroes, but he was also a boor who sometimes ate a dozen hot dogs between games of a doubleheader. This was not heroic or even comical. It was only foolish, and it helped send Ruth to his death at age 53. Millions still follow his example. Don't you.

○ *Drink Plenty of Fluids* Drink minimally a glass of fluid every two hours, and double that if the weather is hot. A liberal fluid intake helps flush the toxins of food additives from our system. It also helps regularity.

Q   **If I want to reduce my caloric intake, what foods should I cut?**

A   First, cut out all of the nutritionally bogus foods — soft drinks, alcohol (which isn't a food at all), ice cream, desserts, donuts, Ding Dongs, and Ho Hos, or anything not true to the four basics.

If you've done that and still want to reduce, then cut equally from the four basics. Don't cut just protein or carbohydrates; remove your 500 calories, or whatever, by eating smaller portions of everything. This way you can be assured of maintaining your balanced diet. We will discuss weight reduction further in the next chapter.

Q   **What if you need to add calories to maintain weight?**

A   Then the smart way is to add equally from the four basic food groups.

Even though I say that, when I was in high school and college, and in the enviable position of having to consume 4000-5000 calories daily just to maintain my humble 135 pounds, I usually piled on the carbohydrates, most of them nutritionally bankrupt, like ice cream and beer. I was already eating three balanced meals a day (planned by mom or Stanford), so I had an adequate supply of essential nutrients. As additional calories, the beer and ice cream probably neither helped nor hurt my health and running.

Today, my diet is back to 2500-3000 calories a day, and I stick pretty closely to the four basics. If I again start running the voluminous mileage to rationalize a diet of more than 3000 calories, I probably will again ignore my own advice and line up at the trough for beer and ice cream.

Q   **What do the top runners eat?**

A   The top distance runners of this country eat more or less typically American diets, which is to say bad. Let's take an amusing but true look at the three marathoners who represented the United States Olympic team in Montreal.

Frank Shorter, the 1972 Olympic marathon champion and 1976 runner-up, says he eats only one balanced meal a day, which is dinner. He says he doesn't have time for other meals because he runs two or three times a day. So instead he munches, whenever he can, on cereals, breads, donuts, cheeses, pretzels — whatever suits his fancy and is convenient. In the evenings, after dinner, he sips on beer. Shorter says his daily caloric intake is between 2000-2500, which is extremely low for a man who trains 15 to 25 miles daily.

Bill Rodgers, currently the best marathoner in the world, eats a lot of pizza and ice cream according to his coach, Billy Squires. And Rodgers himself says he eats everything but large pieces of steak and other red meats. To supplement his diet, Rodgers takes one multi-vitamin pill and drinks large quantities of pure fruit juice.

According to a letter he wrote to *Track and Field News* in late 1974, Don Kardong, who finished fourth in the 1976 Olympic marathon, eats Froot Loops for breakfast, peanut butter sandwiches and cookies for lunch, and pizza and beer for dinner. Something of a Mark Fidrych of marathoning, the ebullient Kardong claims his diet totals more than 5000 calories daily.

So there you have it. Beer, pizza, ice cream, presweetened cereal and packaged donuts — the sustenance of champions.

Learn to run away from the fast food joints.

How can this happen? What justice is there if America's three top distance runners can gobble junk food and still run longer and faster than anyone?

The answer is a paradoxical truth of diet and running. The more miles you run, the more dubious aliment you can toss in your stomach, or to put it another way, the incinerator. Because any food or near food is quickly burned as fuel in the man or woman running 10-25 miles a day. It will not linger, rot or inflict gastronomical distress as it will in the man or woman who runs little or not at all. This is true of all culinary crud, be it Ding Dongs, Ho Hos or Milwaukee's finest — alcohol does not accumulate as poison in the liver of an active distance runner. It quickly burns as fuel.

We have always been told that an athlete has to watch his diet more closely than a non-athlete. Perhaps athletes *do* watch their diets more closely, just as they watch all their bodily functions more closely. But the fact is, athletes can get away with eating junk, at least more than a sedentarian can.

Because bad food doesn't hurt the top distance runners, don't quickly conclude that it helps them, either. The way to think of the whole diet question is: You can't go wrong by eating right, but you may go wrong by eating poorly. And the less you run, the more this is true.

And who really knows if those eating poorly now won't indeed have a day of judgment in the future. Who can say for sure that all the additives of Ding Dongs and Froot Loops, and all the cholesterol of pizza and ice cream won't come back to haunt the Shorters, Rodgers and Kardongs later in their lives.

In fact, maybe I will heed my own advice the next time I train sufficiently to rationalize a high caloric intake. Maybe I'll trade the beer for freshly squeezed apple juice, and ice cream for deliciously ripened papaya.

Q **Does an active athlete require more protein than a non-athlete?**

A High protein diets are both useless and wasteful for anyone. Because muscle is largely protein, we mistakenly conclude we have to eat the muscle of a cow or pig to maintain our own. This is, of course, as silly as thinking we can increase our intelligence by eating the brain of a cow or pig.

Protein is an essential nutrient — without it none of your cells could reproduce, and you would soon perish. But the amount of protein you need daily, even if you're an athlete, is far lower than even the bad American diet contains.

The National Research Council's Recommended Daily Requirement of protein is only 40 grams. Satisfying this requirement with a normal balanced diet of 3000 calories is easy — a good American balanced diet as prescribed by nutritionists contains more than 100 grams of protein.

The minimum of 40 grams is ridiculously easy to attain in this overfed republic. A quart of enriched milk has 40 grams. So do three large eggs. So does just eight ounces of steak, since steak contains about five grams an ounce. So does a loaf of enriched white or natural whole grain bread. And that's enough for the whole day.

Q   **But surely an athlete needs more protein than in one quart of milk
. . .**

A   This is currently being argued among athletes, coaches and nutritionists,
and with no conclusive proof, one way or the other.

I can think of one reason why long distance runners might require more
than the minimum just to stay safe. Every time you run more than 18
miles and deplete your supply of glycogen, you begin to feed off of your
own fats, and to a smaller extent, proteins. So of course your replacement needs would be more than the standard turnover. More on this
later.

The point is, even if you need a little more protein, a good balanced diet
will comfortably assure you of your needs. Any protein over your
personal requirements is either used as energy or stored as fat — the
same as any other food.

Q   **What foods provide the most energy?**

A   All foods — carbohydrates, fats and proteins — can provide energy to
the working muscles, but only when they are reduced by the body into
the two usable sugars, glucose and fructose.

1. *Carbohydrates* Carbos are the primary source of muscle energy,
because they can most quickly be reduced to glucose. Simple
carbohydrates, like honey (which is glucose and fructose isolated)
are ready for immediate use and therefore give the quickest lift.
Table sugar and candies (which is sucrose — glucose and fructose
bonded) are next as available sources of energy.

Complex carbohydrates are slower sources of energy — the
body's process of breaking them down to glucose or fructose takes
a bit longer. Complex carbohydrates include cereals and grains,
fruits and vegetables, and the lactose in milk and its products.

Complex carbohydrates are infinitely better for athletes. They are
stored in the liver as a complex sugar, glycogen, and released as
the simple sugar, glucose, in regulated amounts as the muscles call
for it. Because the flow of glucose is regulated by the liver there is

no chance of hyperglycemia (too much blood sugar), which is always followed by an insulin reaction, which then results in hypoglycemia (not enough blood sugar).

Yet it is just this roller coaster ride of energy and depression that you will feel if you eat a lot of simple carbohydrates.

The liver can store enough glycogen to feed the muscles for about 20 miles of running. After that, the primary source of energy becomes fat.

2. *Fat* During aerobic running, glycogen supplies 75 percent of the muscle energy — fats supply the rest. When the liver runs out of glycogen, fats become the primary energy source.

The body stores fat in three different places — around the organs, underneath the skin, and within the muscles.

Fat stored around the organs is necessary protection, something like the foam rubber in a box of glass panes.

Fat stored underneath the skin — the flabby stomach — is unnecessary beyond a small percentage. The rest is excess baggage, and won't do much good besides keeping you warm and afloat should your plane ditch in the North Sea.

Fat stored within the muscle can be a source of energy. It is a startling fact that lean marathon runners have more fat within the muscles than does a typical professional wrestling fan. The muscles of a Bill Rodgers contain 20 percent fat, compared with the 10 percent of an untrained person. The marathoner's double in-muscle fat levels are a result of training consistently beyond the point of glycogen depletion, and not a result of double ingestion of fats.

Like carbohydrates, fat is converted to energy when mixed with oxygen and reduced to usable sugars. The breakdown of fats to sugar is about eight times slower than the breakdown of carbohydrates to sugar. A fisherman, who doesn't need a large and steady flow of energy, depends on fat as the primary source of energy. He can wait for the slower breakdown process. A runner, though, uses carbohydrates as the primary source and fats as the backup system. When the carbohydrates are gone, fat is the new primary and protein becomes the backup.

3. *Proteins* Protein is the third and most cumbersome and inefficient source of energy, which is why a prerace meal of steak and eggs is of little use. The breakdown of protein to energy happens only when glycogen is depleted and fat can't keep up with the energy demands. What happens is the body's cells actually start self-destructing.

Evidence of cellular breakdown in a marathon is an abnormally long recovery period — a month is often required to fully recover from a marathon. Longer races take still more time.

Tom Fleming, who finished fifth in the 1976 United States Olympic Trials, says he doesn't have to shave the day following a well-run marathon. He theorizes he has exhausted the body's reserves of proteins and doesn't have any left to grow hair. If ever one requires a big juicy steak, it is *after* a marathon, not before.

Q   **What is a good prerace meal, then?**

A   A good prerace meal is one you are familiar with, light and easily digestible, and consisting primarily of complex carbohydrates.

Long a favorite breakfast of Boston Marathon runners is toast and porridge (although we call it oatmeal in the rest of the country). This is cheap, available in any kitchen or 24-hour truck stop, and satisfies all the requirements of a good prerace meal.

Pancakes and waffles are similarly good, but I personally don't eat them before a race, because I like great quantities of milk to wash down the syrup, but don't like to drink milk before a race.

Fruits and vegetables, although rich in complex carbohydrates, should be avoided before a race or hard training run because of the gastric upset they are likely to cause.

Q   **You said you don't like to drink milk. Why not?**

A   Actually, I love to drink milk, but shun it before a race or hard training run for a couple of reasons. One, milk is, besides water, largely protein and fat, neither of which is easily digestible, and which are in fact quite useless as an energy source. My body has all the fats and proteins it currently needs, so any food that is not a carbohydrate is useless weight I have to carry during the run.

Secondly, although I normally tolerate the milk sugar lactose very well, I have trouble digesting it during extreme physical efforts, like a race.

In fact, many adult Americans cannot tolerate lactose very well under any circumstances. As Dr. George Sheehan has pointed out in his books and in numerous *Runner's World* articles, about a fifth of all Europeans and a majority of Asians, Blacks, Jews, Arabs and native Indians of the Western Hemisphere should not drink milk as adults. These people do not have within their bodies the enzyme lactase, which digests lactose. Since the lactose remains undigested in the stomach it draws fluid into the stomach and causes cramping, according to Sheehan.

Even the minority of adults who can tolerate milk should, like myself, avoid it before hard efforts, since the lactose is still digested very slowly.

Q   **What other foods should I avoid before a race?**

A   Avoid fats and proteins — the worst prerace meal imaginable is bacon and fried eggs (yet how sadly typical!). Also avoid large quantities of simple carbohydrates, like sugar on the cereal or candy bars, since they will cause the inevitable insulin reaction and resulting hypoglycemia by the time you toe the starting line. And also avoid fruits and vegetables, which will perform acrobatics in your stomach.

Obviously you might have to fudge a little for convenience. I mean, try to think of oatmeal without milk. Just use common sense, don't stuff, and give yourself plenty of time between eating and racing.

Q   **How long before the race should I eat my last meal?**

A   Three hours is the minimum time you should allow yourself. Four to six hours is safer.

Q   **How should I eat before a regular day's training?**

A   Eat whatever you wish, and give yourself three hours if the meal was
      light, and four to five hours if the meal was heavy and contained a lot of
      meat. Unless you are planning on an unusually long and hard run don't
      upset your normal eating patterns for running. If every meal is planned
      around running, you are sacrificing, and that will kill your interest in
      running quicker than anything will.

Q   **Let's get back to prerace eating. What should I eat the day before
      the race?**

A   For races less than 18-20 miles your normal diet should give you all the
      glycogen you need. Just don't eat a big steak or roast the night before.
      Take two potatoes instead.

      For longer races you should eat a carbohydrate-rich diet for two or three
      days preceding the race. You might want to substitute your meat and
      potatoes dinner with lasagna and garlic bread, or your breakfast of bacon
      and eggs with cereals and pancakes. Don't eat anything terribly radical
      to upset your system, and don't add more calories. Just trade some of the
      protein and fat calories for carbohydrate calories. The idea is to saturate
      the liver with glycogen, so you won't be short of it during the race.

Q   **Is this what is meant by carbohydrate loading?**

A   Partially so. True carbohydrate loading is a dietary trick used to *super-
      saturate* the liver with glycogen, raising the level by 10-20 percent. A
      normally saturated liver contains enough glycogen energy for 18-20
      miles of running. With carbohydrate loading you can raise the depletion
      point to 22-24 miles. This obviously would help you in a 26 mile, 385
      yard marathon.

      Traditionally, a carbohydrate loading plan takes six days. If you want to
      load up for an important Saturday marathon, you would begin the plan
      on Sunday. On Sunday, Monday and Tuesday you train regularly while
      limiting your intake of carbohydrates to no more than 20 percent of your
      diet.

By Tuesday night you will have depleted most of your body's supply of glycogen and glucose. As a result you feel terrible, totally lacking in energy. The Tuesday run was probably completed with great difficulty. Then on Wednesday, Thursday and Friday you drastically reduce your training mileage, and increase your carbohydrate intake to 80 percent of your diet.

What happens is the starving liver overcompensates for the previous glycogen famine. Determined not to be short again, the liver packs in glycogen 20 percent beyond the normal saturation level.

Carbohydrate loading is of value only in races longer than 18-20 miles.

Q   **Then you recommend carbohydrate loading before marathons?**

A   No.

Q   **But why not? I mean, you just said that carbohydrate loading increases the glycogen supply . . .**

A   There are too many things that can go wrong with a carbohydrate loading diet.

For one, you may not fully recover from the depletion phase in time for the race. This happened to me the only time I tried carbohydrate loading. I had the expected blahs on Tuesday night, but never recovered as I should have by Saturday, and hence ran one of my worst races. I really don't know why the plan flopped but it sure did, and upon talking with others who have tried it, I found similarly bad results. The best laid laboratory plans don't always work in reality.

Secondly, I think you can attain the same effects by depleting not with a carbohydrate-less diet, but with a 15-18 mile run the Tuesday before the race. Then on Wednesday, Thursday and Friday you can cut your training to a couple of miles daily, and eat a high carbohydrate diet. This results in the same liver overcompensation, but without the risk of backfire.

This, in fact, is the method preferred by the top runners. Neither Bill Rodgers nor Frank Shorter deplete carbohydrates from their diet. They load by easing their training for a few days before the marathon and letting their glycogen reserves build.

This is the method of loading I recommend.

*   *   *

Q **Would my running improve if I became a vegetarian?**

A There is no conclusive evidence that a properly regulated vegetarian diet either helps or hurts your running.

Yet I would suspect the value of a vegetarian diet increases as you grow older, and therefore might help your running performance later in life. Why? Because the accumulation of cholesterol in a vegetarian will be only two-thirds to a half of that of a meat eater. Since cholesterol lines the arteries and eventually restricts blood flow, a person with less accumulative cholesterol will have better blood circulation, and thus a better oxygen supply to the muscles.

Young runners, as a rule, won't have restricting cholesterol levels, even if they eat large quantities of meat, eggs and fried junk. But over a period of time, the difference between low cholesterol diets, like vegetarianism, and high cholesterol diets is quite apparent, even among runners.

In fact, Dr. Joan Ullyot says non-running vegetarians have lower blood cholesterol levels than do running meat eaters.

I think we can follow the principles of vegetarianism without embracing the practice wholeheartedly. The first thing everyone, runner or not, should do is reduce or cut entirely the intake of red meats — beef, pork and lamb.

In terms of cholesterol and saturated fat, even so-called lean steak is villainous — it is from one-half to two-thirds fat! Hamburger is even worse, although it is true you eat less of hamburger in one sitting. And pork is so bad that, well, can you honestly believe that eating a greasy strip of fried hog is good for you? If you do, take another look at bacon drippings the day after.

Another reason to avoid red meat is putrefaction. Red meat not only sits in the warm intestines longest of any food, but also putrefies the fastest, and becomes a breeding ground for viruses.

And still another reason to avoid red meat is the increasing use of chemical additives used to fatten cattle.

Q **Are poultry and fish as bad?**

A Not nearly so. If beef is a murderer, then poultry and fish are simple thiefs, which is why we can eat them and still keep our cholesterol levels nearly as low as a vegetarian's.

A very good runner's diet, and a good compromise between vegetarianism and meat eating, is the diet of Dr. Alex Ratelle, a St. Paul anesthesiologist who in 1977, at age 53, ran an astounding 2:35 marathon. Big Al eats less than 2500 calories a day, and avoids red meat, white sugar, desserts and coffee.

*   *   *

Q **What about not eating at all? Should runners try an occasional fast?**

A A one-day fast may not be a bad idea, but prolonged fasting is both silly and harmful. For one, it allows a toxic buildup of uric acid. And secondly, how can you repair your own cells without protein? Your body will slowly degenerate during a prolonged fast.

Fasting really has only two uses — to lose weight and cleanse the digestive system. Both of these can be accomplished without fasting.

Losing weight, as we will discuss in the next chapter, is best accomplished when we gradually lower the caloric intake and increase the caloric output. This method maintains our health and energy, and becomes habit over a period of time. Fasting can never become habit, except in the mentally ill, because it is self-destructive and ruinous to health.

As far as cleaning the digestive system, we do this perpetually if we eat a high fiber diet and drink plenty of fluids. Fasting as a purge is necessary only for those chronically constipated, which won't happen if we run and eat well.

*   *   *

Q **Should runners take vitamin supplements?**

A Medical opinion on vitamin supplements ranges from "the secret of health and longevity" to "preposterous quackery."

However, most nutritionists agree that a balanced diet will provide all of the essential vitamins and minerals. If the diet is adequate, no supplements are necessary.

If you accept the nutritionists' premise, three questions remain: 1) Should we take vitamin supplements if we suspect our diet is less than adequate? 2) Do runners need more vitamins than non-runners? 3) What happens if we take more vitamins than necessary?

Supplemental vitamins can never atone for a bad diet, since vitamins are not actually food, but food elements. They are not a substitute for proteins, carbohydrates and fats, and a diet lacking in those essential nutrients cannot be made good by vitamin supplements.

At the same time, it is possible in these days of fast foods and frozen pizzas to eat a diet full of proteins, carbohydrates and fats, and *still* be lacking in one or more of the vitamins and minerals. For that reason, *one* multivitamin pill taken daily may possibly help and certainly can't hurt you.

Q **Why just one multivitamin pill?**

A One multivitamin pill by itself satisfies nearly all of your minimum daily vitamin requirements. Here are the vitamins and their dosages listed on the label of a typical multivitamin pill bottle.

Each Tablet Contains		**% US RDA**
Vitamin A	10,000 Int. Units	200
Vitamin B-1	10 mg.	667
Vitamin B-2	10 mg.	588
Vitamin B-6	5 mg.	207
Vitamin B-12	10 mcg.	167
Niacinmide	100 mg.	500
Vitamin C	200 mg.	333

Vitamin D	400 Int. Units	100
Vitamin E	30 Int. Units	100
Calcium	20 mg.	183
Iodine	0.15 mg.	100
Iron	20 mg.	120
Copper	2 mg.	100
Manganese	1 mg.	**
Magnesium	200 mg.	50
Zinc	10 mg.	67

**US RDA not established

As you can see, one multivitamin pill really does it all.

Q **Can we overdose on vitamins?**

A Vitamin pills are second only to aspirin in childhood poisonings. In overdoses (more than 10 times the RDA), vitamins A and D are toxic, and have caused death on occasions.

The most overused vitamin, C, is commonly thought to be harmless in excess amounts, since the excess is discarded as waste by the body. Yet there is new evidence that shows large amounts of vitamin C causes kidney and bladder stones.

Q **But isn't vitamin C a cold preventative?**

A If not for the fact that history's only double Nobel laureate, Dr. Linus Pauling, didn't support that contention, I think the whole idea that vitamin C is a cold preventative would be dismissed as nonsense.

What C does is alleviate the symptoms of a cold, since in large doses vitamin C acts as an antihistamine. But whether or not it prevents colds has yet to be proven.

If you take a multivitamin pill daily, you certainly don't need more vitamin C. Or any other vitamin.

Q **Do runners need more vitamins?**

A   Numerous tests show that supplemental vitamins do not improve athletic performance. Neither does athletic participation make a special demand for supplemental vitamins. The whole idea is hogwash, but is filling the pockets of more than a few charlatans, who peddle their chemical alphabet on the back of muscle magazines, comic books, and now even *Runner's World*, since runners are proving to be no more suspicious of lies and hocus pocus than are body builders and folks who buy Florida land over the telephone.

Regarding vitamins, here are the comments of three people who know better than to overindulge. They also happen to be three of the most successful coaches in their sports.

Bill Bowerman, coach *emeritus* at the University of Oregon, is generally conceded to be the best distance running coach this country has ever had. Bowerman developed the hard-easy method of training; he was the head US Olympic coach in 1972; he has coached more sub-four-minute milers than anyone else has; and he was a consultant to *Aerobics*. This is what Bowerman says about vitamin pills:

Runners who take them have expensive urine.

James Councilman is the legendary swimming coach at the University of Indiana, where he tutored Mark Spitz and Gary Hall among others. Here is Councilman's opinion of vitamins:

I give my kids small amounts of vitamin C, even though I can prove it's useless. But if they think it makes them swim better, then I'll continue to give them small amounts.

And according to Bob Kiputh, who coached Don Schollander and several championship teams at Yale:

Forget about vitamins. They just detract from the business of swimming.

Perhaps marathoner Bill Rodgers has the best commonsense approach to vitamin taking. He daily takes one multivitamin pill as insurance, and says:

Since one can't hurt you, why take the chance of being low in any area?

         *   *   *

88

Pills and potions – a poor substitute for the real thing.

Q   **Is there any difference between synthetic and natural vitamin pills?**

A   The only difference for your concern is price. So-called natural vitamins
       are a rip-off, often costing five times that of synthetic vitamins, which
       are just as good.

Q   **What about wheat germ oil, bee pollen or liquid protein?**

A   All have been tested exhaustively, and none contribute to athletic
       performance. Liquid protein, which upsets the body's metabolism, is
       downright dangerous, and is in the process of being banned by the FDA.
       Like snake oil and megavitamins, these potions have no business in the
       life of an intelligent runner.

       We can even predict with some degree of accuracy how the next miracle
       food supplement will come into being. Some quack with a bogus degree
       from a mail order college will make a pilgrimage to a remote part of the
       world where people claim to live for 190 years. There he will talk to the
       oldest and wisest of all, the medicine man, who will on his dying
       194-year-old lips impart the secret of a long and healthy life, the milk of
       a duck-billed platypus in heat!

       The milk will then be brought back to the US, to a laboratory once
       occupied by a now defunct brewery, made into pills, and sold by the
       billions to the millions who have not yet used up their bee pollen.

Calories in minus calories out equals . . .

CHAPTER NINE

A Few Words About Weight Control

Q   **Is running a good way to lose weight?**

A   Running is an effective tool for carving pounds, but is not a quick panacea for obesity — it will not make a fat person thin overnight.

Anyone concerned about weight control should be aware of the following interrelationships:

○ *Basal Metabolism* Everyone expends calories at a different rate. Teenage males typically expend 3500 calories in a normal day, and thus need to eat 3500 calories to maintain body weight. A typical teenage female expends only 80 percent as much as her male counterpart — about 2800 calories a day. The basal metabolisms of both males and females drop as they get older.

○ *Pounds and Calories* One pound of body weight represents 3500 calories. So to gain or lose a pound you must have a net gain or net loss of 3500 calories.

○ *Running and Calories* Regardless of speed, running expends about 100 calories a mile for men, and about 80 a mile for women.

So losing weight through your running is strictly a mathematical problem. If you add five miles of running a day, and don't change your diet, you will lose a pound every week. Likewise, if you don't add any running, but remove 500 calories from your diet, you will also lose a pound every week.

Q   **A hundred calories per mile is less than I thought.**

A   The caloric cost of running really isn't much, at least not when compared with the caloric total of some familiar foods and drinks.

Drinks	Calories	Equivalent Miles
Beer, 12 ozs.	150	1.5
Cola, 12 ozs.	150	1.5
Fruit Juices, 12 ozs.	160	1.6
Whole Milk, 12 ozs.	240	2.4
Skim Milk, 12 ozs.	140	1.4
Milkshake, 12 ozs.	400	4.0
Foods		
Steak, 10 ozs.	1000	10.0
Hamburger, 5 ozs.	500	5.0
Frankfurter, average size	150	1.5
Fried Egg	100	1.0
Pizza, average slice	200	2.0
Baked Potato	100	1.0
with oz. of sour cream	200	2.0
Bread, slice	80	.8
Bun, hamburger	120	1.2
Cheddar Cheese, 3 ozs.	375	3.8
Candy Bar, 1 oz.	150	1.5
Cookie, average size	130	1.3
Ice Cream, 4 ozs.	150	1.5
Apple Pie, average slice	300	3.0

Q **In other words, if I drink two additional beers, I've ruined my three mile run?**

A Of course you haven't ruined your run, but you have put yourself back to square one in the calorie war.

Running is not as calorie expending as people think. One bottle of beer, one glass of apple juice, or one chocolate chip cookie is more calories than one mile of running.

An extra slice of apple pie with a scoop of ice cream completely gains back the calories expended in a five mile run.

As you can see, running is not a license to pork out at the dinner table, or even filch at the snack bar. Nor is it the secret to losing 30 pounds in a month.

Q **If I want to lose 30 pounds, how should I do it?**

A Sensibly.

And not in a month.

Seriously, if you want to take off *and keep off* 30 pounds, you want a reducing program you can easily incorporate into your lifestyle, and eventually want to make a habit of. You can do this only when the habit itself is appealing and conducive to good health.

Obviously a fast or any number of nutritionally quack diets aren't healthful, or even appealing. And they keep the pounds off only for as long as you maintain the miserable regimen, which you can't do indefinitely, because in time such preposterous diets will drive you to sickness and ruin.

Instead you need a sensible plan, one you can make habit of, and actually enjoy. Such is the plan of one pound a week.

To lose a pound a week you need to see a net calorie loss of 3500 a week, or 500 a day. If you fight the battle of your bulge on two fronts, with both running and diet, you stand a good chance of winning. If you run but two miles a day, and drop but 300 calories (that slice of apple pie!) from your daily intake, you've already won. Maintain this steady plan five days a week for nine months and you'll have lost 30 pounds.

At the end of the nine months you can move up to three miles a day *and* start eating a slice of apple pie again without regaining weight.

Q **Nine months to lose 30 pounds — that's pretty slow.**

A Not if you can keep it off the rest of your life. And this plan makes it easy to keep it off, because this plan becomes a positive part of your daily life, a pleasant habit you won't give up.

Q **What's the most we should try to lose?**

A   Two pounds a week is the most you can lose with a sensible plan. This means a net loss of 7000 calories a week or 1000 a day. To do this you would have to add five miles of running and drop 500 calories from your diet every day. Of course you could also drop 1000 calories (at quite a sacrifice), or run 10 miles (with great difficulty if you were so obese you needed to lose that much weight that quickly).

In terms of effort and that dreaded word sacrifice, losing two pounds a week is more than twice as hard as losing a pound a week. And there is a much greater chance that you'll quit in frustration. To steadily lose two pounds a week takes more than double the determination, also.

Q   **How can I tell if I need to lose weight?**

A   First off, forget about those puerile height and weight charts — what matters is your percentage of body fat. Pinch the skin underneath your upper arm. If the pinch is more than an inch thick, you need to lose weight, even if the chart labels you normal or thin. A six foot, 160 pounder can actually be quite fat.

Q   **You must be joking.**

A   Not at all.

The average American adult male is 15 percent fat; his female counterpart is 25 percent fat. Since the populace of the United States is largely overfed, underexercised, and hence fat, we will consider as ''needing to lose weight'' anyone higher than average, regardless of height and weight.

More than just thick skin folds, a high body fat index also means high levels of blood cholesterol, since the two correlate roughly. And as medical science has pointed out, a high cholesterol level indicates a future of cardiovascular trouble. The easiest way to tell if you need to lose weight is the forementioned pinch test. For men the pinch should not exceed an inch, and for women, an inch and a half. Skin folds thicker than that indicate a body fat index higher than the precarious national average.

Q   **What is my optimum racing weight?**

A   Some coaches say the optimum is two pounds for every inch — 5′10″ and 140 pounds — but again this is meaningless without knowing the body fat index. At optimum racing weight, males should have less than five percent body fat (Frank Shorter has two percent), and females less than 15 percent.

For younger runners, a low body fat level is easily attainable and mostly a result of high training mileage — 70 miles a week should keep a young runner lean enough.

Older runners, though, may have to count calories in addition to training hard if they want to achieve optimum racing weight. Fifty-three-year-old Alex Ratelle is a good example. The 5′7″ anesthesiologist was running marathons in the high 2:40s while training 70 miles a week and weighing 132 pounds. He assumed his body fat index was low, but a water buoyancy test showed he was close to 13 percent body fat — low enough for good health, but too high for premium racing.

To lose the excess baggage Ratelle cut red meat and desserts from his diet and increased his mileage to more than 100 a week. At a sleek 124 pounds Ratelle successfully dropped his marathon time to 2:35:43, the fastest marathon ever recorded by an over-50 American runner.

What Ratelle's case proves is that a wide range exists between a healthful and an optimum body fat index. Anything below the national average is good, but to race at your best you'll have to go much lower than that.

Q   **Is it easier to lose weight in hot weather?**

A   No. Water loss is not to be confused with calorie loss. The caloric expenditure of running is constant, regardless of weather.

This is why wearing a warmup suit in hot weather is actually counter-productive to losing weight. You overheat faster, abandon the run sooner, and thus expend less calories.

Rubberized sweatsuits and belly belts are worse than warmup suits, and are far more dangerous. You cannot melt fat from the body. You can reduce that flabby belly only with a net calorie loss.

Beer – an acceptable vice for the active runner.

CHAPTER TEN

Vices

Q **Should a runner drink coffee?**

A Open any health or diet book and you'll find a raging condemnation of coffee. Its caffeine causes hyperacidity in the stomach, raises the heart beat and blood pressure artificially, causes in many young people skin eruptions and zits, causes in every drinker a nervous rush of energy followed by a hangover of lingering depression; in brief, a roller coaster ride through your emotions which ends with a dash to the nearest urinal.

Add to the above that caffeine is mildly addicting. What used to be one cup in the morning is now three. When at one time you wouldn't drink coffee past six p.m. for fear of not sleeping, you now sip it while watching Johnny Carson. You no longer feel its euphoric rush, yet without it you can't get out of bed in the morning, much less function during the day.

Yet, who can live without the stuff? Who can think of looking out the window of a warm house on a rainy day without a cup of coffee in the hands? Who can think of waking up next to a Colorado mountain and its icy stream without the smell of coffee brewing on the campfire? How can you even open the morning paper, or finish off your toast, or drive across Nebraska, or stay awake through your pastor's Sunday sermon without coffee?

Alcohol addiction can bring you to ruin in a few years; heroin is faster than that. But the addiction to coffee is more of a kindergarten vice, like the telling of white lies — you tell them to avoid reality, and afterward feel let down. So it is with coffee. But then some runners, like Dr. George Sheehan, prefer the unending psycho-drama of coffee's ups and downs to the steady (and boring) predictability of no coffee at all.

And in all fairness, coffee does have one redeeming value. If you like to run with empty bowels, as you should, what swifter way to accomplish the preliminary task than by gulping a cup of coffee?

Q   **What is tea's effect on a runner?**

A   Tea is the world's most popular beverage. Its caffeine level can be more, but is usually less than coffee. American orange pekoe teas have from one-half to two-thirds the caffeine level of coffee.

Tea is a slower acting stimulation; its caffeine does not quickly elevate, then drop you as coffee's does. Nor is tea abrasive to the stomach and intestines; even ulcer patients can safely drink mild teas.

Yet despite tea's many exotic flavors, plus all the evidence it isn't as harmful as coffee, most Americans, including myself, persist in drinking coffee.

Coffee fits our American tastes. It is fast acting, powerful, briefly exciting, quickly obsolete, and it leaves you depressed and greedy for more.

Tea likewise fits the old Orient. It is slower acting, more respectful of the body, subtly lifting, lingering, and it leaves a warm and mellow glow.

For runners, neither coffee nor tea are especially good. Both drinks, tea more so, are mildly diuretic, which means they steal nearly as much body fluid as they add. Iced tea is actually a terrible hot weather drink, since the net fluid gain is low. Drink it only because you like its taste, and not if you need a lot of fluids.

Q   **What about colas?**

A   Colas are the other major caffeine drink we Americans soak up. As a fluid replacement, colas are better than coffee or tea, since colas are not diuretic. But in all other considerations, colas are worse.

While coffee and tea have no calories, colas, rich with sugars, syrups, caramels and food colorings, have as many calories as beer — about 150 per 12 ounce bottle.

Colas are similar to another household item, not found in the re-
frigerator, but in your woodworking shop. Like sandpaper, colas can
quickly erode your teeth.

*   *   *

Q   **On the other side of the coin, what are the effects of depressants, like
alcohol?**

A   From a nutritional standpoint, pure alcohol is not a food, but a poison
full of empty calories.

Yet alcohol is consumed regularly by 80 million Americans, including
the author.

What role does alcohol play in the life of an active runner?

In recent years the world's top distance runners have hauled their
drinking habits out of closet. Herb Elliott, the great Australian miler of
the 1950s, was one of the first to admit he enjoyed occasional noggins of
ale, but then Elliott was ahead of his time in most everything, especially
in his training and results (Elliott trained naked on a remote beach and
ran a world record 3:54.5 mile in 1958).

Elliott was succeeded by another Australian world record-holder, Ralph
Doubell (800 meters in 1:44.3) who casually remarked he liked to get
drunk on airplanes and "stinkered" with his coach every two weeks.

Meanwhile, the United States failed to provide the world with a drink-
er's hero. Part of it was the teetotaling example of Jim Ryun, but most of
it was the teddybear notion that US athletes were free from vices. When
Marty Liquori admitted to drinking beer before the 1968 Olympic
Trials, some coaches threatened to kick Liquori out of training camp.
And the newspapers wrote derisive stories headlined: Liquori Gets His
Kicks From A Sixpack.

Then in 1972 a new wet-whistled hero, who looked like a sixties
anti-hero, emerged and not only admitted to drinking great quantities of
beer, even the night before Olympic marathons, but also to "popping a
gin now and then." He was an American named Frank Shorter.

The running fold quickly followed Shorter out of the closet, and now beer is being touted by nearly every running notable, including Dr. George Sheehan, who himself drank six beers *during* the 1977 Boston Marathon. And beer is now the official post race beverage at the Honolulu Marathon.

Q   **You mean beer might be good for runners?**

A   If you enjoy beer you can find many ways of rationalizing its use. Some ways actually might benefit runners.

○ *Beer As Carbohydrate Loading* Frank Shorter drank two liters of heavy German beer the night before he won the 1972 Olympic marathon. I once ran 52 miles after a night of copious beer drinking. Dr. Sheehan knows an exercise physiologist who found people ran farthest and fastest on a treadmill after a night of drinking beer.

What all of us have found is that drinking beer, at 150 calories a bottle (or 900 a sixpack) is an effective way of sneaking extra carbohydrate calories into the body without upsetting the digestive system or adding the weight of solid food.

○ *Beer As Instant Energy* Like a combustible engine, the working muscles can actually use pure alcohol as energy. This is one of Sheehan's reasons for drinking beer at Boston.

○ *Beer As An Electrolyte Replacement Drink* This is Sheehan's other reason, and one reason why beer is served as a post race drink at the Honolulu Marathon. Beer has a salt and mineral balance somewhat like the sweat you lose in a run.

○ *Beer As A Muscle Relaxant* The race directors at the Honolulu Marathon found nothing relieves the post marathon muscle cramps as swiftly and effectively (and enjoyably) as beer.

As a sort of proof that the above are true is beer's use as an overtraining preventative. When I am training too hard for my own good and feel on the brink of overstress, I'll drink three or four beers (as fluid replacement), go to sleep for ten hours (muscle relaxant), take the next day off and drink more beer (carbohydrate loading) and always feel strong and refreshed by the following day (energy).

Q **What about wines and hard liquor?**

A Percy Cerutty, who was Herb Elliott's coach, advocated drinking a small (four ounce) glass of wine with meals. He argued that wine drinking would speed along the digestive process. Whether you believe that or not, a small amount of table wine can't do much harm.

On the other hand, hard liquors won't be recommended at all in this book. They are strongly diuretic and it is too easy to overdose on them because they don't fill your stomach as beer does. And who can really admit to enjoying the taste of pure alcohol? Don't you inwardly repulse at the smell of vodkas and whiskeys?

No matter what you drink, don't get drunk. Aren't you past that stage? And never, ever, get behind the wheel of a car if you are at all tipsy.

Q **What effect does smoking marijuana have on running?**

A In a thousand users, marijuana induces a thousand different reactions, from euphoria to paranoia, from sexual excitement to sleepiness. Its direct effect upon running is medically unknown at this time, but athletes who have smoked dope and then run say they feel a lack of concentration, an inability to run more than a mile or two simply because so many other things seem interesting.

As with alcohol 20 years ago, none of the top athletes seem willing to talk about their grass usage. Does this mean the top athletes don't use marijuana? Far from it — many younger athletes use it as commonly as beer.

Among dope smoking runners I have known are world record holding sprinters, sub-four minute milers and sub 2:20 marathoners. The distance runners, though, use it more sparingly, like once or twice a month. They don't feel the drug itself is especially harmful — they dislike having to *smoke* the stuff to get high. Which, I think, is one of the three best arguments against its common usage.

○ *Smoking* The way most people get high on grass is to inhale its smoke and hold it in the lungs for as long as possible. What makes it worse is that most joints, pipes and bongs are not filtered — look at the filth and grime left as residue in your pipe. Do you want your lungs to look like that?

○ *Long Term Effects* The effects of lifelong marijuana smoking still aren't known, although heavy smokers may sustain permanent brain damage, as they do in the Tangiers hashish pits. What if the tars and other leftover filth turn out to be as carcinogenic as tobacco? Or asbestos?

○ *Paraquat* Did you know the United States Government has spent 40 million dollars spraying Mexican marijuana (America's biggest source) with a poisonous substance called paraquat, which in a brief time inflicts permanent lung damage in the smoker? Paraquat is believed to have caused one death already, to a young high school baseball star. Apparently there are some people in this country who think death or mutilation is the proper penalty for smoking something currently known to be less harmful than alcohol.

Q   **What about smoking cigarettes?**

A   I am not going to waste my efforts telling you about the effects of smoking cigarettes. You smokers have been a lifelong inconvenience to me — now I'll be an inconvenience to you. Go elsewhere to find out what havoc your miserable cancer sticks wreak.

New sights and friends await the intermediate runner.

CHAPTER ELEVEN

More Words On Training — Intermediate Levels

Q **What do you consider an intermediate level of running?**

A Again, it is an arbitrary definition, but in this book an intermediate level of running will be considered the ability to run comfortably for an hour.

Q **I just learned to run comfortably for 20 minutes — why should I want to go for an hour?**

A Only you know the answer to that.

In Chapter Five we set a goal of learning to run comfortably for 20 minutes, three times a week, a level which would satisfy your aerobic requirements and give you a small taste of what running is all about. Since you spent money to buy this book, I felt you *should* train your body and mind to do that much.

In this chapter the words "goal" and "should" will be dropped from further discussion. You've now reached a point in your training where you "should" be insulted if I tell you what "goals" you need to have.

The two new buzz-words in this chapter are "suggestions" and "guidelines." If you want to progress to an intermediate level of running — three weekly runs of 30 minutes, 45 minutes, and one hour — this chapter can suggest how.

The best argument for going longer is the proportionate increase in enjoyment. Experienced runners know the fun and pleasure of running really only begins at 20-30 minutes. As long as you sweated to get this far, to 20 minutes, you might be interested in seeing what adventure lies beyond.

It will take you just two weeks to improve to 30 minutes, and if you decide to stop there, fine. This chapter will suggest, again with the seven-step method, how you can improve your running range to one hour. But somewhere between the first and seventh step, you very well might find your satiation point. This chapter can help you find that, too.

Q   **What are the cardiovascular benefits of running longer?**

A   There are mixed reactions to this question.

Dr. Thomas Bassler of the American Medical Joggers Association claims that regular runs of an hour will give any person almost complete immunity from coronary trouble. In fact, Bassler doesn't stop there. He goes on to say that the ability to run a marathon — 26 miles, 385 yards — gives the runner absolute cardiovascular protection.

Most medical authorities think Dr. Bassler well-intentioned, but rather extreme. The Aerobics Institute concedes that additional running might contribute to coronary immunity, but so far this can't be proved. Dr. Cooper himself is content to run two miles, three or four times a week.

Dr. George Sheehan, the runner-cardiologist-philosopher-writer, admits to not knowing if an increase in running gives you increased cardiovascular protection. He thinks the change in a runner's lifestyle might be more significant to health than the actual increase in running. As he says in *Dr. Sheehan On Running*:

"One who embarks on these efforts tends to leave other loyalties behind. He becomes a completely new person living a completely new lifestyle."

I tend to agree with Sheehan. The increased amount of running by itself would increase your coronary immunity only negligibly, since those three 20-minute workouts already put your cardiovascular fitness level among the top 10 percent.

More importantly to your health, when you start running longer you also start gravitating toward the marathoner's lifestyle. You begin to think as a runner and start treating your body as others treat their motorboats and sports cars.

You less frequently associate with people who think fun is dressing in a suit and tie, paying 20 dollars to eat two pounds of undercooked meat, and spending the rest of the evening looking for entertainment in smoke-filled cabarets.

You more frequently hang around people who think fun is spending a weekend in Tahoe or Vail running and backpacking on the mountain trails.

Q   **What would be your motivation to run for more than 20 minutes?**

A   My motivation would be purely hedonistic. Only when I can run comfortably for longer distances do I enjoy running.

Only when I can run for more than 30 minutes do I feel the amazing rebirth of power. Only then do my muscles loosen and do I feel the sensual rhythm of all the moving parts. Only then do I forget my body's limitations, and instead concentrate on its potential.

Only then do I again feel like a teenager training for high school cross country.

Only then do I really think and feel and live as a runner.

Dr. Sheehan says something to the effect that the first few miles of running are for your body and the rest is for your soul. To the latter I would add exquisite pleasure.

Q   **So the benefits of running longer are more mental than physical?**

A   To be sure, the physical gain is significant. While your coronary immunity isn't greatly improved, your cardiovascular fitness to perform any aerobic task, including racing or running for great distances, certainly is.

And your net weekly calorie loss from running at an intermediate level is 2½ times that from running at a beginning level.

But all of the physical benefits of running longer seem of less importance than the changes in attitude and perception. Your motivation to get out there and run for 30-60 minutes is not for better health, but simply for the love of what you are doing, and the pleasure you know you will receive.

Your motivation is now no different than that of the eight-year-old who wakes up on Saturday morning, and after grabbing a baseball glove, skateboard and fishing pole, goes out in the world to seek adventure, fun and pleasure.

What could be more simple or charming than that?

*   *   *

Q **How can I increase my running range to one hour?**

A My suggestion again would be to use a seven-step method of graduated improvement:

Seven Steps to Intermediate Running

○ *Step 1* Run three times a week, using alternate days — 20 minutes, 20 minutes, 20 minutes.

○ *Step 2* Three times a week — 20, 20, 30.

○ *Step 3* Three times a week — 20, 25, 35.

○ *Step 4* Three times a week — 20, 30, 40.

○ *Step 5* Three times a week — 25, 35, 45.

○ *Step 6* Three times a week — 30, 40, 50.

○ *Step 7* Three times a week — 30, 45, 60.

Q **What kind of pace are we talking about?**

A The longest run of the week must be done entirely at a slow and comfortable pace. This is the run in which you are trying to increase your range, so you hardly need the additional strain of a fast pace.

For the other two runs, do the first 20 minutes slowly and comfortably. Then as the muscles loosen and you start to feel alive, run at whatever pace you wish. On some days you might feel like testing yourself with a spicy pace — then do it. On other days you might choose to maintain the slower pace all the way. That's fine, too. After the first 20 minutes of easy running, be open-minded about what will happen next. Try to let your choice of pace be spontaneous, based simply on how you feel. If during an impulsive burst of speed you quickly drain yourself of energy and have to quit the run before its completion, think nothing of it. You can always be more cautious and level-headed during the longest run of the week.

Q   **What difficulties might I expect when trying to stretch that longest run?**

A   Physically, you won't have any trouble with breathing, as you probably did when learning to run for 20 minutes. Instead, the fatigue you will feel in a long slow run is of the muscles, tendons and joints. The feet, ankles, achilles, calves, knees, upper legs, hips and lower back will all send two-word telegrams to your brain: Please Quit.

At this stage in your running you must learn to distinguish between muscle-tendon-joint fatigue and m-t-j pain.

Fatigue is a dull ache — pain is a sharp hurt. Fatigue aches constantly — pain hurts only when the affected area is supporting the body weight. Fatigue is the result of hard effort — pain is the result of injury. Fatigue is to be tolerated if you are to improve as a runner. Pain is never to be tolerated, unless you desire to injure yourself further.

The distinction is important, because in both cases your brain will want to heed the message and implore you to quit running.

Two other problems indigenous to long running are blisters and rashes. Blisters can be prevented in most cases by wearing either snugly fitting socks or blister repellent insoles, and by *never* wearing new shoes on a long run. Try your new shoes on the shorter runs for at least two weeks. If you do get blisters, treat them this way: puncture and drain; wash and disinfect (I use Chloraseptic mouthwash spray), and let the skin peel by itself — don't tear it off.

Rashes appear most often in the groin and armpit, and on the nipples. Groin and armpit rashes can be prevented by wearing shorts, jocks, bras and tee shirts of chafe-resistant material like nylon tricot, or by rubbing vaseline onto the affected area before running.

Nipple rashes can be dealt with by wearing quarter-sized bandages over the nipples. I know of a runner who estimates he has used more than 10,000 nipple bandages over the years. I don't know if he gets a discount.

Mentally, it is not uncommon to have fears of going longer, especially if you were unable to run at all three months ago, and were forced to start your running with a walk. But like the fear of waterskiing or learning a foreign language, the real problem is fear of the unknown. The solution is simply to get your feet wet.

The other mental difficulty of going longer is boredom. For this I don't have a solution, nor do I think there *should* be a solution — if running longer distances bores you, then don't do it. Either you have already passed your satiation level, or you don't belong in running at all. There are plenty of fitness sports you might find far more interesting.

Q   **You recommend running on alternate days, but also within the framework of an odd-numbered seven-day week. If my math is correct . . .**

A   If your math is correct you will discover you have a two-day rest period once a week.

The principle of training works best when you have a balanced dosage of stress and adaptation. At this level, a good balance is one day of work followed by one day of rest.

But double any one dose of stress, and your body is going to need roughly twice the time to adapt. Make one of your weekly runs significantly longer than the others, and you would best benefit with a following two-day rest.

Working within a framework of a week not only makes your scheduling easier, but also allows that two-day rest after the week's longest run.

Q   **Let's say I am at step seven. Might a good schedule not be: Monday - 30 minutes; Wednesday — 45 minutes; and Friday — 60 minutes?**

A   It's not a bad schedule, but I would switch Monday with Wednesday for the simple reason that by sandwiching the shortest run between the two longer runs, you get the same stress, but with slightly more adaptation time. The weekend rest will refresh you adequately for the 45-minute run on Monday, and the short Wednesday run won't leave you tired for the long Friday run.

Of course this is only a guideline, and not a set of rules, but if I were following it, I would also move everything forward so that I could do my long run on Saturday. I like to make a lengthy production of my runs — that is, I like to reward myself afterward with a long swim or sauna and several beers. Weekdays never seem appropriate for this.

Q **How fast might I expect to move from one step to the next?**

A Try a new step every two weeks — in most cases you will be able to handle it. In fact, you'll probably discover that improvement is easier here than it was during the first seven steps.

Q **When I was learning to run for 20 minutes, you recommended that I do it alone. What about now?**

A One of running's many attractions is that you can alone, in pairs, or with any number of people.

I would hope that you are cultivating a taste for running alone, both for the intrinsic joy that it brings, and for the fact you will never feel lost without a training partner.

At the same time I think it both fun and valuable to occasionally run with others. Under few other circumstances will you ever see people more clearly than you do when running together.

If there is a time most appropriate for running together, it would seem to be during the longest run of the week, when the pace is slow enough for easy conversation, and the length of the run makes it worthwhile for runners to get together. Joe Henderson says the social and running highlight of his week is a Saturday morning group run in his hometown of Los Altos, California.

In my hometown of Bismarck, North Dakota, the group runs are always organized by a 50-year-old gynecologist, and include at various times myself, a college job-placement counselor, a nurse, a few high school cross country runners, a junior high track coach, a theology student, a high school drama teacher, a country-western disc jockey, and even on occasion an American record-holder in the marathon and a world class steeplechaser.

I mention this group because it succeeds despite huge differences in age, occupation and even running ability. In fact, the very disparity might indeed be its strength — I think we all enjoy the opportunity to step outside of normal routines and be with people with whom we have little in common except a singular love of running. But then, that's all that is needed for a successful running group.

Q   **Is there a general increase in stress when I begin to run at an intermediate level?**

A   By running only three times a week, and at a comfortable pace, your body is given sufficient time to adapt to the increase in stress. In other words, since your fitness level is increasing as fast as the additional stress, the net stress level stays constant. You should feel no more stress at an intermediate level than you did in the beginning.

However, if you have any of the common muscle-skeletal faults as described in Chapter 13, an increase in running might very well precipitate your first running injury.

Q   **If my stress level stays constant, why might an increase in running cause me to get injured?**

A   General overstress is only a secondary cause of running injuries. The primary cause is any number of muscle-skeletal faults — weak arches, muscle-tendon inflexibility, etc. — which disrupt your alignment and symmetry.

How quickly you suffer injury depends upon 1) the number and severity of your muscle-skeletal faults, and 2) how much running you do..

If your muscle-skeletal faults are legion — if you have a short leg, flat feet, turned-in ankles, a swayed back, and you can't even get close to touching your toes — you might have already suffered your first injury in the beginning levels.

On the other hand, if you are Frank Shorter and have been described by Kenny Moore as "mechanically perfect," you can run 140 miles a week, as Shorter does, and stay quite free from injury.

Most of us, though, have a fault or two (mine are bowed legs and Morton's feet) which significantly increases our chance of injury at the intermediate level.

Q   **What can be done to reduce the risk of injury?**

A   For one, learn the difference between pain and fatigue. Pain warns you of injury. Fatigue says only that you are tired.

Secondly, learn to identify your muscle-skeletal faults, and then learn how to correct them. Do this, and you should have an almost unlimited range of injury-free running.

Q   **Where can I learn more about injuries?**

A   You will find a lengthy discussion on injuries in Chapter 13.

Marty Liquori, 1978 USA-USSR 5000-meter winner, Berkeley.

CHAPTER TWELVE

The Danger Of Overdoing It

Q **Is it possible to do too much running?**

A Quite definitely.

Although most medical authorities believe it impossible for a healthy runner to overdo it on one or two runs, it *is* possible to let the accumulative physical stress climb too high over a period of weeks, months or years, a common mistake made by competitive runners.

When the accumulative stress mounts too high, all kinds of calamity can result.

Q **What sort of calamity?**

A If you have any number of the biomechanical faults as described in the next chapter, the usual result is injury.

Other predictable results are illnesses, from colds (very typical), flus, and streps to mononucleosis, which is the rather heavy price many of us have paid when straining to reach our maximum performance.

If you escape without illness or injury, the result may simply be a drop in performance, lingering dysphoria, disenchantment with running; in short, staleness.

Q **What causes too much stress to accumulate?**

A Basically, overstress results from not allowing your body adequate time to adapt from each dose of stress, from letting the balance of stress run amok.

Specifically, there seem to be four causes of overstress most common among runners.

○ *Running Too Hard Too Often* The principle of training is making an organism stronger by giving it balanced doses of stress and recovery time. Give your body too little stress for its current tolerance, and the training effect will be less than optimal.

But give your body too much stress without enough recovery time, instead of adapting and becoming stronger, the body just gets worn down.

○ *Too Much Anaerobic Running* The other balance vital to your upward mobility as a runner is that between aerobic (easy breathing) and anaerobic (difficult breathing) running. Anaerobic running is vastly more stressful than easy volume training, yet those hard fast runs must be indulged in regularly if you are to improve. Adding anaerobic running to your training program is a bit like adding a turbocharger to your car's engine — it sucks gas (your energy), but boosts performance. If your turbocharger is too big for the engine, your increased performance (ability to run fast) is more than offset by the increased time you must spend in the pits (in bed) refilling your tank. And if the race is long, you will lose to the more efficient cars.

Physiologically, doing too much anaerobic running will, in time, actually lower your red cell count (the measure of your ability to carry oxygen to the starving muscles), and you will begin a drop in conditioning, despite the fact you might have been in the best shape of your life before adding the speedwork to your training.

Finding the right balance between aerobic and anaerobic running is tricky at best, but is one secret to maximizing your potential. Chapters 18 and 19 discuss how you can find the right balance.

○ *Too Many Races* The physical effect of racing too often is almost identical to that of doing too much anaerobic running. But racing also imposes enormous mental stress, and so must be done even more sparingly.

As Joe Henderson points out in *Jog, Run, Race*, racing doesn't always demand payment upon delivery. Too much racing now may not cause trouble until the following season.

In 1971 the top American middle distance runners were Marty Liquori and Mark Winzenried. Both raced prodigiously that year. Liquori gunned down Jim Ryun in their famous Philadelphia race in May, and then went on to beat all of the best European milers and earn the number one ranking in the world.

Winzenried raced a phenomenal 70 times during 1971, and strung together more world class times in the 800 meters (below 1:48) than any half-miler has done before or since.

Both were top Americans in their event. But neither made the US Olympic team in 1972. Liquori injured his foot in late 1971 (during a cross country race) and never recovered sufficiently to even try out for the team.

Winzenried, after racing madly again during the 1972 indoor season, and after recording fast outdoor times during March and April, came up with a sore achilles tendon and got bounced from his opening round heat in the Olympic Trials.

More recently, Frank Shorter crossed the line of too many races. During 1977 Frank toured the country in search of road races, and on some occasions, even raced twice within 24 hours. But as it always does, the quantity of Frank's races stole from the quality. In two of 1977's most important races, the World Cup 10,000 and the New York City Marathon, Shorter, normally the consummate big meet performer, faded badly in the late stages.

○ *Not Enough Sleep* I am of the opinion that you can flagrantly violate all of the above — do too much volume, speedwork and racing — and still escape unharmed *if* you get enough sleep. Sleep is the catch-all, the elixir. It can make good all kinds of stupid training errors and overenthusiastic binges.

George Young, the four-time Olympic steeplechaser, and Jim Ryun both violated all standard training wisdom. Both ran hard every day. Both overdosed on interval training. Both, especially early in their careers, raced too often.

Yet both succeeded in keeping their health (as much as that's possible at a world class level — Ryun had a mild case of mononucleosis in 1968, and Young periodically battled an ulcer) and for years were the top Americans in their event.

Ryun and Young, you see, were also world class sleepers. In high school and college, Ryun often conked out shortly after dinner, and sometimes right after practice. He wouldn't awake until his 6 a.m. workout the following morning. Thus Ryun spent most of his career sleeping 10-12 hours a day.

In *Always Young*, George Young expounded on the importance of sleep. He said nine hours a day was the minimum sleep time needed to recover from each day's hard training.

Today, Mt. Olympus is still filled with heavy sleepers. When Marty Liquori came within a tick of breaking the indoor mile world record in 1975, he said the key to his success and improvement over the two previous years was less training and more sleep. How much sleep? Whenever possible, 10-11 hours said Liquori.

Bill Rodgers, the American record-holder in the marathon, is also a firm 10-hour-a-day man, while Shorter, when he can fit it into his hectic racing-business schedule, also tries for double figures.

Q   **Sleeping for 10 hours seems quite a luxury. If I added 10 hours to my working and commuting time, I'd have little left for anything else.**

A   For most runners, any sleep past eight hours is wasted time. But for Shorter, Rodgers and Liquori, hard training athletes who want to win gold medals in the 1980 Olympics, 10 hours is more than a luxury. If you computed the time-value and the cost-benefit of their extra two hours of sleep, you would find that those two hours are most wisely spent in bed.

Q   **So, eight hours is the right amount of daily sleep for most?**

A   Eight hours is a recommendation that has stood the test of time, and should be the right amount for most runners. Just to play it safe, I try to sleep for an extra hour the night following the longest run of the week. But this might be nothing more than an excuse for "sleeping in" on Sunday morning, and thus avoiding church service.

Q   **What if I sleep less than eight?**

A   If you sleep for only seven hours a day, including naps, you are inviting disaster into your running. If you sleep for less than six, you should forget about being an athlete. You should forget about enjoying life, too.

Q   **Eight hours might sound easy to you, but I just plain don't sleep very well.**

A   Insomnia, rampant in this country, has two basic causes: tension and drug abuse.

If your insomnia is purely tension-related, running should provide the cure (see Chapter 14).

Even with running, though, you still might have trouble sleeping if you have a dependence on drugs. Drug abuse, of course, isn't limited to heroin addicts. Here I include people who drink more than three cups of coffee or consistently take more than two alcoholic belts each day. I'm also talking about people who depend on cigarettes, tranquilizers, pot, diet pills and sleeping potions to get through a normal day.

Insomniacs come not from the fit, pure and wholesome, but from the out of shape and chemically polluted. Get in shape and cut your drug habits, and your chances of sleeping soundly each night will be very good.

Q   **If circumstances cheat me out of sleep, should I alter my running?**

A   While some of the best races have been run after a night of insomnia, your everyday training should be reduced if you are not getting enough sleep. Remember again that training is a two-part definition — stress and rest. Since lack of sleep adds to the stress, you must reduce your training to keep the critical balance.

In college, the distance runners always seemed to get sick or injured during the last two weeks of each semester, when the pressure of papers and finals cut daily sleep time to six or seven hours. In these cases, training should have been cut in half. Disaster could have been avoided.

Q   **How can we tell if our accumulative stress is too high?**

A   Fortunately, there are several warning signs of overstress. Among these are:

       Aching legs and/or lower back
       Swollen glands
    * Blood in urine
       Runny nose
       Irritable and quick-tempered
       Loss of appetite
       Loss of weight
       Sexual disinterest or dysfunction
       Tired, but don't sleep well
       Growing dissatisfaction with running
       Growing dissatisfaction with everything

* Usually results from the overstress of running. However, consultation with a physician is advised.

Q   **What should I do if I have these symptoms?**

A   Because I see only disaster looming ahead if you continue to overtrain, what I would recommend is for you to immediately take three days off, and follow that with a week of light training.

Furthermore, during the abstinence I would go on a hedonistic binge — for three days warmly embrace a lifestyle completely antithetical to Dr. Thomas Bassler. During the day I would take my sun lotion, sixpack and waterpipe out to the swimming pool and shock others with my decadence. Tired of that, I would go back to my apartment and take a snooze.

Upon waking I would take a lengthy shower, perhaps a bubble bath, while sipping from a mai tai or mint julep. That finished, I would dress in my tightest white pants, pastel shirt and gold medallion, and head for the most lavish restaurant in town. After feasting on two pounds of Chateaubriand (dark on the outside, pink on the inside) and asparagus tips, I would drive to the nearest singles bar, break several hearts, and depart with my lady of the evening.

For the next week I would train lightly, and after that, gradually increase my running until I found the right balance of stress and adaptation. Such a plan never fails to revive my interest in running, as well as other delightful things in life.

A better plan, though, is avoiding overstress in the first place. This you can do, of course, by carefully avoiding any of the four causes.

○ *Run Hard Just Often Enough* For most runners, this means only three hard workouts a week. And to play it safe, skip running completely at least one day a week.

○ *Maintain A Sensible Aerobic vs. Anaerobic Balance* For general training, don't let anaerobic training exceed 10 percent of your total running. To find the right balance for specific race training, read Chapter 19.

○ *Race Infrequently* Don't let the number of miles you race exceed five percent of your total running. This means you need to space each one-mile race with 19 miles of training. You need nearly 500 miles of training between each marathon.

○ *Get Enough Sleep* This means you should consistently get eight hours a night. If circumstances cut your sleep, reduce your training accordingly.

*   *   *

Q **Should we attempt to run with a cold?**

A Running with a mild cold won't kill you, but I suggest resting for a couple of days, at least until the cold peaks. At that time you can start running gently until the cold vanishes.

The reason I am against running with a cold is that your virus was probably first invited by overstress. So what you need now is not more stress, but a heavy dose of rest and adaptation. If you continue to overtrain while nursing a cold, you leave yourself vulnerable for further viral invasion — things like flus, streps and mono find their victims not among the strong and healthy, but among the weary and ragged.

Q **So I shouldn't run with the flu?**

The strain of racing is a major cause of overstress.

A   Absolutely not.

Q   **What about returning from an illness? When is it safe to start again? How much running should I try?**

A   Since a virus leaves no itinerary, it is hard to say when you can safely start running again. In the first place, don't even think about exercise until the disease peaks. After that, wait until the first day you can resume normal non-running activities. After you reestablish your routine, you might try a gentle, every-other-day running schedule, and see how your body reacts. More than anything, returning from illness takes a vigilant monitoring of your feelings, and an abstinence from any schedule planning until it is quite clear you are free from the clutches of disease.

Although cause for great frustration, most running injuries are highly treatable, as well as avoidable.

CHAPTER THIRTEEN

Injuries

Part One: General Causes

Q **What causes running injuries?**

A Most running injuries result not from getting sacked by a middle linebacker, or even tripping over an untied shoelace, but instead from running too many miles with a less than perfect body.

Running injuries are actually diseases, since their occurrence is not traumatic, but slowly degenerative. Because disease is a frightening word, though, we will call them overuse injuries. Among the many and interrelating causes of overuse injuries are:

1. Excessive Foot Pronation
2. Skeletal Imperfections
3. Muscle-Tendon Inflexibility
4. Muscle-Tendon Strength Imbalance
5. Poor Running Style
6. Running On Hard Or Uneven Surfaces
7. Inferior Running Shoes
8. Stress and Overtraining

1. *Excessive Foot Pronation* The feet of most runners strike the ground on the outside edge of the heel. As the foot rolls forward, it also rolls inward as the weight of the body shifts to the center of the foot. This rolling inward from the outside of the foot to the center is called pronation, and is a natural part of proper running mechanics.

In *excessive* pronation, your foot rolls from the outside edge to the center, but instead of stopping there, as it should, it keeps rolling toward the inside. The body weight shifts past the center to the inside of the foot, and in extreme pronation you can actually tear through the inside upper of the shoe.

Q   **Other than possibly tearing through my shoes, why is excessive pronation a problem?**

A   When the body weight shifts suddenly from the outside of the foot to the inside, the whole leg must torque inwardly to compensate.

To see how this works, stand with your weight focused on the outside edge of your right heel. Now quickly shift your weight to the front and center of your foot, just behind the second and third toes. Notice how the knee bends forward with only a few degrees of inward lateral motion. This is normal pronation.

Now, try it again, but this time shift your weight from the outside edge of the heel to the inside edge of the forefoot, where the longitudinal arch inserts into the first metatarsal bone. Notice the difference — this time your knee rotates inward as it bends forward. This is excessive pronation, and the strain caused by its inward torque and twisting will cause, in over thousands of strides, a whole catalogue of overuse injuries.

Q   **How can I tell if I am pronating?**

A   If you toe off of the inside of your foot, you are pronating.

If your shoe uppers look as if they are ripping apart on the inside edge, you are pronating.

Another way to tell if you are a pronator is to walk barefoot on a hard surface. How well does your longitudinal arch hold its shape when supporting your weight? If it flattens easily, you are a pronator.

Q   **So, a weak arch causes pronation?**

A   Weak or flat arches are one of the several causes of pronation.

Another cause is bowed legs — with bowed legs your feet strike the ground at an angle, and thus far to the outside edge. Your feet have to pronate excessively just to arrive at the center for a normal toe-off.

A third cause of pronation is a narrow and rounded heel, which rolls easily from outside to inside during foot contact.

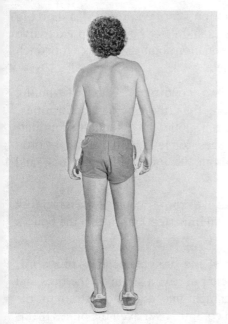
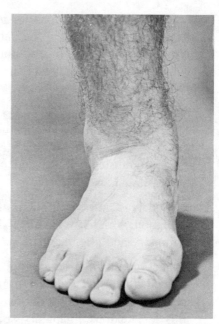

Skeletal imbalance, turned-in ankles, and flat feet are three common causes of injuries.

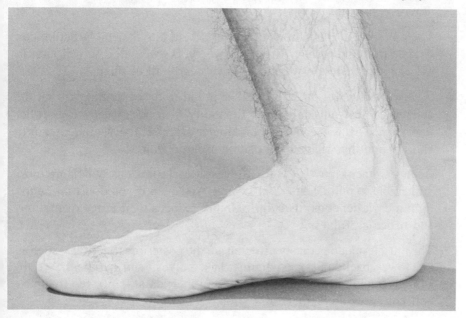

And a fourth cause of pronation is Morton's foot syndrome — a short big toe. A normal sized big toe acts as a stabilizer bar to stop excessive pronation. But a short big toe stops pronation about as well as a four-inch curb would stop a runaway fire truck.

2. *Skeletal Imperfections* This is the second major cause of running overuse injuries, and includes more than the obvious deformities. Skeletal imperfections also include such subtle, but potentially debilitating flaws as bowed legs, knocked knees, leg length differences as little as an eighth-inch, misplaced bones in the foot, Morton's foot, and turned-in ankles.

Bowed legs and Morton's foot, as we know, cause excessive foot pronation, which like the other skeletal imperfections, affect the body's symmetry and alignment.

Perfect running motion is symmetrical and straight ahead — in a word, aligned. Just as a car out of alignment puts extra strain on the tires and steering system, a body out of alignment puts additional strain on the muscles, tendons, ligaments, spinal column, over even the bones themselves. In a matter of time and miles, some part of the body will break down.

There are literally hundreds of places where our skeletal structure can deviate from the perfect. But don't worry. As we will discover later in the chapter, there are ways to correct nearly all of them.

3. *Muscle-Tendon Inflexibility* The grand irony of running is that the runner has less muscle-tendon flexibility than does the average roller derby fan. That is because any endurance exercise, like running, tends to shorten and thus tighten the used muscle-tendons.

As any trainer knows, it is the tightest muscle-tendons which are most vulnerable to pulls, tears, and strains. And even if you don't injure the tight muscle-tendons, their inflexibility reduces their range of motion, and hence usefulness.

The muscle-tendons thusly affected are the posteriors (backside) such as the lower back, buttocks, hamstrings, calves, and achilles. A tight achilles tendon is not only delicate, but inefficient, since the tightness will not allow a complete and strong push-off of the stride.

4. *Muscle-Tendon Strength Imbalance* As Dr. Sheehan says, three things happen to the muscles when you start running, and two of them are bad. Along with the previously mentioned inflexibility, you develop a muscle-tendon strength imbalance — increased strength of the posterior muscle-tendons, and a relative weakening of the little used anterior muscle-tendons. While the lower back, buttocks, hamstrings, calves and achilles grow stronger through running, the anterior shin muscles, quadriceps, groin, hip adductors and abdominals stay the same, or grow weaker.

This imbalance occurs mostly in long slow distance runners. Middle distance runners have the best muscle balance since at faster speeds they use the quadriceps, groin, hips and abdominals to push and lift. Sprinters have a polar opposite imbalance —since sprinting is more pushing than pulling, the sprinter's anterior muscle-tendons are stronger than his posteriors.

The danger of developing a muscle-tendon strength imbalance is, according to physiotherapist, Joseph Zohar, "That when one muscle group is excessively stronger than the opposing muscle group, the odds of injury in the weaker muscle are greatly increased."

This is why a sprinter often pulls a hamstring muscle while a distance runner hardly ever suffers that. On the other hand, a distance runner is more susceptible to a strained groin muscle.

·5. *Poor Running Style* In its own chapter, proper running style is discussed exhaustively, but a few words need to be said here on how poor running style can cause injuries.

When you run properly, exerting strength and control from the trunk area, your foot will touch the ground lightly and with an absence of shock. There should be no thudding or slapping — if there is, you are striking the ground too hard and with too much shock. The chance of stress injuries is increased.

Overstriding is another style fault which invites injuries, especially in the achilles tendon and calf muscle. You are overstriding if your foot touches the ground in front of your center of gravity. Ideally, it should touch directly underneath your body's weight.

A third style fault is running with feet either toed-in (pigeon-toed) or toed-out (duck foot). Both of these faults throw the entire leg out of alignment. Pigeon-toed runners often have problems with their achilles tendon, while duck-footed runners usually suffer knee injuries. For good alignment and running efficiency, toe straight ahead.

6. *Running On Hard Or Uneven Surfaces* Running on asphalt or cement, inevitable for city runners, produces shock, as well as causing the arch to flatten and the foot to pronate during each stride.

These problems are made worse if you run on the side of a sloped road, which artificially makes one leg longer than the other and destroys the balance and symmetry.

Yet, the alternatives to asphalt and cement can be just as bad. A grassy surface often hides dips and mounds, gopher holes, and general unevenness. Dirt and gravel roads, when they can be found, are usually filled with chuckholes and tire tracks. And beaches have a sharper slope than the side of a road.

7. *Inferior Running Shoes* As we learned in a previous chapter, a bad running shoe is a breeding ground for running diseases.

Shoes with a weak shank and inferior arch support do nothing to prevent excessive pronation, as a good shoe will.

Shoes with a stiff forefoot will make the achilles and calf work harder during the toe-off. So will a shoe with a low heel. Since the achilles and calf are vulnerable to injury in a good many runners, the last thing needed is additional strain.

Shoes with a thin, paper-like sole do little to absorb shock. Metatarsal stress fractures and forefoot strain are likely results.

Sometimes even the quality brand shoes have faults which precipitate injury. The ultra-wide flares of the original Nike LD-1000 are a good example. The wide flares were supposed to add stability, but instead worked as a lever to quickly and harshly bring the runner into a flat-footed position. Nike realized its mistake, and has modified the LD-1000 — it now adds stability without manipulating the foot.

8. *Stress and Overtraining* Even if you have some or all of the above

problems — if you pronate, limp, are tight and out of balance; if you run like a duck, always on cement and wear K-Mart Specials — you can *still* stave off most running injuries if you give your body proper rest.

On the other hand, you may have none of the above faults, yet be constantly injured because you don't get enough sleep or else run too much too often.

Stress and overtraining not only magnifies overuse injuries, it also creates them.

Part Two: Cure and Prevention

Q   **Does this mean we should treat the causes, not the symptoms, if we want to cure and prevent running injuries?**

A   You've summed it perfectly — if only Western medicine understood that concept as well as you do.

Yet, how often does a coach, trainer, or even doctor attempt to treat your shin splints with rubdowns, tape, whirlpools, stale encouragement to "run through the pain," and finally, if none of the above work, total rest?

Unfortunately, it happens all of the time. It happens on nearly every high school and cross country team in the country. It happens in the office of nearly every doctor who himself doesn't run. It happened to me at a major university with an athletic department stocked with four full-time trainers and a team orthopedic surgeon considered one of the best in the country.

In my own case, my bowed legs and short big toes cause me to pronate excessively. During high school and the first three years of college I escaped significant injuries because my teenage flexibility allowed me to absorb the torque and twisting of excessive pronation.

It wasn't until the summer before my senior year at Stanford, when I was running 90 miles a week, that the pronation finally caught up with me. The trouble began in August, with a painful spot no bigger than a thumbnail three inches above my left ankle. Since it didn't hurt during the run — only before and after — I continued to train maximally. This was to be my best cross country season yet, so I could hardly afford to rest. Instead I gulped aspirin and iced my leg after each run.

But the shin steadily got worse, and during the first week of team practice I began to notice a changing wear pattern on my left shoe. Both shoes had the usual wear on the outside heel, but the left only showed peculiar wear on the inside edge of the upper, near the arch and heel. In fact, a week after I noticed this I tore through the heel counter. And a week after that an x-ray determined I had a tibial stress fracture, which necessitated a two month layoff. My cross country season was ruined.

What I didn't know at the time, but what was clearly indicated by the unusual wear pattern, was that I was pronating excessively. I was landing on the outside of my heel, and then completely rolling to the inside before I could manage a feeble toe-off.

Regrettable is that my shin splints and eventual cracked tibia could have been prevented or reversed, right up to the time of the fracture. All I needed was something to stop the excessive pronation. All I needed was something to keep my left foot from rolling inside the shoe. As I know today, all I needed was a pair of orthotic arch supports.

But instead the coach sent me every day to the trainer for alternate ice rubdowns and hot whirlpool baths, before and after practice. When that failed to cure my aching shins, the trainer had me stand in line with the football players for an ankle taping. And after a training session in which I was unable to bend the ankle, the trainer cut the tape (and sometimes my skin), and I spent another 30 minutes taking alternate hot and cold.

None of the trainer's methods made my leg feel better, and so the next step was an appointment with the team orthopedic surgeon. After I waited in his office for more than two hours, he examined the leg for 20 seconds and pronounced tendinitis. He said I should take a few days off and double the amount of time spent in the whirlpool. As a final bit of advice, the doctor diagrammed what he called a "revolutionary" way of taping the ankle. This I was to give to the trainer when I resumed running.

As the doctor ushered me from his office, I remembered to ask him what he thought had caused the injury in the first place. I'll always remember the good doctor's answer. He said: "It doesn't really matter now, does it?"

Q   **You sound bitter.**

A   Not bitter, but angry. And not over my own past, but for the millions of runners, mostly unwitting high school kids and beginners of all ages, who are getting similarly bad advice from coaches, trainers and physicians, who through their ignorance or laziness in keeping up with their professional standards, are betraying their professional trust.

Yet how utterly simple is the cure and prevention of running overuse injuries. With the knowledge available today in human physiology and podiatric and orthopedic medicine, there are really no excuses to suffer needlessly. All we have to do is treat the cause of a running injury. And as we know today, for every cause there is a simple cure.

Q   **What are the simple cures?**

A   Let's go back to part one of this chapter and look at the eight general causes of running injuries. Then let's list them here, along with their cures:

Injury Causes	*Injury Preventatives*
1. Excessive Foot Pronation	1. Corrective Shoe Inserts
2. Skeletal Imperfections	2. Corrective Shoe Inserts or Shoe Alterations
3. Muscle-Tendon Inflexibility	3. Static Stretching
4. Muscle-Tendon Strength Imbalance	4. Strengthen Opposing Weak Muscle-Tendons
5. Poor Running Style	5. Good Running Style
6. Running On Hard or Uneven Surfaces	6. Run On Softer and More Even Surfaces
7. Inferior Running Shoes	7. Quality Brand Running Shoes
8. Stress and Overtraining	8. Rest and Reduction In Training

1. *Excessive Foot Pronation* What is needed to prevent excessive foot pronation is a shoe insert which allows the foot to roll from its outside edge to its center, but no more. Any number of inserts will work, depending on the severity of pronation.

Says Dr. George Sheehan: "Most runners need some support inside their shoes. I sometimes make the analogy to eye problems. If you have a minor reading problem, you can do quite well with a pair of glasses you buy at Woolworths. If your problem is more serious, you need prescriptive lenses."

The same is true of pronation. If you pronate slightly in excess, you can do quite well with a three dollar drug store arch support. If you pronate quite excessively, as I do, you may need a prescriptive heel and arch support called an orthotic.

Here is a list of available shoe inserts, from the simplest to the most complex:

— *Arch Cookie* An arch cookie is shaped like a quartered orange, with the flat edges placed against sole and inside upper of the shoe. The support inside most shoes is a small foam rubber cookie, but if this isn't enough support, you might consider replacing it with something larger and stiffer, like a Dr. Scholl's leather cookie. Most shoe repair shops and drugstores sell them for two or three dollars.

— *Full Foot Arch Support* This is a one-piece longitudinal and metatarsal arch support made of leather and foam. They are available in sizes to match your shoe — just toss them in and they are ready for wearing.

The cheapest and most flexible full foot arch support is the Dr. Scholl's Flexo, sold in nearly every drug store for three or four dollars.

Similar to the Flexo, but stiffer and made of better leather, are the Pro Comfort Support and the Dr. Scholl's Athletic A and 610 supports. They cost about twice as much as Flexo's, and are found in most well-stocked running and shoe repair shops.

— *One-Piece Heel and Arch Support* These are similar to the inserts already built into all Eaton shoes, and are the kind of support you need if a narrow and rounded heel is the cause of your pronation. Bike and Pro Comfort make these, but they are new on the market, and hence difficult

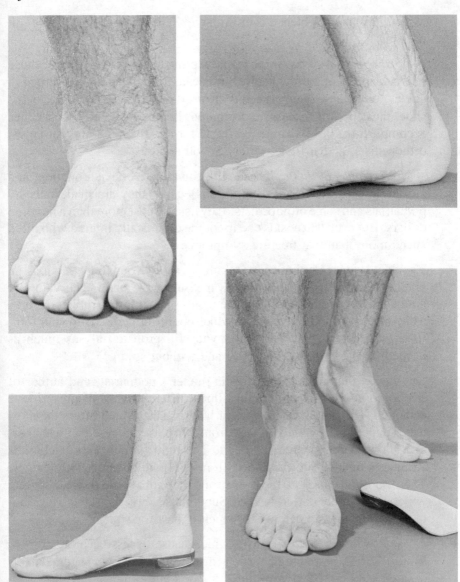

Top: The unsupported foot. Note the pronation and flattened arches.

Bottom: The supported foot. Note how the orthotic aligns the lower leg and builds the arch.

to get. Try an enlightened running shop. They cost from six to eight dollars.

— *Orthopedic Wedges* Some runners pronate excessively not because of weak arches or narrow heels, but because of bowed legs or turned in ankles. What these runners need is an insert which raises the inside of the shoe, thus checking excessive pronation. Leather-covered cork wedges accomplish the task, and are available for about ten dollars from most orthopedists, podiatrists, and Dr. Scholl's stores.

— *Prescriptive Orthotics* These will stop any excessive pronation, and are the last answer in arch supports. Because they are made only by podiatrists and some orthopedists, they usually cost more than a hundred dollars. But even that cost is cheap for the chronically injured who often spend more than that treating symptoms.

The doctor makes orthotics by taking a cast of your foot, much as an optometrist makes contact lenses by measuring the size and curvature of your eyeballs. From the foot cast he molds out of plastic, rubber or cork, a one-piece heel and arch support which conforms perfectly to your foot. Run with them in your shoe and you will pronate only as much as needed; in other words, naturally and without strain.

Dr. Steven Subotnick, a California runner's podiatrist, and author of *The Running Foot Doctor* makes three different types of prescriptive orthotics. The first is made of clear hard plastic, which offers the most rigid support. The second is made from thin plastic covered with leather, and allows a few degrees of bend. The third, which Subotnick calls "runner's molds" are fashioned from cork and covered with leather. These conform closely to the foot during the entire stride phase, a feeling which many runners find best of Subotnick's three prescriptive orthotics. The doctor can determine which is best for your needs.

2. *Skeletal Imperfections* Flaws which cause excessive pronation — Morton's foot, bowed legs, turned-in ankles, and narrow rounded heels — are easily corrected with arch supports and orthotics.

The other major skeletal flaw which causes a good many running injuries is a difference in leg lengths. Differences of more than an inch are quite obvious and result in a noticeable limp. Differences less than an inch are equally bad for a runner, since the very slightness stays hidden.

Sore hips and lower back are the usual results of uneven legs. Instead of waiting for the inevitable injuries, though, check your legs for possible length difference. Stand barefoot with your legs together. Do the knees match evenly? Is the pelvis level?

If the difference is less than a quarter inch, put a felt heel pad of the same thickness in the shoe of the shorter leg.

If the difference is between a quarter- and a half-inch, you need a lifting wedge. A pad alone has too large a drop-off. If you also wear orthotics, put the wedge underneath the orthotics.

Differences more than half an inch necessitate shoe alterations, as well as internal support and lift. This gets complicated, so you are best off consulting a runner's podiatrist.

3. *Muscle-Tendon Inflexibility* The simple remedy for inflexibility is stretching — something we've known for years. The recent flexibility breakthrough has not been in stretching *per se*, but in the way we should do it.

In the old days we stretched a muscle by bobbing on it. We stretched the back of our legs by touching the toes 100 times.

Current studies find this practice to be counterproductive to flexibility. According to physiologist Dr. Herbert de Vries, bobbing and bouncing invokes a reflex opposing the stretch, which actually makes the muscle tighter in the long run.

The solution to inflexibility, then, is yoga, or, if you prefer to do without that connotation, static stretching. A static stretch works best when you stretch a muscle-tendon as far as you can without pain. Stretch slowly, and at the same time, breathe deeply. Feel yourself become limp and relaxed. Stretch the muscle a little further with each exhaled breath.

Yogis call proper stretching "playing the edge," since a well executed stretch is close to the edge of pain, without actually crossing into that unpleasant region. With each exhaled breath, you move the edge further back. Yogis hold their stretches for ridiculous lengths of time, sometimes for hours, but for a runner seeking increased flexibility, 30 seconds is an adequate stretch. The muscles and relating tendons most likely to tighten from running are the posteriors — the achilles, calves, hamstring, buttocks and lower back. For all-around flexibility, you also need to stretch the anteriors — the shin muscles, quadriceps, groin, hips and trunk.

Stretch each muscle-tendon group for 30 seconds and twice daily — before and after the run. Here's how:

— *Achilles and Calves* Stand five feet from a wall, then lean against it, bracing yourself with your hands. Keep your feet flat on the floor. This is called a wall pushup. To stretch further, bend at the knees, and place your body weight on the balls of your feet.

— *Hamstring* Sit on the floor with both legs extended in front of you. While keeping the legs straightened, reach to grab your toes. If you can't manage that, grab your ankles. Extend the stretch with each exhaled breath.

— *Buttocks* Stand on your haunches, in a squat, for 30 seconds.

— *Lower Back* Lie on your back and roll over backward until your knees touch the ground close to your head. If your knees don't quite touch the ground, let them hang at the edge of their stretch. Breathe slowly and hold for 30 seconds.

— *Shin Muscles* The most effective shin stretch is not static, but a slow ankle rotation in both directions. Point the toe as you rotate the ankle for 30 seconds in each direction.

— *Quadriceps* This is the classic hurdler's stretch. Sit on the ground, extend the left leg, pull the right leg back and grab its ankle with the right hand. Now lie on your back and feel the right quadricep stretch. Hold for 30 seconds and switch legs.

— *Groin* Stand with legs as far apart as you can comfortably manage. Bend forward at the waist and try to touch the floor.

— *Hips* Sit with legs crossed in the classic lotus position for 30 seconds.

— *Trunk* Find a chin-up bar, and hang from it for 30 seconds, or as long as you can.

If you stretch the above muscle-tendon groups twice each day you run, and once each day you don't, you'll be adequately flexible for running, and hence avoid many injuries and much misery.

Six stretches for injury prevention:

a) *Achilles-calf*
b) *hips*
c) *groin*

d) *lower back*
e) *hamstrings*
f) *quadriceps*

4. *Muscle-Tendon Strength Imbalance* Since most distance runners have disproportionately weak anterior muscles, we must strengthen them to achieve a healthy balance. This may be done in two ways.

The natural way is to add a little speedwork to your slower paced runs. We learned earlier in this chapter that middle distance runners, because of their variety of training paces, develop equally the anterior and posterior muscles. Even if you repulse at the thought of interval 440s, you would be wise to spice the end of your run with a few 30-60 second pickups. These don't have to be flat-out sprints, just fast enough to feel yourself lifting from the hips and pushing strongly off of the stride.

Another way to strengthen the anteriors is with the following exercises:

— *Shin Strengthener* Sit on a table and hang your legs from the edge. Strap the handles of a suitcase or dufflebag filled with books around your right foot. Move your foot up and down, until the shin muscles say quit. Rest and repeat. Then switch feet and do the same.

— *Quadricep Strengthener* Leave the dufflebag hanging from your foot, and swing your lower leg forward and backward. Feel your quadriceps flex. Do this until you become tired. Rest and repeat. Switch legs and do the same.

— *Groin, Hips and Trunk Strengthener* The best exercise here is bent-leg situps, preferably on an inclined board. Women, this will also tighten that protruding tummy. Do as many as you can — yes, it should hurt. Rest and repeat.

Since a strong trunk is essential to good running style, every runner should do situps three times a week, religiously.

5. *Running On Hard Or Uneven Surfaces* An asphalt road, especially during the hot summer, is not a bad running surface, providing you wear good shoes and avoid running on the slanted edge.

Better, if available, are the dirt and gravel shoulders, or entire roads of gravel and dirt, as long as they are free of ridges, tire tracks and chuckholes.

The best surface imaginable is a smooth forest trail covered with pine needles. The "Joggers Capital of the World," Eugene, Oregon, has constructed such a path, ten feet wide and five miles long.

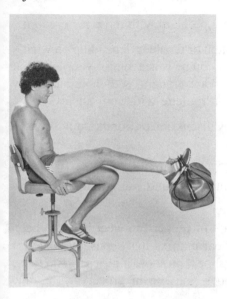
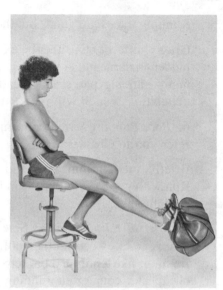

Four strengthening exercises for injury prevention:

a) *hips and quadriceps* c) *stomach*
b) *shins and ankles* d) *trunk*

Running tracks are good, but the big problem with those is boredom.

Grassy surfaces can either be excellent or terrible, depending on what's hidden underneath. A well kept golf course is heaven for your legs, but many enticing parks and meadows are fraught with holes and tiny undulations which will play Russian roulette with your ankles.

6. *Poor Running Style* For a lengthy discussion on good running style, I refer you to Chapter Six.

Briefly, the four things you should keep in mind regarding style are: 1) Run with good posture; 2) Run lightly; 3) Don't overstride; and 4) Toe straight ahead.

7. *Inferior Running Shoes* Selection of proper footwear has also been discussed elsewhere in the book. Bear in mind that shoes not made for running, like tennis and basketball shoes, promote injuries. So do those cheap and counterfeit running shoes you see in grocery stores and discount centers.

Wear a top brand shoe for your running. Any of them are good.

8. *Stress and Overtraining* This subject also has its own chapter. The two things to remember here are: 1) Don't run hard every day. Proper recovery is a necessary part of the whole training process. If you wish to run hard, do it every other day. 2) Don't cheat on your sleep. Eight hours isn't just for children. You need it, too.

Part Three: Specific Cases

Q   **How can we apply the concepts of cause and prevention to specific injuries?**

A   It's simply a matter of identifying each specific injury, knowing its cause or causes, and then applying the proper prevention techniques.

Starting with the lowest part of the anatomy, the feet, let's identify the most common injuries, their causes and their cures.

○ *Forefoot* The most common forefoot injuries are stress fractures of the metatarsals, the small bones connected to the toes. The symptoms are general swelling and tenderness in the forefoot, with local pain at the

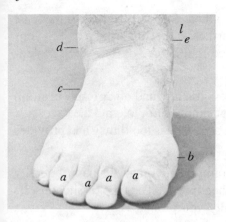
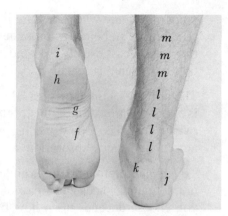

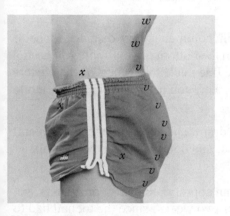
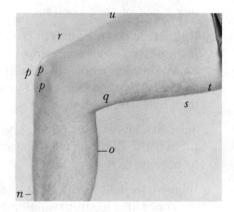

Common injuries:
a) *metatarsal stress fractures*
b) *bunions*
c) *ankle pseudo-sprain*
d) *fibula fracture*
e) *posterior shin splints*
f) *metatarsal arch strain*
g) *longitudinal arch strain*
h) *fascitas*
i) *heel bruise*
j) *heel bumps*
k) *heel spurs*
l) *achilles tendinitis*

m) *lower calf strain*
n) *anterior shin splints*
o) *upper calf strain*
p) *chondrolamacia of the knee*
q) *lower hamstring tendinitis*
r) *lower quadricep tendinitis*
s) *hamstring pull or strain*
t) *groin pull or strain*
u) *quadricep pull or strain*
v) *sciatic nerve irritation*
w) *lower back strain*
x) *hip strain*

point of fracture when pressure is applied. Stress fractures are the least crippling of all bone fractures, nevertheless they do bring a halt to your running. A cast usually isn't required, but a three or four week abstention from running usually is.

The primary cause of metatarsal stress fracture and other forefoot strain is excessive pronation — the forefoot simply can't tolerate the excessive twisting. This is made worse if your shoe sole is too flimsy and provides not enough shock absorption.

To prevent forefoot fractures and strain, then, you need a pair of quality brand running shoes and a pair of shoe inserts. The type of shoe inserts you choose depends upon how badly you pronate.

Painful bunions, swelling in the first joint of the big toe, are also caused by pronation, and by wearing shoes too small. Move up a half size and buy a pair of shoe inserts.

Blisters are another forefoot problem common among distance runners. If the blisters consistently appear on the bottom of your foot, you need a blister repellent insole, like the fine one made by Spenco. If the blisters regularly appear on the top of your feet, you need to wear socks, move up a half size, or both.

To treat a blister, puncture it, let it drain, and apply disinfectant several times daily. Don't rip the skin loose, and don't allow the popped blister to become dirty.

Ingrown toenails hardly seem like an appropriate injury for runners, yet they once kept me from running for two weeks, since the toenail had to be lanced, and the toe bandaged. To avoid this, cut your toenails regularly and straight across the toe.

As well, almost every veteran distance runner has lost a toenail after a particularly long run. Don't be alarmed if it happens to you. Just keep the affected area disinfected.

Runners with Morton's foot often form calluses on the tip of their second and longest toe. Keep the callus regularly filed down with an emery board. Don't try to cut it off with a razor blade. You can easily cut too deeply.

O *Arch* A common and very hard to treat problem occurs at the point where the longitudinal arch inserts into the heel — the problem is that the straining arch pulls, tears and can eventually detach from the heel. This is called the plantar's fascia syndrome, and is the injury which kept Marty Liquori from trying out for the US Olympic team in 1972.

Since the cause of this injury is an overstrained arch, an arch support is the cure. And you need more than a cookie here — you really need full foot arch support, if not an orthotic.

I myself wear orthotics, and the one day I forgot to wear them, I suffered a mild fascia strain. The pain didn't start until hours later, but when it did, it hurt like hell. Every time I put weight on the injured foot, I felt as if I were stepping on a sharp rock, yet there was no protuberance, just mild swelling. I had to rest for two weeks, but since I've religiously worn my orthotics, the fascitis hasn't returned.

○ *Heel* Three injuries affecting the heel are bruises, bumps and spurs.

Bruises on the bottom of the heel are almost always a result of wearing improper shoes without at least a half-inch of heel padding, and cupped heels which further absorb the shock of heel-first impact. If you have a heel bruise, don't monkey with your stride — that will only throw you out of alignment and cause other injuries. Just buy a pair of good running shoes.

The other two injuries, spurs and bumps, occur where the achilles tendon inserts into the heel. Spurs are sharp points of calcium deposits which irritate the achilles. Bumps are red swollen bursa at the outside point of tendon insertion. In time the bumps can become bony protuberances which might have to be surgically removed, as they were in the case of long-time *Runner's World* editor, Joe Henderson.

The spurs, like heel bruises, are mostly a result of shock. Good shoes are the preventative answer.

Heel bumps, though, are caused by our old friend, excessive pronation. Proper shoe inserts are the answer.

○ *Achilles-Calf* Achilles tendinitis and chronically sore calf muscles are caused by short, tight tendons and muscles, a situation made worse by running.

For immediate relief of sore calves and achilles, place a quarter-inch felt heel pad in each shoe. This artificially lengthens the diseased muscle-tendons. Secondly, check the flexibility of your shoe's forefoot sole. An overly stiff sole puts additional strain on your calves and achilles each time you toe off.

The long term cure of sore calves and achilles is endless static stretching of that muscle-tendon group. Do your wall pushup stretch several times a day. Aim for significant improvement over time.

○ *Ankle* Unlike the achilles and calves, the ankles become more resistant to injury the more you run.

Unless, that is, you suffer severe pronation — then you are subject to ankle injuries at any time of your running career. Pronation causes problems on the inside of the ankle. Arch supports will cure this.

A classic beginner's ankle injury, as Dr. Joan Ullyot has observed, is "pseudo-sprain," which has the same symptoms as a traumatic ankle sprain (pain and swelling in the front and outside of the joint), but which occur over a period of time. Good running shoes and a slowly progressing training program will prevent the pseudo-sprain.

○ *Shins and Lower Leg* There are two types of shin splints, and their causes differ.

Anterior shin splints are marked by soreness anywhere along the front of the leg where the tibia and shin muscles meet. The first pains usually occur about four inches above the ankle, and from there they creep upward toward the knee. Anterior shin splints hurt most when the forefoot slaps to the ground after initial heel-first impact.

There are two causes of anterior shin splints. The primary cause is a muscle strength imbalance — the anterior shin muscles are relatively weak (and thus susceptible to pulls and tears) compared with the overly strong calves and achilles. To alleviate the imbalance, regularly do the shin strengthening exercise as described in part two.

A secondary cause, and which makes the above situation worse, is overstriding. Your feet should strike the ground not in front of your center of gravity, but directly under it.

Posterior shin splints are also called inner-leg shin splints, since the pain occurs along the inside edge of the tibia. The source of pain is tendinitis of the posterior tibial tendon, which runs between the tibia and the achilles-calf.

These are the shin splints which ruined my senior cross country season at Stanford, and which eventually led to a tibial stress fracture.

The cause is excessive pronation. The cure is a proper pair of shoe inserts.

Another lower leg overuse injury is pain along the outside of the lower leg. This is fibular tendinitis, and sometimes in extreme cases, fibular stress fracture. This injury ruined the 1971 track season of Dave Wottle, the man in the white golf hat who, of course, recovered and went on to win the 1972 Olympic 800 meters.

The cause of fibula-related injuries is striking the ground too heavily, and too far to the outside edge of the foot. Run lightly and toe straight ahead!

O *Knees* The most common of all running injuries is chondromalacia, appropriately called "runner's knee." Its symptoms are pain and tenderness around the sides and bottom of the kneecap.

Runner's knee is a classic result of excessive pronation.

Also a result of pronation is soreness on the inside of the knee joint. Again, anti-pronatory shoe inserts are the solution for such injuries.

Pain above the knee is an equally classic result of a muscle-tendon strength imbalance — the lower quadricep muscle and tendon are relatively weak compared to the opposing muscle, the hamstring. The solution, then, is the quadricep strengthening exercise as described in part two.

Another knee injury is inflammation of the tendons in back of the knee. This problem is more closely related to the next affected area — the hamstring muscle.

O *Hamstring* A pulled hamstring muscle is usually the injury of sprinters, although it occasionally happens to distance runners attempting too much speedwork. This is what struck Marty Liquori as he was sharpening for the 1976 US Olympic Trials. The hamstring tear kept Liquori off of the team for the second consecutive Olympiad.

More susceptible to injury in distance runners are the sinewy tendons which join the hamstring to the back of the knee. Again, excessive speedwork is the cause.

The hamstring trouble most common to distance runners is a chronic and nagging tightness. The result is less muscle efficiency as well as a feeling of heaviness. If the muscle is severely tight, and actually aches throughout the day, an irritated sciatic nerve is the likely culprit.

If your hamstrings are tight — and they are if you can't touch the floor without bending your knees — begin an immediate and disciplined program of static stretching. Do it now, because once sciatica develops, your problems multiply.

Further discussion of sciatic nerve trouble is found in the section on the lower back and buttocks.

○ *Quadricep* This muscle is relatively injury-free among runners of all speeds. If the lower quadricep becomes injured, it is from disproportionate weakness, and strengthening exercises must be undertaken.

Upper quadricep injuries are more a result of inflexibility. The solution is static stretching — the hurdler's stretch.

○ *Groin* Australian Ron Clarke, perhaps the greatest long distance track racer in history, said the worst injury he ever had was a pulled groin muscle that made every step of his running agony during the entire summer it took for the muscle to heal.

Groin muscle pulls and general tightness are almost always a result of inflexibility, since almost all runners are not adequately flexible in that area. How far apart can you spread your legs? If less than 120 degrees, you are too tight and hence vulnerable to groin injuries. Start stretching right away.

○ *Hips* Among runners, the two familiar hip injuries are hip pointers and bursitis.

A hip pointer is a pain along the top ridge of the pelvis. Its two causes are hip inflexibility and a difference in leg lengths.

Leg length difference and inflexibility are also responsible for inflammation of the hip bursa, located in the joint where the femur attaches to the pelvis.

To stretch the hips, sit in the lotus position for at least 30 seconds. To check for leg length difference, stand barefoot in front of a full-length mirror, and see if your knees match, and if your pelvis is level. If not, place a lifting pad or wedge in the shoe of the shorter leg.

○ *Lower Back and Buttocks* The more you run, the tighter and more swayed your lower back becomes if you don't regularly stretch it, and also strengthen the opposing abdominal muscles. Of course, an inherently swayed back, lordosis, accelerates the looming disaster.

The disaster facing runners with tight and swayed backs is sciatica, or irritation of the sciatic nerve, which descends from the base of the spine through the back of the legs. The sciatic nerve becomes irritated when pinched and pressured by the sagging back.

The symptom of sciatica is a dull aching pain from the lower back to the heel. Running doesn't loosen the legs, either. The pain only gets worse as the run continues.

Fortunately, sciatica has several warning signs. The first is a chronically tight lower back, which grudgingly loosens during the run.

The second step is soreness in the back hips and butt, or, as the late Steve Prefontaine described it: "like someone is kicking your ass."

After that, sciatica creeps down your leg until you are rendered a running cripple. This ruined the fine career of Buddy Edelen, America's top marathoner in the early 1960s.

Before sciatica strikes you (scare tactic — cheap, but effective) embark on a daily routine to stretch the lower back, buttocks and hamstrings, and to strengthen the opposing trunk muscles.

○ *Trunk and Abdominals* In my long personal history of running ailments, none was more mysterious and frustrating than the stitch, that gripping and knifelike pain along the bottom of the rib cage on the right side. What made the stitch so frustrating was that it struck only during races, when I was exerting maximum effort.

Although my best race in high school was the two-mile, I was forced to run the mile, since the stitch predictably assaulted me after five or six laps. The most embarrassing attack occurred when I was leading an indoor two-mile, and had just passed the first mile in 4:50. I ran the

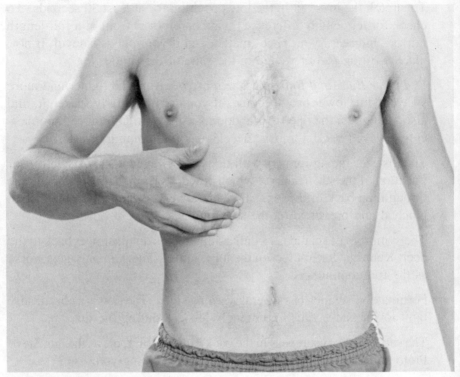

The dreaded stitch occurs in the diaphragm, located underneath the right rib cage.

second mile, doubled over in pain, in six minutes.

Since this was the dark ages of running medicine, the half dozen doctors I saw were unable to find a cause, although some of their guesses now seem amusing: Cracked ribs, pneumonia, an ulcer, intestinal blockage, a misplaced liver, and gas (my coach told me that a laxative would "flush" the stitch away).

Finally, one doctor who suspected a case of prerace jitters prescribed valium, and miraculously the stitches disappeared, although neither the doctor nor myself knew exactly why.

Because the stitch happened only in races, I gradually reasoned it had to be related to maximal breathing. And in a human biology class I found what muscle moved the lungs during breathing — the diaphragm. Could a stitch possibly be an overworked diaphragm, which was straining or even cramping during a race?

To test the theory I daily strengthened the diaphragm by lying on my back and breathing with two 20 pound sandbags on my stomach. This I did for three months, and have since run all kinds of distance races without being stabbed by the dreaded stitch.

As a satisfactory postscript, Dr. George Sheehan three years later wrote in *Runner's World* that a stitch was caused by improper breathing which caused the diaphragm to cramp. Learn how to breathe correctly — filling the lungs from the bottom to the top — by lying on your back and breathing with weights on your stomach, said Sheehan.

Whether or not you are plagued by the stitch, an inordinately strong trunk is essential. Good posture and running style is possible only with a strong trunk. As well, strong abdominal muscles prevent your lower back from sagging.

As mentioned in part two, bent-leg situps are still the best trunk strengthener. Do as many as you can, rest, and repeat. Don't cheat. Situps is the runner's single most important strength exercise.

To stretch the abdominals, hang limply from a chin-up bar. Growl and bare your teeth at the inevitable joker who may try to tickle you.

Part Four: Running While Injured

Q **Can we run while injured?**

A That depends upon two factors.

The first thing you must do is determine the cause of the injury, and then apply the preventative solutions. If you have posterior shin splints or runner's knee, have you yet bought a pair of adequate arch supports? If you have lower back stiffness and mild symptoms of sciatica, are you stretching and performing situps?

Only after you've determined the cause and applied the standard preventions should you run while injured. The next question, then, is how badly are you injured?

Joe Henderson, the long-time editor of *Runner's World* describes four different levels of injury, based upon the level of pain.

During the first level, pain is mild at the outset, and actually goes away during the run, but then reappears afterward. First level injuries are more annoying than actually constricting.

What Henderson calls a second level injury is one in which pain is present, sometimes increasing throughout the entire run. Yet the pain is still tolerable, and doesn't interfere with your running style.

Problems really begin with third level injuries. The only manageable runs are those which are short and slow, and sprinkled with stops. The pain of the injury is present throughout the day.

The fourth and last level of injuries is that which makes running without a limp impossible. There might also be visible swelling around the injury.

Q   **Why do you judge the severity of an injury by its pain? Isn't there a more scientific way to do it?**

A   I suppose you could have a muscle or tendon biopsy, and in that way determine how badly the muscle or tendon is injured.

But a pain reading is just as good, and is certainly less expensive. Besides, a constant pain reading can let you know exactly what movements are aggravating the hurt, and whether the injury is getting better or worse.

Pain is Nature telling you something is wrong. Pain is destruction. Without a sense of pain, some people have unknowingly burned or bled to death.

Q   **Assuming I've taken preventative measures, how bad does an injury have to be before I should stop running?**

A   If you've corrected the cause of the injury — if you bought arch supports for those shin splints — it should be quite safe to run through first and second level injuries. As extra precaution, though, stretch beforehand and begin the run very slowly, with much interspersed walking and jogging. And avoid the kind of running which hurts the most — speedwork, running up steep hills and around sharp corners, and long hard road runs.

Third level injuries must be handled more delicately. Henderson suggests using jog-walk intervals in your training. Says Henderson: "Start very slowly and cautiously. When the pain increases to a (running style) disturbing level, walk and perhaps do some stretching exercises."

To this I would suggest you move your training to a soft and level surface, like a football field. After thoroughly stretching and warming up, slowly jog from one end of the field to the other. Stop, walk for a while, stretch a bit more, and return upfield when you feel ready. Never allow the pain to become so bad that you limp. When that happens, it's time to quit.

Fourth level injuries require a total abstention from running. Instead, try walking, cycling or swimming as an alternate activity to maintain your fitness. And don't worry. Remember what George Harrison said: "All things must pass."

Q **If an injury forces us to stop running, how can we tell when the injury has healed enough to start running?**

A If an injury has healed, but you haven't yet corrected its cause, any kind of running is a risk. Your muscle-skeletal flaws will cause, sooner or later, a repeat of the injury.

Once you've taken the necessary preventative steps, there is no clear answer to when you can safely resume running. You can't wait forever, but neither should you, as Bill Bowerman says, "pull up your carrots to see if they are growing." Do that, and you might have to start the recuperation period all over.

As a minimum standard, wait until the swelling and tenderness disappear. Secondly, check how the injury feels during your normal activities. If your knee hurts when you retrieve the morning paper, it is hardly prepared for the demands of running.

When the swelling and tenderness have subsided, and the pain of just walking around has disappeared, then treat the injury as third level. Cautiously begin a program of jog-walk intervals. Closely watch how the injury responds. Back off if it still hurts badly.

Even if the injury shows signs of improvement, don't expect too much too quickly. Your recovering knee might feel increasingly better for three days in a row, and then on the fourth day, feel terrible again. Don't worry or panic. Muscles and tendons heal at their own speed. Rest a day or two if the injury gets worse. Reexamine the cause and your cure — you might have corrected the pronation, but failed to see the leg length imbalance. Or you just might be trying too hard, and not allowing yourself enough rest or patience.

Don't be bound to any schedule, and don't be discouraged if each day isn't better than the previous. Notice instead your week to week improvement. Don't compare today's pain with yesterday's — compare it with last week's. Gradual improvement is more important.

Also, as you recover, don't be surprised if early morning running hurts more than running later in the day.

Q **Why is that?**

A It's simply a case of the muscles and tendons being their tightest right after you wake up. Bob Anderson, the owner and publisher of *Runner's World*, reports that all of his injuries have occurred during times when he ran before breakfast.

If you like to run in the morning, know that you must spend more time stretching and walking before each run.

*   *   *

Q **Does it do any good to treat the symptoms of an injury?**

A Some methods make sense, but others don't, and are actually quite harmful.

Many runners, including Drs. Joan Ullyot and George Sheehan, recommend taking two aspirin tablets before each run if you have the slightest symptoms of injury. Both claim aspirin slows inflammation, and therefore retards injury.

I am not about to get into a debate with two MDs whom I respect greatly, and who have either directly or indirectly influenced much of my thinking. Still, aspirin, because of its well-known anticoagulant properties, would seem to make worse the inflammation and internal bleeding of muscle-tendon damage. This became apparent to me the day I was taking two aspirin tablets every four hours, and accidentally banged my head against the cupboard door. Although the cut was miniscule, I bled for half an hour. I began to wonder if maybe I was a long lost heir to the British throne.

Secondly, aspirin dulls your monitoring of pain, which is your only way of telling whether or not your running is causing further damage.

Thirdly, aspirin upsets the stomachs of many runners, including myself.

Q **What about heating ointments? Shouldn't I rub a bit around the injury before I run?**

A Heating ointments are good elixirs for stiff muscles — I sometimes use them on my lower back before running.

At the same time, heating ointments should not be used for treating injuries. Like aspirin, the analgesic balm will only speed internal bleeding.

Q **What about ice and cold-packs?**

A Now there's a symptomatic relief which makes sense, and for the same reason ointments and aspirin don't. Applying extreme cold to an injury stops or reduces inflammation and internal bleeding. Since a sore shin continues to bleed internally after the run, some of the damage occurs while you're soaking in the hot tub. By icing an injured muscle or tendon immediately after each run, you've reduced the damage.

Yet, in a backhanded way, even ice and cold can cause harm. When I suffered my pronation-caused shin splints, I was able to continue running as long as I did because each night I vigorously massaged the shins with ice blocks from a frozen milk carton. I thus put off finding the real cause and enacting a real solution. I fooled myself thinking my sore shins would get better. Of course they didn't, because I failed to stop the excessive pronation.

Ice relief should be considered a treat to be indulged in only after you've found and corrected the injury's cause.

Part Five: Doctors

Q **When is it time to see a doctor about an injury?**

A   It's time to see a doctor about a running injury when you either can't determine the cause of your injury, or you can't find a way to correct it.

In other words, treat yourself as best you can before enlisting the help of a doctor.

(Important note: The above advice applies only to overuse injuries. For traumatic injuries, like a suddenly sprained ankle or broken leg, consult a physician immediately.)

Q **What kind of doctor should I see for an overuse injury?**

A   There was a time when all injured runners went to see orthopedic surgeons, who presumably knew more about the working machinery of an athlete than did any other physician. But that was back in the days when the cause of all running injuries was thought to be traumatic, the result of stepping in a hole and thus twisting the knee, rather than what we currently know the cause to be — the overuse of a faulty body.

Then about 10 years ago a few podiatrists who themselves were runners began independently to discover that imperfect feet may actually be the cause of running injuries. To prevent such injuries, the podiatrists began fitting runners with corrective shoe inserts.

At first, the sports orthopedists laughed off podiatry as a psuedo-medicine that had only temporarily risen above the ranks of voodoo and the laying on of hands, and would soon, after some well-known runner had been maimed at the hands of a podiatrist, sink back to where it really belonged.

Such was the pontifical opinion of conventional sports medicine. But the podiatrists surprised everyone — their results with treating runners were undeniably successful, considerably more so than their critics. The runners began to flood the podiatrists' offices, and even Dr. Sheehan admitted that if he could do it again, he'd choose podiatry over cardiology.

Since then, the enlightened orthopedists of the sports medicine community have accepted podiatry, and have added to the field research in flexibility, muscle-tendon strength imbalances, and so on. The runner has benefited enormously from the combined knowledge and practices of orthopedics and podiatry.

Q **What you're saying is, both podiatrists and orthopedists are good people to see for running injuries.**

A Before one can answer yes to that, a further qualification must be made. Since the numbers of unenlightened doctors in both fields still run rampant in the backwaters, and even cities, it is vital to see a doctor of either specialty who himself is a runner. Dr. Sheehan would agree to this. The *Runner's World* medical editor and author of *Running And Being* says he has learned more about the runner's body through his own running, than from journals, textbooks and his own medical practice.

The stresses of running are unlike anything else, and there is still a paucity of published research available for the non-running doctors who must find their information in a book.

At this time, all things being equal, I am slightly biased toward podiatrists. Part of it is the romantic notion that podiatrists made the first breakthrough in preventative running medicine. My other reason, more practical, is that podiatrists generally have a wider selection of, and more experience in making corrective shoe inserts, which are the solution to a good majority of all running injuries.

Q **How much do orthotics or other corrective inserts cost?**

A The first-time cost of fitting and making orthotics is, like contact lenses, quite steep. My first pair of orthotics cost nearly a hundred dollars, but that included a preliminary casting and several office consultations. If I lost my orthotics, it would cost only twenty dollars or so to have them replaced.

Q   **That first-time cost is pretty expensive.**

A   Well, try buying a new set of tires for less. Try eating dinner for four at a
high fashion restaurant for less. Try pinching the leg of a high fashion
woman for less.

As a one-time cost to drastically reduce the misery of chronic overuse
injury, it's a raging bargain.

Q   **How can I find a doctor who has successfully treated runners.**

A   For starters, ask the veteran runners in your town if they know of such a
doctor. If that fails to produce a name, call all of your local orthopedists
and podiatrists, and ask them if they regularly treat runners. Grill them
with questions, and force them to provide satisfactory answers. It's
going to be your legs and money.

If you still aren't satisfied, look in the last chapter of this book, which
lists the addresses of sports medicine organizations that can refer you to
doctors experienced in treating runners.

Drinking is essential when running in high temperatures.

CHAPTER FOURTEEN

The Four Blights
(And Bowser, Too)

Q   **Why is summer the dangerous season for runners?**

A   Hot summer weather can kill even the most experienced of runners. Heat does not kill suddenly, or even accidentally, as a car does, but slowly, sneakingly, and with the full, unthinking cooperation of the runner.

Q   **Does the heat actually kill many runners?**

A   Heat stroke killed at the 1973 Boston Marathon, it kills every late summer on a high school football practice field, and, though one doesn't like to predict such things, it will continue to kill a half dozen runners or more each summer.

Q   **How does heat have the potential to kill even the fastest and healthiest runners?**

A   High temperatures cause the runner to quickly run out of fluids, which as sweat evaporating from the skin, is the body's only means of cooling itself. If one continues to run after the fluid is gone, the body's temperature will quickly rise past 106 degrees, heat collapse level, up to 108 degrees, a deadly level.

Q   **How much fluid can a runner lose before overheating?**

A   On a typical summer day of 85 degrees and 50 percent humidity, a 150 pound runner loses about six ounces of body fluid *every mile*. Eighty percent of the body fluid is lost through sweat; the other 20 percent is expired in various ways, chiefly breath vapor.

Once a runner loses three percent of his body weight in fluids, without replacing any of it, he is flirting with heat exhaustion or stroke. Since body fluid weighs about a pound for every pint, a runner can lose his three percent, or four to five pounds, in ten to twelve miles of running on a hot summer day.

Ten to twelve miles of hot weather running is the absolute limit if the runner doesn't make up the fluid loss by drinking.

Q   **So you recommend drinking a lot of fluids during summer running?**

A   Absolutely.

Q   **What kind of fluids should I drink?**

A   Water is good enough for most of your drinking. If your diet is well balanced, your body will produce an adequate electrolyte (salt) supply. An overheated body runs short of water long before it runs short of electrolytes.

Electrolyte replacement drinks — Gatorade, Sportade, ERG, and Body Punch — might be marginally better than water, since they already have the rough composition of sweat, and therefore are more quickly absorbed and used by the body. These drinks also contain glucose, a broken down sugar giving quick energy.

Such a drink might therefore be slightly advantageous during all-out performances, like races, but for your everyday running, water is fine.

Fruit juices are good replacement fluids, since they contain fructose, another broken down sugar. Fruit juices, though, are expensive.

Coffee and tea should be avoided. For one, caffeine is the last drug you need in hot weather. Secondly, both liquids are mildly diuretic, meaning that some of the fluid can't be used and is discarded in the urine.

For the same reason, alcohol should not be taken before or during the run. Beer, though, especially when mixed with lemonade as a shandy, is a good post-run drink. Beer contains a good electrolyte balance, as well as iron. And since beer is only mildly alcoholic, particularly when cut with lemonade, it is only mildly diuretic.

Q   **When should I drink?**

And for those who don't like water . . .

A Drink whenever you can. For starters, drink a pint to a quart of fluid before beginning the run.

Q **Won't that give me a side ache?**

A It might if you aren't accustomed to running with fluid in the stomach. Learn to do so, even if you must suffer through the first few runs. The reward is well worth the price.

Q **And then?**

A And then drink at least eight ounces of fluid every five miles. This is minimum hot weather drinking. In extremely hot weather, or on long runs, you should drink 16 ounces every five miles. Remember, you are losing six ounces every mile, and once you've suffered a net loss of 60-70 ounces you run a significant risk of heat exhaustion.

If you run 15 miles in hot weather, you will lose about 90 ounces. If you drink minimally, eight ounces every five miles, you'll have consumed only 16 ounces over the 15 miles, since you drink only twice, at five and at 10 miles. The result is a net loss of 74 ounces, well past the limit of safety.

If all this sounds like hocus pocus, the point is that even though drinking eight ounces every five miles sounds adequate, it really isn't.

Here is a chart showing the net results of fluid losses and fluid gains typical of a hot summer day.

Miles Run	Fluid Loss 6 ozs./mile	Minimal Drinking 8 ozs./5 miles	net loss	Recommended Drinking 8 ozs./2 miles	
2	− 12		− 12	+ 8	− 4
4	− 24		− 24	+ 16	− 8
6	− 36	+ 8	− 28	+ 24	−12
8	− 48		− 40	+ 32	−16
10	− 60	+16	− 44	+ 40	−20
12	− 72*		− 56	+ 48	−24
14	− 84*		− 68	+ 56	−28
16	− 96*	+24	− 72*	+ 64	−32
18	−108*		− 84*	+ 72	−36
20	−120*	+32	− 88*	+ 80	−40
22	−132*		−100*	+ 88	−44
24	−144*		−112*	+ 96	−48
26	−156*	+40	−116*	+104	−52
28	−168*		−128*	+112	−56
30	−180*	+48	−132*	+120	−60

* = danger

Q   **Should I take salt pills with my fluid?**

A   Taking too much salt makes useless the fluid you drink. This is why you can drink gallons of ocean water and still die of thirst. Because salt pills are so easily abused, they will not be recommended in this book.

The replacement of fluids must come first. If you feel the need for salt, then salt your food. But don't fool around with salt pills.

                              *   *   *

Q   **Is it ever too hot to run?**

A   That's a complicated question to answer because of the many variables: temperature; humidity; length of the run; condition of the runner; the runner's tolerance to heat; and, of course, the fluid loss and replacement.

In plugging all these variables into some kind of rough formula, we are going to have a wide margin of error. The important thing is to err on the side of safety.

For starters, here is a standard temperature and humidity safety chart.

Heat Safety Chart — Normal Training

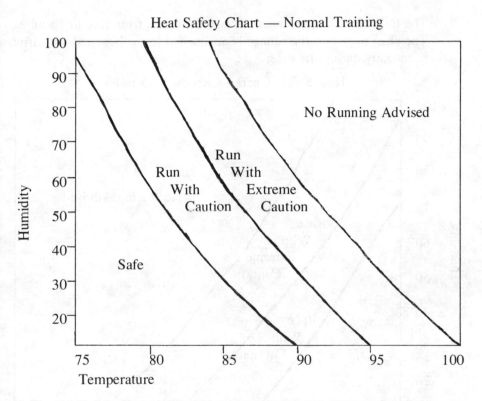

(Chart Revised from U.S. Weather Service Operations Manual)

The above chart gives us a starting point for safety consideration. Yet, safe for some is quite unsafe for others. To determine what is safe for each runner, we must consider the other variables. How far is the person running? How much fluid will he lose and drink back? What shape is he in? Is he acclimated to the heat?

An 80 degree day with 50 percent humidity may be listed as safe, but is it really safe for a novice running his first marathon? If he drinks no fluids during the race? If his longest training run has been seven miles? If he came straight from the North Pole?

Obviously not.

Q   **What if the runner is racing?**

A   The following chart has been revised for races, from five to 15 miles. The chart presumes the runner is acclimated to the heat and will drink adequately during the race:

Heat Safety Chart — Races, 5-15 miles

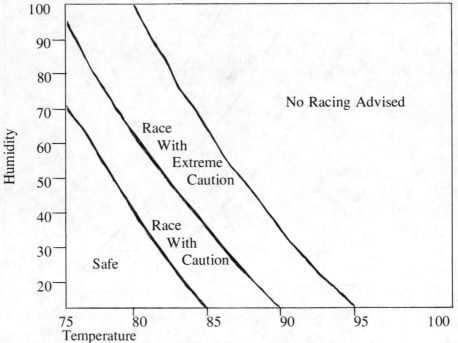

Q   **Can heat safety charts tell us anything at all?**

A   The above chart is a good guideline for a trained runner, acclimated to the heat, running within his limits (not racing) and never allowing a fluid debt of more than 50 ounces.

For races of more than 15 miles, here is a further revised safety chart:

Heat Safety Chart — Races More Than 15 Miles

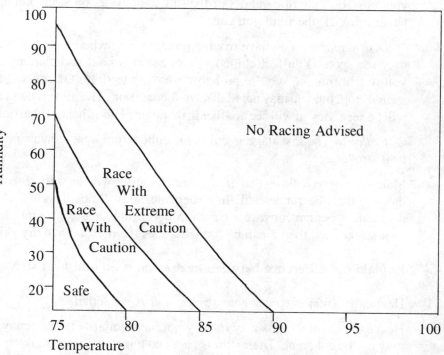

Q **How can a runner tell if he is becoming overheated?**

A The symptoms of overheating occur in predictable order, which gives the knowledgeable runner sufficient warning. These are:

○ *Dry Mouth* In high school we called it cotton mouth, since the saliva felt no more watery than cotton. Coaches and other ignoramuses will tell you a dry mouth is natural — don't believe them. Being unable to spit isn't natural. Your fluid debt at this stage is probably 40-50 ounces (a debt of 65 is dangerous, 75 is critical). An immediate 20 ounces of fluid should be taken, and the run should be continued with caution.

○ *Hot Head* This is the next warning signal. The inside of your head feels slowly boiling. The pulse can be felt at the temples. You need a quart of fluid immediately, and you need to wet your head and skin. If you can't do both on the run, abandon the run.

○ *Dizziness and Loss of Coordination* You can no longer keep a rhythm, and unless you concentrate, can't run a straight line. In order, you must: quit the run; get out of the sun; keep water on your skin and head; drink all the fluid you can.

○ *Disorientation* You have trouble remembering where you are. You may see spots. You feel chilled — your skin is cold and clammy. If you're still running, you're probably weaving terribly. Of course you should stop, but you may not realize your condition. The hope is that you will be seen, or you will see another in this state. This is heat exhaustion.

○ *Collapse* The last stage is collapse, either from heat exhaustion or heat stroke.

Many wrongly believe that if a runner is still sweating, there is no danger, that the runner still has adequate body fluid. This belief is damned. A person can sweat right through heat exhaustion. Only in a heat stroke, and then it can be too late, does the person have dry skin.

Q **Explain the difference between heat exhaustion and heat stroke.**

A Heat exhaustion precedes heat stroke, and is not lethal.

Heat exhaustion victims may or may not have collapsed. They may or may not be coherent. Their skin is pale and moist — sickly looking. A heat exhaustion victim must:

1. Be taken out of the sun.
2. Be sprayed continuously with water or placed in a swimming pool to lower body temperature.
3. Drink as much fluids, preferably electrolyte drinks, as can be tolerated.
4. Be kept in a cool place for a few hours.

Heat stroke victims usually collapse and are unconscious, although that is not true in all cases. The skin tells the difference — the skin is hot, dry and red. Here is what should be done for a heat stroke victim:

1. Body temperature must be lowered immediately, with any means available. An ice water bath is ideal, but any liquid thrown on the skin is good. The immediate lowering of body temperature makes the difference between life and death.

2. Have someone call an ambulance.
3. Tell the doctor the victim is a runner. Runners have abnormal hearts and EKGs, which are easily misinterpreted among those not trained to look for it.

Q **Can the symptoms of overheating occur after the run?**

A Yes, they can. Heat collapse can occur hours after the run, which is why you should always take a long cold shower or swim after any hot weather run. You must also replace your fluid loss, which can be up to a gallon.

Both precautions are important to your health. Even if you didn't experience overheating symptoms during the run, your temperature could still be as high as 105-106 degrees. This is not well-tolerated for more than a few hours. So, get that body temperature down.

And drink those fluids. If you don't urinate within two hours after a run, you haven't taken enough fluids. When you do urinate, observe its color. Dark yellow urine is a sign of dehydration. Light yellow or clear colored urine is much better for your health.

Q **In what ways can a runner cope with the heat?**

A First of all, the runner should never try to fight the heat. Heat will not adapt to the runner; the runner must adapt to the heat.

Always know before you run, the temperature and humidity. An unexpected rise of 10 degrees and 10 percent humidity can turn a warm day into a dangerously hot day.

Never let the lure of the race tempt you to run in unsafe conditions.

Wear the right clothing.

Keep wet when you can.

And drink fluids liberally.

Q **Why should I keep wet?**

A Wetting the skin is the best way of keeping cool. Your sweat wets the skin naturally, but to conserve body fluids, apply water directly to your skin. On a hot day, run through every sprinkler you can find. If you really get hot, ask a homeowner to use his garden hose, and then thoroughly douse yourself. Soak your head and hair. Soak your clothes.

In some races, like the Boston Marathon, the spectators line the course and squirt water on the runners. Accept their gift.

Q **What should a runner wear in the heat?**

A If there is little or no sun, expose as much of the body as you modestly can. Men, wear only shorts and shoes. Women, wear shorts, shoes and a sleeveless top cut to expose the stomach.

If the sun is shining high in the sky, both men and women should wear a loose-fitting white cotton tee shirt, and soak it in cold water before running. You might wear a white golf or tennis hat, and soak it, too.

Q **How long does it take to acclimate to the heat?**

A Acclimation to heat takes three weeks. If your local weather changes suddenly to the hotter, or if you move to a hot climate, lighten your training by a third for three weeks. The reason for this is, acclimation will increase your body's tolerance to heat by a third.

Be patient, and never race in heat unless you are thoroughly acclimated.

*   *   *

Q **Is it ever too cold to run?**

A If a runner takes adequate precaution — dressing properly and staying on well-traveled roads — there are few days too cold for running in North America. I ran through five North Dakota winters, worst in the continental United States, and missed less than a handful of days because of foul weather. The temperature, even 40 degrees below zero, was never too cold by itself. The wind, though, sometimes drove the chill factor down to 100 below. Below is a temperature, wind and chill factor safety chart:

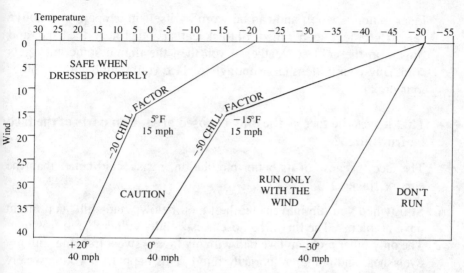

Q **What are the dangers of running in cold weather?**

A The biggest danger is having to stop, unable to continue, and having no one see your plight. This is why you should never overextend on a cold day. This is also why you should run only on well-traveled roads.

Of course, never run in a blizzard or otherwise poor visibility. Blizzards kill because people get lost in them.

The nagging danger, unless you dress properly, is frostbite, mostly in the fingers and ears. Runners usually don't freeze their toes as long as they keep moving. When walking in cold weather, one may need heavy socks and boots to keep the feet warm, but runners stay quite toasty in ordinary sweat socks and running shoes. Just stay out of deep snow.

The ears and fingers are another story. The ears should be covered with a heavy, snugly fitting stocking hat pulled down past the earlobes. If you normally wear your hair long, wear it longest in the winter. Hair is great ear protection.

The hands and fingers should be covered with mittens, not gloves. Gloves divide the fingers, and cold conquers.

The best mittens are those two piece affairs worn by woodchoppers. The inner mitten is wool, and can be worn by itself in temperatures above zero. The outer mitten is made of thick leather and protects the hands and fingers in the coldest weather. Even then the thumb sometimes gets cold. Buy your mittens large enough to place your thumb with the other four digits.

Q **That leaves the face as the only exposed area. Can parts of the face be frostbitten?**

A The face, because of its better circulation, resists cold better than the ears or fingers.

Still, when you run into the teeth of a 60 below wind chill, you might have problems. The tip of the nose is especially vulnerable to frostbite. The only other problem I've had with my face is sweat freezing shut my eyelashes, and being temporarily blind. This happens if you unwisely run with the wind at first, build a sweat, and then turn to face the wind.

The best facial protection is a ski mask. Buy one in addition to your stocking hat.

Q **How should we dress the body in cold weather?**

A The rule is, the warmer you are in the extremities — your head, feet and hands — the less you need to wear on the body. In temperatures around 40 degrees, marathoner Bill Rodgers wears in races only light gloves as additional protection.

Another rule is, several thin layers of clothing are warmer than one thick covering. Space between the layers traps body heat.

Here is a recommended list of winter running clothes:

○ *Stocking Hat* Buy one thick and snugly fitting. Wool is best. They cost two to five dollars.

○ *Ski Mask* Own a ski mask in addition to a stocking hat. On coldest days you'll need both. The cost is two to five dollars.

○ *Turtleneck Shirt* Fashion doesn't count, so buy one at the discount store. Buy it loose-fitting, and of cotton polyester. Don't spend more than three dollars.

Dressing for the weather – the secret of winter running.

○ *Thermal Underwear* You can buy both the top and bottom for five dollars.

○ *Warmup Suit* For ten dollars you can buy an adequate cotton sweat-suit. However, a nylon polyester suit breaks the wind much better. They cost from 25 to 70 dollars, although 50 and up is purely for fashion.

○ *Windbreaker Jacket* You can buy one with cotton lining for ten dollars.

○ *Athletic Socks, Over-the-Calf* These will cost two dollars a pair.

○ *Woodchopper Mittens* Good mittens cost ten dollars, but buy them anyway. In the long run they are cheaper. Good leather lasts for years.

You now have everything you need to run comfortably on a January day in Bismarck, North Dakota. Here is a recommended dress chart for various winter temperatures:

70°	50°
Tee Shirt Shorts Shoes	Tee Shirt Shorts Shoes + Turtleneck worn over the tee shirt. + Socks

30°
Turtleneck
Tee Shirt
Shorts
Socks
Shoes
+ Thermal Underwear worn
  under the tee shirt and
  shorts, or
 	
Warmup Suit worn over
the turtleneck and shorts.
+ Stocking Hat
+ Inner Mittens
	10°
	Both Warmup Suit and
	    Thermal Underwear
	Turtleneck
	Tee Shirt
	Shorts
	Socks
	Shoes
	Stocking Hat
	Inner Mittens

$-10°$	$-30°$
Warmup Suit	Windbreaker Jacket
Turtleneck	Warmup Suit
Tee Shirt	Turtleneck
Shorts	Tee Shirt
Thermal Underwear	Shorts
Socks	Thermal Underwear
Shoes	Socks
Stocking Hat	Shoes
Inner Mittens	Stocking Hat
+ Outer Mittens	Full Mittens
+ Windbreaker Jacket	+ Ski Mask

Q **Do I need to wear special shoes in the cold?**

A No, but some find leather shoes slightly warmer. Whatever you decide to wear, buy your shoes big enough to wear with thick athletic socks. You might have to move up a half size.

Q **Within my locality, where are the warmest places to run?**

A The temperature won't vary much within any locality, but the wind will. The following are the calmest places in any locale:

○ *Lower Elevations* Wind grows stronger with increased elevation.

○ *Older Residential Areas* The fully grown trees in these areas act as wind buffers.

○ *Downtown* The taller buildings are good wind buffers, too. Be alert for traffic, though.

○ *Parks* The older parks have the taller trees.

The most important tip to remember when running in the cold and wind is: *Plan your courses to run the first part against the wind and the last part with it.* This is both physiologically and psychologically advantageous.

Q **I have one further question. Can cold weather running damage the lungs?**

A   No, that's another myth perpetuated by non-runners. The fingers, toes, and ears are your body's bell-weathers — they will freeze before any vital organ, including the lungs, will.

*   *   *

Q   **Should we run in the rain?**

A   Some of the choicest runs are those taken in a warm summer rain. Just wear shoes you aren't afraid of soaking.

A cold winter's rain may not be quite as much fun, but it certainly can be enjoyable if you stay warm. Runners from the University of Oregon like to wear thermal long underwear, turtleneck shirts and windbreaker jackets in the rain. They find warmup suits too baggy and bothersome when wet.

If you are too shy to parade outside in your long underwear, you might invest in a nylon shell rainsuit to be worn over the warmup suit or directly over the skin. Don't mistakenly buy a rubberized rainsuit. Never, at any time, should you wear a rubberized suit — not in the rain, not to lose weight, not ever. Rubberized suits create their own weather conditions — 98.6 degrees (and rising) and 100 percent humidity. If you read the first part of this chapter, you know how dangerous that can be.

Q   **Is it safe to run during an electrical storm?**

A   No. Certainly the odds are against ever being struck by lightning, but why take a chance on something over which you have no control?

If you are caught in an electrical storm, seek the lowest elevations and run for cover.

*   *   *

Q   **Is it dangerous to run on the streets and roads?**

A   It is if we aren't careful. Like heat, cars can kill the healthiest of runners. Unlike heat, cars strike quickly and without warning.

Out of convenience, most of us run on the road. Yet we are not its king. The car is, and to avoid its merciless wrath we must observe the following safety reminders:

You might have to change directions or even stop, but always heed traffic.

Getting Bowser where he can't bite you.

1. Run facing traffic. This is both the common sense and legal rule of all pedestrians, including runners.

   There is an exception to this rule, however. Don't run facing traffic around a left turn. The opposing traffic is making a tight right, and often can't see pedestrians until it is too late.

2. Stay close to the side of the road. Even if you are proud of your new shoes, don't run in the middle of the street. The gravel shoulders are better for your legs anyway.

3. Even though you, the pedestrian, usually have the right of way, always yield to cars. Consider the possibilities if you don't. Does it matter if you win a court case posthumously?

4. If a driver challenges you for the right of way, let him "win." Pride has no place here.

5. Heed traffic signals. This takes will power when you have momentum, but do it anyway.

6. It hardly needs to be said, but look in all directions before crossing a road.

7. Realize you are most vulnerable to bad judgments at the end of a long, hard run, when you are not thinking clearly, feel invincible, and think you have won by your sterling effort, the right of way.

8. Run defensively. Never assume anything of the driver.

9. Don't run where you know traffic is bad or where there is no room on the shoulder.

10. As a group, don't run more than two abreast. Go to single file at the slightest crowding.

11. Don't run on a street divider unless it is amply wide.

12. Wear bright colors, at least in the shorts and shoes. Don't be embarrassed. Would you rather have traffic not see you?

13. At night, either run where the street is well lit, or wear a reflector vest. Doing both is safer.

Think of the above as the 13 ways to increase your luck against the car and its driver.

* * *

Q **When I'm running, and a mean looking dog approaches, what should I do?**

A Most dogs, unless they have been trained to attack, are bluffers and cowards.

If you approach a hostile dog, slow your pace, raise your clenched fist, and stare at the mutt. This will, in almost all cases, stop the mangy beast in his tracks.

Once you have passed the dog, he might, as cowards do, run at you from behind. If you hear the following footsteps and barking, stop, turn around, and again raise your fist at the dog. This should stop him for good.

In the few cases a dog carries out the attack, reach for the nearest stick or rock and go to it. You don't want to fight more than you have to, but if the dog tears your flesh, kick and beat the living hell out of him. It is your perfect right to do so; the owner is clearly negligent, and the courts will back you in 100 percent of the cases, even if you kill the dog.

If you do get bitten, get immediate medical attention. Then call your lawyer and proceed to wring all the money you can from the negligent owner. Tell your lawyer that dog bite wounds heal much faster on the French Riviera.

Running – the ideal family affair.

CHAPTER FIFTEEN

The Age Factor

Q   **At what age do we reach our peak as runners?**

A   Well, that depends on how you want to define peak. If it's peak of enjoyment, that can be attained by runners of all ages who approach the sport with a judicious blend of common sense and spontaneity.

As far as peak of performance, the physiologists tell us that it's all downhill after age 20*, yet extremely rare is the distance runner who reaches world class level at that tender age.

In actuality, most of the world's top distance runners hit their peak of performance somewhere between their early 20s and early 30s. Lasse Viren, at 23, was considered quite young when he captured his first Olympic 5000/10,000 double in Munich in 1972. Far more typical among the best were the ages of the three marathoners who represented the United States in Montreal — Frank Shorter, 28, Bill Rodgers, 28, and Don Kardong, 27.

Of course there are exceptions, but, interestingly, most of them occur *above* the norm. Gaston Roelants, the Belgian who won the 1964 Olympic steeplechase, was 35 when he won the International cross-country championships in 1972. George Young, another steeplechaser, was a winner on the pro track circuit at 37, while amazing Jack Foster of New Zealand ran a 2:11 marathon (faster than Frank Shorter's winning time at the Munich Olympics, and faster than the great Abebe Bikila *ever* ran) at age 41.

* Based on maximum oxygen uptake as measured by J. L. Hodgson of the University of Minnesota in a study entitled "Age and Aerobic Capacity of Urban Midwestern Males."

181

Q   **Why is there a discrepancy between a runner's age and performance peak?**

A   That is a good question, because in some strength/endurance sports, like swimming, athletes do reach their peak of performance around age 20.

A large part of the answer is that in both swimming and running it seems to take 5-15 years of constant practice and regular competition to reach the peak. Most world class swimmers began training for competition well below the age of 10. Most distance runners, though, don't begin regular training until they are 15, freshmen or sophomores in high school.

Q   **Then why don't runners start planning their careers at age 10?**

A   This in fact was the plea made by a Baltimore physician, Dr. Gabe Mirkin, in a 1971 letter to *Sports Illustrated*. In the letter Mirkin said that runners in the future who waited until their teens to start could never catch up with those who started as small children.

Mirkin himself led the children's crusade by enlisting his sons, age seven and nine, in strenuous training programs.

Q   **What are the boys doing today?**

A   At last report, both no longer run. They decided they'd rather enjoy childhood while they could, and so both retired from the sport before age 10.

Hundreds of unfortunate children have since been driven (by fanatical parents with visions of Olympic gold medals floating before their eyes) along the trail blazed by Dr. Mirkin. And almost without fail, they have quit running before reaching high school, much less their physical peak. A lot of them get injured, more fall disinterested, and all of them are cheated out of normal childhoods.

The whole idea of strenuous training for the young seems preposterous. And it doesn't even produce good runners — it hasn't so far, nor, I'm betting, will it ever. I would further wager that future world class

Running – for the young-minded of all ages.

runners will not be younger, but older, as we constantly learn more about diet, injury prevention, stress and rest, and longevity.

It must be said here that there is a whole continent of young distance runners who do not burn out, and do have later success. These are the Africans, who as children run long distances not as training, but as their only way of getting to school. But curiously, the African track stars are among the *latest* blooming athletes in the world. Rare is the African who reaches world class status in his 20s, but common is one in his 30s. Kip Keino, Ben Jipcho and Abebe Bikila all enjoyed their fastest times and biggest wins after their third decade.

Q   **What is the earliest age one should begin running?**

A   Children are the most natural of runners, and should be given every opportunity to run, *but only at their own whims and desires*. The natural habitat of a child is the playground, not the roads or the tracks. If you bring them along on training runs, or to races, fine, but never force the kid to enter a race or run *x* number of miles in training. Follow the example of Bob and Rita Anderson, the publishers of *Runner's World*, who bring their five-year-old daughter and three-year-old son to the local fun-run races, and let the children decide if and what races they wish to run.

Q   **When is the earliest one should begin "training" as such?**

A   Junior high school age is the absolute earliest anyone should begin running systematically, and then only if the coach places strong emphasis on fun. The successful junior high coach isn't always a winner, but *is* one who makes sure his athletes enjoy running and will want to continue in high school and beyond.

If a young runner thus has a solid background in fun and enjoyment, he or she will be ready for more strenuous training and competition in high school. And even then there is no rush to get started — Frank Shorter didn't start track until his senior year.

Q   **Then the earliest you recommend hard training is in high school?**

A   Correct.

Q   **But if it takes 5-15 years of hard training to reach one's performance peak, very few will reach it in time to coincide with their physical peak. The discrepancy remains.**

A   That's also correct, but what is the alternative? The grand theory of childhood training and future success has totally washed out in reality.

Plus I suspect that peak performance in running consists of many variables, training and peak physical age only two among them. I suspect that our sport is vastly more technical than people give it credit for — that rhythm, body-mind coordination and concentraion are essential to success, and take years to properly develop. Finally, I have a suspicion that older runners, by and large, have more of a sense of urgency in their running. They know the opportunities for peak performance won't last forever.

Q   **If we start running much later than high school, say at 30, can we still expect to reach our performance peak 5-15 years later?**

A   Yes, 5-15 years is a good rule of thumb at any age. Dr. Joan Ullyot started at 30, and at 35 began to enter the top ranks of women marathoners, where she still remains now in her late 30s. Jack Foster didn't start until 33, and then ran his best times in his early 40s.

Dr. Alex Ratelle, the marathoner, bloomed later yet. He began in 1965 at age 40, and in 1977 ran his fastest marathon to date, an American over-50 record of 2:35:43. He thinks he has a crack at breaking 2:30 in the next year or two, and I wouldn't bet against him.

Q   **What happens after the performance peak?**

A   If you take care of yourself — if you eat right, train right, practice injury prevention, and maintain freshness and enthusiasm — you should be able to turn the peak into a plateau that will last another 5-10 years, especially if you reach the peak early, in your 20s or 30s.

One trouble is that many runners, once they've reached their peak and know it, will let up. The other trouble is the increasing likelihood of injury as you grow older. A well-tuned car may be able to run just as fast as a new model, but the chance of breakdown is much greater.

Mike Manley, the Olympic steeplechaser, was a late peaker, and didn't reach his best form until his late 20s, despite a long and intensive career. As his racing times continued to improve with each passing year, Manley claimed that his training became more difficult, because his muscles wouldn't snap back from a hard workout as quickly as they did in younger days. He also said that injuries, when they occurred, took longer to heal than before. In short, said Manley, age was making world class training a real drag.

But Manley, who learned much of his running from the Bill Bowerman school of thought, was smart enough to make the necessary compensation in his training — more stretching, hard/easy, etc. — and thus was able to earn a spot on the 1972 US Olympic team.

Q   **What happens after the plateau?**

A   When you do start the inevitable slide, it is actually quite slow if you maintain your current training and stay free of injuries. If you reached your performance peak early, in your 20s, the dropoff in your racing times in your 30s will be only about a half percent a year. In your 40s and 50s, the slide is about one percent, and after that, about two percent.

That is to say, if you started running and training for the marathon at 30, you might hit your peak, say three hours, at age 40. If your training stays constant, you can maintain the peak for aother 5-10 years (or even improve, as Dr. Ratelle has, by losing weight and training harder) before you begin a drop of one percent a year — about two minutes each year in the marathon.

By your middle 50s you might be running the marathon in the 3:10-30 range, and after that, lose about four minutes a year. By age 60, you will probably be running the marathon 30-45 minutes slower than you did at age 40. Unless, of course, you didn't start running until age 40!

Q **At what age should we begin to curtail our running?**

A When we no longer find it enjoyable.

Q **That's a pretty vague answer.**

A That's because age is quite irrelevant to the amount of running one should do. At all ages, runners should not exceed their individual levels of stress tolerance and enjoyment. To be sure, your stress tolerance lessens as you grow older, but this is gradual, and so your reduction in running will also be gradual, so much so that it will probably go unnoticed. There is certainly no magical point when you must reduce or stop your running. This is nonsense.

No longer a strange sight – at seven million, the number of women runners is outgrowing the men.

CHAPTER SIXTEEN

For Women Only

Q **What percentage of people running today are women?**

A An October, 1977, Gallup poll revealed that 11 percent of all Americans run at least a mile a day, two days a week. Sixteen percent of the male population call themselves runners, compared with seven percent of all females.

In raw numbers, this means there are 23 million Americans who run. Approximately 70 percent, or 16 million, are male and seven million are female.

These figures compare to 1975-76 estimates of 10 million runners, with only one to two million women. So, the number of female runners is increasing numerically as fast as the men, and proportionately much faster.

Q **Is running a feminine activity for women?**

A Running is as feminine or masculine or androgynous as the runner likes it to be. Unfortunately, the Soviet track women of the 1950s created such a strong public image of running as unfeminine that the myth still lives. Those women, and their East German counterparts today who take anabolic steroids (male hormones) should be discarded from any argument, comparison or consideration.

Chief of the myths is that running will make a woman's muscles hard or unsightly. The fact is, the predominance of estrogens in a woman will keep her muscles from bulking up. The East German women are bulky and hard because they take male hormones. A woman's natural estrogen level will allow her to almost double the strength of any muscle without adding an inch of bulk.

189

And because running is such an effective calorie eater, the chance of gaining muscle anywhere is almost nil.

What running does, since it heightens the physical and mental awareness, is heighten one's sexuality. Male runners feel even more masculine; female runners feel even more feminine.

If a woman has ever been questioned about the propriety or femininity of her running, she should consider the motivation of the questioner.

Often as not, men who impugn the femininity of women runners are threatened by running. They are threatened by the time their "ladies" spend away from them. They are suspicious of the men their women might see while running, since they know secretly men runners are more healthy, robust and *virile* than themselves. The most petty of men are jealous of their wives or girlfriends, who are experiencing increased health through running, while the men themselves are growing ever more fat and unsightly.

Such men are those pathetic souls who like their women soft and pampered, shopping for groceries, and bawling over the latest soap opera. Such men are often themselves smokers, heavy drinkers, obese, overly aggressive, addicted to television, constipated, irritable, impotent, and in otherwise precarious and miserable health; in brief, the most *unmasculine* of men.

*   *   *

Q   **Should a woman's running style differ from a man's?**

A   No, good running style is the same for both men and women.

However, it seems that women are guilty of more style faults in the beginning. Unlike most men who competed in high school sports, most women have not run regularly since childhood. As well, women have been brainwashed to run femininely, delicately, or in other such erroneous, contrived and unnatural ways.

As a result, many women think they look graceful if they run with long stride and pointed toes. This style looks only like it really is — affected and inefficient.

Other women, in the beginning, spend more energy prancing up and down, going nowhere, rather than moving straight ahead. Many mistakenly believe jogging (Isn't that a dreadful word? Let's call it *running*.) is a stationary movement, and that it is a bonus if you really go somewhere. This is doubly foolish, and women who run this way have watched too many television commercials where "jogging" is perceived as a silly preliminary before the truly important business of fixing corn flakes for the husband and kids.

Many women, too, carry their arms and hands too high, as if protecting or hiding their breasts. A high arm carriage, as discussed in the chapter on style, upsets the critical balance. Your resting hands should be no higher than waist level.

Lastly, women, because of different hip structure, tend to swing their trail legs around the side to the front, rather than lifting them forward. This is inefficient, and a habit that must be overcome. Learn to lift from the hips and at the knees. Learn to make all your motions straight ahead.

Q **What can women do to run correctly?**

A First, read the chapter on style; it applies to everyone. Secondly, observe the more experienced runners, both male and female. See how their motions are directed forward, and not from side to side or up and down. Watch how they run with a natural flow and efficiency. Good running is existential. It simply is. For both men and women.

Q **Should women run with men?**

A There is no reason not to, if the man and woman are of roughly equal ability and they enjoy running together.

Running with someone is a superb way of getting to know them; running gives a short, quick and honest assessment of a person. Your approach to life is manifested in the way you approach running. Competitive people will try to compete, somehow, if only by words and their implications. Aggressive people will attack their runs. Impulsive people will speed and slow. Thinkers will think, talkers will talk, complainers will complain. Running so isolates a person from the usual inhibitions of modernity, that the inner self is cut loose. So, run with a man or woman only if you want to know them more intimately.

Certain problems arise when a woman chooses to run with a man. A woman just starting running is going to be significantly slower than her male equal. The average untrained 40-year-old male can still, if pressed, run a mile in less than eight minutes. An untrained 40-year-old female usually cannot. A mile, or any distance shorter than 20 miles, strongly favors the stronger man.

In the beginning women are advised not to run with men. Wait until you can run two or three miles at a pace under nine minutes a mile.

As the woman increases her ability, a second problem arises. Her adaptive ability to run longer distances will increase faster than the man's. Say both the man and the woman are running three miles in about 25 minutes. In two months, the man will want to run the three miles at a faster pace, while the woman will want to run the same pace at a longer distance. Women adapt most easily to distance, men to speed (the reason for this is discussed later). Improvement rates are different. This doesn't necessarily make running together impossible, or even difficult. It is something a man and woman running together regularly should know, however, to avoid conflict.

A third problem is a bugaboo of all coed sports — male jealousy when the woman is a better athlete or runner.

It is a fact that women have run the equivalent of a 4:14 mile. It is also a fact that women are now running the marathon — 26 miles and 385 yards — at a pace faster than six minutes a mile, and soon, when the fastest women track stars move up to that distance, will be running them at a pace of 5:30 a mile.

Of the 16 million men running in this country, only 500 or so can run a marathon faster than the fastest woman.

Training, far more than sex, determines how fast and comfortable one will run in longer distances. There is no sound reason for a man to feel threatened by faster women.

If a man feels threatened by your faster performances, he is either ignorant of the facts or petty. If he is ignorant, inform him. If he remains threatened, avoid him. You are much too wonderful to waste your time with petty people.

Another problem similar to all coed sports is male irresistibility to coach the poor, helpless female. Men somehow feel protective and fatherly, and won't miss an opportunity to dole out advice to women. If this is annoying to you women, as it should be, give the man his own advice. If he persists, tell him what he is doing, and tell him to stop. Is there any reason why a man should know more about your running than you do? And if he does, so what? Experience is your best teacher, remember?

Q   **Are women at a disadvantage to men?**

A   Compared with women, men contain more muscle and less fat in relation to body weight, and therein lies their advantage. Of an average sized, middle aged, untrained man's weight, 40 percent is muscle and 15 percent is fat. His female equivalent has 25 percent muscle and 25 percent fat.

A woman can, by running more and eating less, lose fat, but never as much as a man can. A highly trained female runner has fat levels of 10-15 percent. A similarly trained man has levels of five percent or less.

The man has, in effect, a bigger engine carrying less baggage. In any sport demanding muscular strength or a high muscle-to-body-weight ratio, the trained man will outperform the trained woman. This is true for all running events up to 20 miles.

Q   **Do women have any advantage over men?**

A   Paradoxically, they do.

Both men and women runners can store enough glycogen (blood sugar) in their livers to supply energy for 18-20 miles of running. After that, the body feeds off of its own fat for energy.

Male runners do not burn their own fat efficiently unless they have been trained to do so (and that involves fasting or long runs). This is why so many men complain of hitting the wall at the 20-mile mark in the marathon. They've run out of one fuel, sugar, and can't switch to the other, fat.

Women, even though they may not have been specifically trained to use their own fat, can still do so more easily than men. The reason for this is not entirely understood, but it remains circumstantial fact. Women marathoners rarely complain of hitting the wall. In fact, in a few ultra-marathons, such as the 1973 Pacific AAU 100-Mile, a woman has beaten all the men, and without post race suffering and long recovery period felt by men.

Body fat, a woman's handicap at the shorter distances, is actually her secret weapon at races more than 20 miles. This might also explain why a woman adjusts to training long distances more quickly than a man.

*   *   *

Q   I've recently read some alarming reports that too much running can damage a woman's fertility. Is this true?

A   This isn't a recent finding, much as the papers would have you believe. Serious women runners have known about this for years, and none of them are alarmed.

Hard training, fifty miles a week or more, may precipitate in some women secondary amenorrhea, the irregularity or complete halting of menstruation.

In 1968 and 1972, Dr. Kenneth Foremen, a physical education instructor and women's track coach at Seattle Pacific University, studied the nation's top fifty female distance runners, and found that 17 percent of them were experiencing missed or irregular periods.

Foremen's control group of physical education students showed no cases of menstrual irregularity or cessation.

Similarly, in 1977, women distance runners training at the Olympic camp in Squaw Valley, California, were asked if they were missing periods. These women were running twice daily at high altitude, and predictably, a third of them reported missed periods.

The women who resumed less stressful training schedules after leaving Squaw Valley reported a resumed and regular menstrual cycle.

Whenever a woman trains severely and loses fat, there is a definite possibility of menstrual irregularity or cessation. At worst, the condition is temporary. Cease the hard training, gain weight, and the periods return.

Competitive women runners don't seem worried about possible menstrual irregularity. A group of Stanford runners expressed envy for women who were able to get down to such a low fat content.

The present alarm stirred up by the mostly non-running press is just another in a long series of scare tactics directed at runners. Five years ago it was the ruinous effect running had upon one's joints. Ten years ago it was the damage sustained by the body's organs because of the bouncing one did when running. Fifty years ago it was the dreaded athletic heart. A century ago it was . . .

If you are nonetheless concerned about amenorrhea, write to the Institute of Environmental Stress at the University of California, Santa Barbara, where the most and best research on this is done. Their address is in the last chapter.

Q **Should a woman run during her period?**

A Unless the menstrual cramps are by themselves debilitating, there is no reason to stop running during the period.

Q **Can a woman run a good race during her period?**

A World records have been set, and gold medals have been won during all phases of the period. However, both the cramping and added water weight suffered by many women would probably hinder performance. Extra water can be gotten rid of by taking diuretics, such as strong tea or water pills. Cramping can be relieved by muscle relaxants, but that would also have a side effect negative to racing; downers and athletic performance are not compatible.

Many women runners, when expecting a race and period to coincide, skip the period by taking a birth control pill. If you don't object to birth control pills, this might be the easiest solution.

Q **Should a woman run during pregnancy?**

A   There is no reason to stop running, if the woman finds running still comfortable, and if the cervix is strong. A weak cervix poses the only danger to the pregnant runner; in such cases, all jarring activities must be ceased.

    If the cervix is strong — and your doctor will tell you if it isn't — the fetus can't be damaged by running. The fetus floats comfortably on a cushion of amniotic fluid, and sustains no shock.

Q   **How far into her pregnancy can a woman run?**

A   There is no magical point in the term of a pregnancy when running must be stopped. Mostly, it is a matter of comfort and what the doctor says. Some women have run until labor. Many, however, find running uncomfortable after the fifth or sixth month, and at that time switch to swimming.

Q   **What other health considerations are peculiar to women runners?**

A   Anemia, an insufficiency of red blood cells resulting from the periodic blood loss, is, of course, an ailment shared by millions of women, whether they run or not. Because red blood cells carry oxygen to the muscles, a lack of red cells limits running ability.

    The percentage of red cells in the blood, or hematocrit, should be 40 in a healthy female. Severe anemia, where the hematocrit is below 32, will make itself apparent early in a woman's running career if it hasn't been detected already. A woman with a red cell count that low will never progress beyond the lightest running, if she is able to do even that.

    Moderate anemia, 33-36 hematocrit, may go unnoticed longer, and may never be noticed in non-runners or women who run less than a mile or two a day. The runner's symptom of mild anemia is a premature leveling off of her performance. If she runs and runs, but never progresses beyond a few miles a day while her companions are improving much faster, the answer could be anemia.

    Mild anemia, 37-39 hematocrit, goes undetected in most women, even runners who don't train hard or race. It may not make itself apparent until maximum oxygen uptake is required — the race. If a woman feels her racing performances are not commensurate with her training, if she races no faster than she trains, she might have mild anemia.

Q   **What is the cure for anemia?**

A   A woman who thinks she has anemia should first see her doctor in case the red cell loss is not related to the period.

If it is a periodic blood loss, the doctor will usually tell the woman to take iron supplements, from 100 milligrams a day for mild cases, up to 500 milligrams a day for severe cases. The standard multi-vitamin with minerals pill has only 10-20 milligrams of iron, but is a good preventative for non-anemic women.

Q   **Do women get injured more often than men?**

A   According to Dr. Steven Subotnick, women, because of their usual incidence of wider hips, strike the ground at an angle less perpendicular than male runners. This precipitates pronation, that internal twisting which is the leading cause of stress related injuries. Ergo, a woman might theoretically be subject to more stress related injuries like shin splints, runner's knee, heel bumps, and so on.

As yet, not enough women train maximally to prove or disprove this theory. At any rate, pronation is easily corrected with proper shoe inserts and orthotics (see Chapter 13).

On the other hand, women are less susceptible to muscle pulls and strained tendons. The reason is that women, on the whole, are more loosely strung together than their male counterparts. Any random woman is much more likely capable of touching her toes than is any man. Tight muscles and tendons, more common in men, are those most easily pulled and strained.

With the knowledge runners have today about podiatry, orthopedics, overstress and stretching, it is senseless for anyone, male or female, to get injured unaccidentally.

Q   **How should a woman cope with catcalls?**

A   Ignore the offenders, who are looking for a reaction, particularly anger or embarrassment. Don't give them the pleasure.

Preventing those often lewd, always unwelcome comments is better. Appearing like a serious runner, perhaps an Olympian, usually shuts up most catcallers. If you aren't a fast runner, fake it and dress as one. Wear, as Dr. Ullyot suggests, a tee shirt that says Boston Marathon or AAU Women's Nationals. Don't wear an old fashioned physical education uniform or a bikini top.

Wear real running shorts, too. Don't wear bloomers or a tennis dress. If you wear a warmup suit, don't let a lacy tennis dress hang out from under the top.

This advice is not a plea to dress androgynously, but as a woman runner who knows what she is doing.

Q   **Does a woman have to worry about her safety when running?**

A   Women runners should always be aware of the potential danger of male attackers, especially in the cities, and even their suburbs.

To play it safe, a woman should never run alone at night. Even another woman companion is protection; two women together will deter most attackers.

Watch for men running parallel to you, on the other side of the street, especially if a man doesn't look like a runner (check his shoes and clothes), or if he keeps glancing at you. If you slow or speed and he does the same, run to the nearest store, restaurant, or crowd of friendly looking people. Don't waste time thinking about it; you are not overreacting.

Keep away from signs, bushes, alleys, etc., particularly if you don't know the area or see anyone suspicious lurking.

If you hear footsteps behind you, look to see who it is.

Opinions differ as to the best action for a women to take if she is caught and attacked. Many authorities say loud screaming or a shrill whistle works best to dissuade the attacker. Loud noises, though, do no good if no one hears, or, as is the unfortunate case in some cities, if no one cares. That is why a woman might be safer carrying a small tube of mace or dog repellent, which she could spray in the attacker's face if need be.

Q **Are there special running shoes for women?**

A All of the major brands either make women's shoes, or narrow sizes that fit women. Some of the top, everyday training flats are:

> Adidas Country Girl
> Brooks Victress
> Brooks Women's Villanova
> Converse World Class Trainer (the narrow size)
> Etonic Street Fighter (narrow)
> Etonic KM (narrow)
> New Balance 320 (AA to C)
> Nike Lady Waffle Trainer
> Tiger Tigress

Racing flats available are:

> Brooks Texan (narrow)
> Converse Marathoner (narrow)
> New Balance Super Comp (AA to C)
> Nike Mieka

Q **Do many women race?**

A Yes. One of the pleasant stories of road racing in the last ten years has been the public acceptance and official sanction of women's distance racing.

Only 11 years ago, in 1967, a New Yorker named Katherine Switzer had to sneak into the Boston Marathon, and during the race, had to push and shove the officials trying to remove her.

Today, thanks to the acceptance of women as athletes and runners, and especially to the early marathoners like Switzer, Nina Kuscik, Beth Bonner, Cheryl Bridges, Doris Brown and Dr. Joan Ullyot, women's distance racing has won the sanction of every official American road racing body.

As nearly as can be estimated, a half million runners ran in some kind of road race in 1977. At least 100,000 of the runners were women.

More than 300 women ran in the Boston Marathon in 1978.

Women can race at all levels, but must train accordingly.

Q **What are the racing opportunities for women?**

A Today, women are allowed in almost every American road race with the exception of the men's national championships. In such cases, there are equivalent national championships for women.

In the majority of races, like the Boston Marathon, there is just one event for all runners. Women are counted and awarded trophies separately; thus a woman who finished 789th out of 4000 could be the first place finisher.

Some of the competitions today are actually a series of races. An example would be the Gopher Junction 20 and 10, where a 20-kilometer race is open to anyone, but usually men, and a 10-kilometer race is held just for women, masters (over 40 years old) and juniors (under 20). If a woman wants to compete in her official race, she would have to run the 10-kilometer. But if she wants to run the 20, that's fine, too. No one will stop her; she just won't be official.

Recently, races for Women Only have blossomed around the country. The AAU and Road Runners Club stage women's national championship races at all distances, from 10 kilometers to 50 miles. These are prestigious, attract the best women, and often reward the winner with an expense-paid trip to Europe, Asia or Australia.

Bonne Belle Cosmetics and Pepsi Cola each sponsor a series of 10-kilometer road races held all around the United States. Expense and travel money for these races has been liberal, and so they, too, have become big and prestigious.

Q **Where can I find a schedule of women's races, as well as a list of books and publications for women runners?**

A See the last chapter of this book.

CHAPTER SEVENTEEN

Is Running A Natural High?

Q   **Some of my friends claim running is a natural high. They say they feel tranquility and euphoria during their runs, and for a time afterward. Yet, all I feel is the pain of hard effort. What am I doing wrong?**

A   You probably aren't running long enough. How far do you run?

Q   **Two miles a day during the week, and up to three miles a day on the weekends.**

A   There is your answer. Experienced distance runners have always known, and now medical science is just discovering that the euphoria of running does not occur until after 30 minutes (about four miles), and then only if the running has been aerobic, which is to say relatively slow and comfortable.

During the first 15 to 20 minutes (two to three miles) of running, the body is trying to adjust to the sudden activity. Every cell demands its share of oxygen. Though the lungs are working hard to meet the demand, the production and rationing is slow. At the end of 15 to 20 minutes, not every part of the body yet has the oxygen it needs.

The whole body rebels at the change in inertia. The muscles are cold and stiff and without adequate oxygen. They fuss during the first mile, argue during the second, and implore you to retreat to your sedentary position during the third. This happens regardless of ability.

Somewhere between the third and fourth mile the worst feeling of the entire run occurs, and peaks. Dr. Thaddeus Kostrubala, author of *The Joy of Running* calls the rotten feeling dysphoria (the opposite of euphoria). It is at this point you are stopping, and beyond which a

203

majority of runners like you never go. You think if running three or four miles feels this bad, five will be ineffably worse.

Q   **Well, isn't it?**

A   If you are conditioned to handle it, running distances beyond four miles is where the euphoria, peace, tranquility and sensory journey begin.

Q   **What does a runner's high feel like? Can you describe the transition from dysphoria to euphoria?**

A   There is no end to the ways the transition can be described. In one sense, it is religious, because at the depths of your despair you are miraculously born again with new power.

Another (and overused) way of describing the transition is as the light at the end of the tunnel. To the old athletes, it is second wind. To the experienced runner, it is nothing more exotic than the warmup. In fact, most running coaches recommend a prerace warmup of 30 to 40 minutes in order to dispense with the blahs and arrive at the starting line with a feeling of power and freshness.

The first change you notice is in the breathing — it becomes easier. The lungs suddenly seem to fill more deeply, all the way to the bottom, into every crevice. The breathing becomes an unconscious action.

The next to become subliminal is your rhythm. Suddenly you don't have to think of placing one foot in front of the other — before you can order it has already been done. Your whole body takes on its own rhythm, which is why running longer distances is such a great learning tool for your running style. Only now are you free and loose from the inhibitions and false teachings to run as you should.

Mentally, you feel the great release from tension, from the fatigue of the first four miles, from everything stressful in your daily life. The tensions aren't shot orgiastically, but are flushed as bad oil from a car.

There is a paradox in the release. On one hand you feel all your barriers breaking. You feel open and trusting. You feel as a babe in your mother's arms.

Yet, you are not vulnerable, as this implies. Quite the contrary, you feel in control, no longer at the mercy of your less than perfect body. You feel parental, as if you could support all the world's babes. You feel invincible, indomitable. Though your barriers are down, nothing bad can get to you. You have enough love and power to conquer the world.

After the mental and physical transition there is a sensory change, and this is when you have altered the consciousness, and are truly, gloriously high. Colors take on magnificent hues — did you ever notice how green the early summer is? How utterly blue a fresh sky? How red a stop sign?

And colors aren't the only perceptual change. Once, after running for an hour, I noticed a flag blowing in the wind. *Blowing?* No, it was struggling to free itself of the pole and fly with the migrating Canadian geese. Then suddenly the flag became a belly dancer, thrusting and folding. And then it was a stripper — Old Glory was voluptuously shedding her clothes.

Which lets free the secret shared by all long distance runners. Running, in this euphoric, altered stage is incredibly sensuous. Your thinking is very body oriented; you are one with it, and want to share it with others. Close to where I live in Palo Alto, California, there is an exclusive high school for girls. Katharine Ross is a graduate. Sometimes I pass the school at the end of an hour's running, and, well . . .

The perceptual changes unveil the final change in the euphoric stage — an understanding and acceptance of the different ways man and nature work and interact. You hear the gulls chattering, and you understand why they do so, if not the language itself.

While running on a gravel road in North Dakota I once saw a hawk swoop down and snare from the tall prairie grass a gopher. In the few seconds this happened I saw life, death and the unbreakable, unforgivable chain of nature. I wasn't alarmed over the gopher's fate. I didn't feel anger at the hawk. I only understood and accepted.

You see and understand how the world of man works, too. You see the industries where he produces, the shopping centers where he sells, the schools where he learns, the homes where he is fed, nurtured, loved and sustained. You see where he has fought against nature, and at best won a battle and lost himself. You see where he has fought with nature and has won for that his own right to exist.

And lastly, you see and understand how *you* work, how you overcame your silly fears and worries by simply plunging beyond. You come to understand your real limits, which are far beyond what you had imagined, and which can be extended even further.

*   *   *

Q   **Is the high you speak of tangible? Are there any physical or psychological reasons for it?**

A   I don't think a runner's high can be proved any more than the relief at the conclusion of a boring sermon can be proved.

However, certain measurable changes, both physiological and psychological, might indeed alter the runner and contribute to his euphoria. They are offered here as probable explanations, and are accepted by a growing minority in the medical sciences.

○ *Oxygenation* This explanation is based on the fact that when you breathe pure oxygen, you feel euphoric.

In sustained aerobic running, you raise the supply of oxygen to the cells one percent each minute. This peaks at 30 percent, thus taking 30 minutes. The result is a mild, lingering feeling of euphoria.

○ *Meditation* Running and its unvarying repetition of movements — breathing, the pendulum-like swinging of the arms and legs — produces the same effect upon the brain as does the mantra chanting in transcendental meditation.

In TM the student is taught to repeat over and over a single syllable, the mantra. The teachers give various religious and quack reasons for doing this — the real reason is that the repetition temporarily wears down the left side of the brain's cerebral cortex, the center of logic, sequence and order.

When this happens, as Dr. Kostrubala explains in *The Joy of Running*:

> The repetitive running mode, just like the repetitive mantra, wears
> out the left cortex and allows the consciousness to take a peek at the

functions of the right side of the brain, which are essentially intuitive, aesthetic, creative, nonlogical, nonsequential, and which seem to escape the temporal order of things.

Why does this take 30 minutes? Kostrubala says the left cerebral cortex can take only 30 minutes of sustained sensory bombardment before it quits and lets the right side take over. He draws an analogy to studying, and says it is impossible to learn anything after 30 minutes of concentrated studying. At that time the student must take a break if he is to continue. In a world that rewards its logicians with MDs, JDs, and MBAs, running can provide a safe and reversible journey to the other side. For that insight alone, running more than 30 minutes is worth it.

○ *Body Chemistry Changes* Dr. Jack Greist, a University of Wisconsin psychiatrist, and co-author of an enchanting book called *Run To Reality*, recently found that sustained exercise of only 15 minutes doubles the body's amount of epinephrine, a hormone closely related to adrenaline. Epinephrine, according to Dr. Greist, is the hormone of "happy feelings."

At the time of this writing it was not known what directly causes the level of epinephrine to double. The logical guess is that it is a reaction to an action — the call to flight triggers the boost in epinephrine.

This would go back to the days when man ran either because he was chased or chasing, and the rise in epinephrine either helped him catch dinner or avoid being caught for dinner. Nature didn't dream man would run long distances for the fun of it or that he could learn to cope so well. The shot of epinephrine still remains, and is a pleasant bonus.

Q **If the epinephrine doubles after 15 minutes, why don't I feel its pleasant effects then?**

A The body is still under increasing stress after 15 minutes, so the rise in epinephrine goes unnoticed. It is only after the muscles loosen and the body is thoroughly oxygenated, which takes about 30 minutes, that the high level of epinephrine makes itself apparent.

Q **Does the high stay with the runner after the run is finished?**

A Most find the high remains for 15-20 minutes after the run. This is how long it takes the body to expire the increased oxygen, for the left cerebral cortex to recover, and for the epinephrine level to drop.

Q   **And after that?**

A   After that your body and mind return to pre-running levels, although a reduction in tension can last for hours.

*   *   *

Q   **Is running addictive?**

A   Dr. William Glasser, a Los Angeles psychiatrist, calls running a positive addiction, and has written a book of the same title.

Addiction to running, if there is such a thing, would seem to happen only to people who are running more than 30 minutes at a time, and get hooked on the high.

If there is an addiction in its true sense, the runner would become tolerant to the high, and require larger and larger doses of running to attain the same feeling. Does this happen?

Not in my case, nor, do I believe, in the cases of any distance runners. Even during times when I am routinely running for two hours, I still find a 45 minute jaunt capable of producing a wonderful high. I don't feel any need to increase the dosage.

The second way running might be considered an addiction is if withdrawal symptoms are suffered if the running is stopped. Does this happen?

In this case, yes, it happens to me and to most every runner I know. When circumstances bring my running to a sudden halt, I suffer insomnia, tension, constipation, irritability and a fat increase. Some runners, for whom daily training has been an integral part of their life, report severe depression when unable to run. Tracy Smith, a 1968 Olympic distance runner who trained more than 100 miles a week, said he had to seek medical help for tension when an achilles tendon injury forced him to stop running for two years.

When I am unable to run, I have to drink several cups of coffee to wake me in the morning, and several beers to wind down in the evening. Doses of distance running, though, regulate my body naturally. I awake refreshed and go to bed ready for sleep.

Running, then, is somewhat addicting, but the addiction is unique — not a slow slide to ruin as with drugs, but a steady push upward to health and well-being. For that reason William Glasser calls it a positive addiction.

Q **I'm aware tension is lowered during the run, but is there any carry-over effect? Will running help me stay relaxed during the whole day and help me sleep better at night?**

A An overwhelming majority of runners think so.

In the early part of 1978 Jim Lilliefors, an editorial staff member at *Runner's World*, polled 500 of its readers, and asked them what was their primary reason for running.

The results were startling. Seventy-eight percent said they ran primarily to combat the stresses of everyday life and thus lower tension. Other reasons — cardiovascular protection, weight reduction, getting in shape to race — were often the impetus to start, but after a few months were secondary to the stress reduction.

From the medical viewpoint, there is almost no argument to this premise. Says Dr. William P. Morgan, a professor of psychology at the University of Arizona:

"The link between exercise and tension reduction is so clear that it is no longer questioned by most researchers. It is a dead issue."

Presumably, then, running would help you sleep better, since insomnia and tension are closely related. I always sleep much better when I'm running regularly.

Q **How does running compare with other natural ways of reducing tension, such as quiet meditation?**

A All natural means of reducing stress and tension are good, and are certainly superior to the chemical ways, such as the cocktail, tranquilizer or sleeping pill.

A half hour of aerobic running is probably no better or no worse than a half hour of quiet meditation in a dark room.

Running alone, though, accomplishes two tasks with the same effort. It contributes to the lungs, arteries and heart as well as the overstressed mind.

Q   **Can running cure depression?**

A   It might.

Examine some of the non-recurring causes of depression. Might some of them not be:

○ *Stress and Tension* Ringing telephones you can't escape? Having to please others or having to be pleased? Scolding others or being scolded? Commuting in traffic? The whole rat race?

○ *Boredom* Mindlessly flipping television channels, not enjoying it, but having nothing else to do?

○ *No Feeling of Power* Having no say in the world? Being at the mercy of others? No sense of choosing your own destiny?

○ *No Self-Control* Having no will-power (whatever became of that word?)? Being at the mercy of your weaknesses? Stopping at the first resistance?

○ *No Accomplishments* Doing nothing that everyone couldn't do? Doing nothing at all?

○ *Lingering Ill-Health* Because you smoke and overdrink? Because you never get outside? You're always fighting a cold or plain lack of energy and the doctor can't tell you why?

○ *Unattractiveness* Feeling fat, because indeed you are? Getting more depressed each time you look in the mirror?

Now, examine some of the positive things running does. Does it not:

○ *Reduce Stress and Tension* Remove you from ringing telephones?

Relieve you from having to please others, or having others please you? Relieve you from scolding others or being scolded? Separate you, at least temporarily, from the whole rat race?

○ *Alleviate Boredom* Get you away from the television and out in the wonderful world? Give you an hour of physical pleasure, sensual contact and sensory enlightenment?

○ *Give You Power* At least over yourself? Take you away from the mercy of others? Let you choose, for your hour, any pace and distance you want?

○ *Give You Self-Control* Teach you that you do have will-power? Teach you to overcome your weaknesses? Show you that first resistances are usually bluffs?

○ *Accomplish Something* Give you the pride of knowing 95 percent of the people can't run as far as you can?

○ *Give You Robust Health* Because your lungs are clean as a child's? Because you get plenty of fresh air and sunshine? Give you the strength to quickly dispense with mere colds and give you new levels of energy which your friends and family can't explain?

○ *Make You More Attractive* Reduce unsightly bulges and triple chins? Give you a year 'round suntan? Show the definition of your hundreds of wonderful muscles and tendons? Make you happy and satisfied each time you look in the mirror?

Here is an interesting point: Dr. Robert S. Brown, a psychiatrist from the University of Virginia says he has never treated a physically fit depressed person. Dr. Brown refuses to draw conclusions from this, but I, being a layman with no reputation to lose, will. I say physically fit people are too busy feeling good about themselves to get depressed.

Q   **Do any psychotherapists actually use running as treatment for depression?**

A   In 1977 Dr. John Greist, of previously mentioned epinephrine fame, experimented with running and walking as therapy for people who came to the University of Wisconsin outpatient clinic and complained of depression.

After 10 weeks of walking/running therapy, Dr. Greist found his patients improved at rates similar to those undergoing traditional psychotherapy. But none of the depressions were severe, and so Dr. Greist is hesitant to draw conclusions.

He told writer Hal Higdon in a January, 1978 *Runner's World* interview:

> "I think it is possible that emphasis on running as a treatment for depression at this time, without proper understanding of its limitations as well as its benefits, could actually be dangerous to many depressed individuals. It seems highly probable that the most seriously depressed individuals will not respond to running. These individuals are often suicidal, and a failure to improve from a highly touted running therapy might be the sort of failure that would lead to a suicide attempt."

Still, the belief among most psychiatrists active in this new therapy is that running is a quite simple, inexpensive, but effective tool for the treatment of the garden varieties of depression that from time to time afflict a majority of Americans. This is the kind of depression not necessarily debilitating, but which keeps people from functioning at the top and enjoying life to the most. At the very least, running provides a safe escape from the symptoms. And at best, it might alleviate the causes.

Q **Will running give me a higher energy level throughout the day?**

A For reasons already discussed, moderate long distance running presumably would add to your energy and productivity.

It reduces tension, thus making less cluttered the hours you have.

It contributes to physical well-being, which is closely related to energy and productivity.

It seems to relieve mild depression, which then makes the available hours positive and productive.

But at the same time, an excessive amount of running, such as training for high level competition, can drain the body and reduce your productivity.

Hard training makes enormous time demands. If you are running 15 miles a day, that can easily cost four hours — a half hour for dressing and stretching, two hours for running, another half hour for showering and dressing, and an additional hour's sleep at night to help restore the energy. It is doubtful you can lose four hours and remain as productive. It is also doubtful you would have much extra energy.

In my own case, I find running contributes to my work and energy level if I run no more than four days a week, and make only two of those days long or hard. If I train much more than that, the running begins to dominate my life. I go to bed earlier, sleep later, plan my whole afternoon around running, and after the run, sit catatonically in front of the television and drink beer or eat ice cream as I try to recover. That isn't a very productive or otherwise fulfilling life, but it was exactly the one I led in high school and college, when I trained maximally, when I raced to my best times, when I was a hopeless running junkie.

Anyway, my schoolday experiences point out that optimum running condition and high energy levels do not run parallel. In my own case, 80 miles a week puts me in the best racing shape, but just 20-50 miles a week gives me the highest energy level.

Q **Will running enhance my sex life?**

A I speak only as an amateur sexologist, but I presume running would enhance an already healthy sex life.

Running keeps the athlete in touch with his body. He is aware as never before of all of its functions and capabilities.

Running improves physical appearance. Fat is lost and muscle definition is unveiled. The self image is improved. Confidence rises.

Tension is reduced through running. Tension, say the psychiatrists, is a major cause of sexual inadequacy.

As an amateur, I also am aware that running probably cannot cure a bad sex life. Other help must be sought.

Advanced training means some anaerobic running – hills, intervals, and sprints on the grass.

CHAPTER EIGHTEEN

Advanced Training

Q **What do you define as an advanced level of training?**

A I think there are two equally important definitions of advanced training.

The first is doing a sufficient amount of running to adequately prepare you for all racing distances between a mile and a marathon. What this means is a gradual increase in volume, speedwork, and number of days run, so that you wind up with a weekly schedule with more than double the stress intensity of that of the intermediate level.

The second definition of advanced training, often neglected, but of ranking value, is the ability to train yourself without depending on coaches, friends, or even books, including this one.

For that reason, this chapter will purposely gloss over a few points outlined meticulously in previous training chapters.

Q **What are you going to gloss over?**

A For one, there won't be a seven-step method in this chapter.

Q **Wait a minute. That schedule has helped me to reach this far — why do you abandon me now?**

A I'm not abandoning you. In fact, I think I am respecting your intelligence by letting you figure it out by yourself. Besides, you already know everything you need to. You already know about the balance between stress and adaptation. You already know that you should run hard only three times a week. You already know about a graduated method of stress increase.

Q   **Yes, but you know all of that better than I do — that's presumably why you are writing this book.**

A   Perhaps I've accumulated more knowledge, but that's only because I've been in the sport longer than you have. You already know the principles of training — the details you will pick up quickly.

Where your knowledge is far superior to mine is about yourself — your personal interest in running, reaction to stress, how easily you get injured, how convenient or busy your schedule, how badly you want to run. You see, if you understand the principles of training, you can fit whatever program you wish into whatever lifestyle you lead.

Q   **Well, I can still try to coax a seven-step method from you, can't I?**

A   You can try. But if I give you a seven-step method to advanced training, you might learn to run great distances without ever learning how.

Q   **Is that so important?**

A   Sir Roger Bannister, the first man to run a mile in less than four minutes, thinks so. Bannister spent a great deal of his career defending his non-use of coaches, concluding that running served no purpose whatsoever when "someone always must tell us when to do what."

From a practical standpoint, a dependency on others can ruin your interest and shorten your career, as it did to Jim Ryun.

During an outstanding high school and college career, in which he set two world records in the mile (3:51.3 and 3:51.1) and one in the 1500 meters (3:33.1), Ryun was coached by one man, a tough-minded ex-Marine named Bob Timmons. Timmons planned all of Ryun's workouts *months* in advance, and so all Ryun had to do was attend practice with his willing body. Did Ryun ever rebel, or ask for a hand in his training? No, he commented several times that Timmons "makes it easy for me by relieving the pressure and worry of planning."

In 1969 Ryun graduated from the University of Kansas, and from that point, the brilliance and magic of Jim Ryun seemed to end. Weeks later, at the NCAAs, he lost his first domestic mile in years, to Marty Liquori.

A week after that, at the AAUs, Ryun dropped out of the mile and began a two-year retirement.

Ryun's comeback years, 1971-72, were marked by erratic performances and an unending search to find the right location, right training facilities, and the right coach. He moved from Kansas to Eugene, Oregon, to Santa Barbara, California. While living in Santa Barbara, Ryun received weekly schedules from Timmons, but the futility of this became apparent when Ryun ran an embarrassing 4:19 mile in the Los Angeles Coliseum in March, 1972. Not wanting to risk further disaster in the upcoming Olympic Trials, Ryun moved back to Kansas and Timmons.

The Ryun-Timmons teamed worked, and Ryun made the 1972 Olympic team. A few weeks before the Games he ran a 3:52 mile in Toronto and appeared to be the favorite in the 1500 meters. But it was the last good race Ryun would run, for in the Olympics he met with disaster and tripped in his first-round heat.

The lesson to be learned here is that Ryun spent three years of pain and frustration because his coach had not taught him how to train himself and be independent. Ryun was a world-class runner only when Coach Timmons was close at hand.

Q   **But Ryun was best in the world. Don't all the great runners have stiff coaches?**

A   Not at all. Marty Liquori and Frank Shorter were taught to coach themselves near the end of their college careers, and as a result, they were able to continue training hard and consistently through their middle and late 20s — the most productive years for a distance runner — despite both changing their events and moving all around the country.

Because Shorter and Liquori were not dependent upon coaches, both have realized their potential as runners, and both have the immeasurable satisfaction of doing it on their own. I don't believe Ryun saw his best, nor is fully satisfied with his career.

Q   **I still don't see the analogy. I'm not a world-class runner like those guys.**

A   Neither am I. But I'm also not dependent on a coach or running book, and not vulnerable to every new quack training theory that comes down the road.

I know how to get myself in shape for a marathon, as well as a mile. I know what the right mix of volume and speedwork is for each. I know the proper balance of stress and rest, and how I can gradually increase the former, and decrease the latter. I recognize when I am overtraining, and I know what to do about it.

When I am injured, I know how to alter my training. If I miss a day due to bad weather or an infrequent cold, I know my schedule isn't shot to hell, because my schedule serves its inventor, and is always flexible.

Because I understand *why* a schedule works, I can constantly alter it to meet my current enthusiasms and desires. If I weren't so independent, I would have to change coaches and schedules each time the wind blew.

Q   **That wouldn't be too good.**

A   More than that, it wouldn't be very much fun.

*   *   *

Q   **What is gained from running at an advanced level?**

A   Physically, probably little is gained except specific fitness to run longer and faster. The gain in cardiovascular protection is negligible over what you were doing at an intermediate level.

Of most significance to your general health and appearance is the high calorie expenditure of advanced running — it will likely be more than 5000 calories a week, which represents nearly a pound and a half of body weight.

Mentally, your gain in enjoyment depends upon whether you like to run that much.

Q   **How much is much? You mentioned previously that advanced training would have more than twice the intensity of intermediate train-**

ing, which you said would be accomplished by increases in volume, speedwork and number of days run. Can't you be a little more specific? What does an advanced training program look like?

A   When I am training hard, my weekly schedule might look something like this:

○ *Day One* 30 minutes of easy running.

○ *Day Two* 90 minutes of running, divided into two parts: first 30 minutes easy; last 60 minutes at hard pace, but under control so that I could run faster if I had to.

○ *Day Three* 30 minutes of easy running.

○ *Day Four* 90 minutes of running, divided into three parts: first 30 minutes easy; second 30 minutes at any pace I decide to run — how fast or slow depends solely upon how I feel at the moment of decision; last 30 minutes in fast-slow intervals of one minute run at a mile race pace, followed by two minutes of slow recovery running. Thus in 30 minutes I get 10 one-minute bursts.

○ *Day Five* 30 minutes of yoga or swimming.

○ *Day Six* 2-2½ hours of slow running, preferably with a group of running friends, followed by swimming and copious beer drinking.

○ *Day Seven* Rest.

I say my schedule might look like this, but it hardly ever does in actuality. I only follow its principles.

Q   **Then why do you give it to me?**

A   Because I want you to look at it, and see if you can determine what makes it a good advanced training schedule. I want you to pull the principles out of that schedule, so that you can always adapt them to your convenience and interest, and so that you will always be independent of coaches and training books.

Q   **I notice a few basic principles in that schedule. For one, despite including five days of running a week, you still have only three hard**

days. I understand that, but why are the three days all so different?

A   The differences, of course, are in pace and volume. One of the hard days is a slow run of 2-2½ hours. This is the run in which you are trying to increase your range, and so it must be done slowly.

Two other interesting training effects occur when you run for more than two hours. One is that your body learns to function without glycogen, and instead learns to use its own fat as a primary source of energy. This kind of training will be invaluable should you ever run a marathon, in which you invariably run out of glycogen after 20 miles and are forced to run the last six miles on fat power.

The second training effect unique to long runs is an increased development of capillaries — the smallest and most numerous blood vessels — within the muscle tissue. This concept was first utilized (at least in the running world) by that great New Zealand coach, Arthur Lydiard, who sent all of his runners, including half-miler Peter Snell, on 30-40 kilometer runs once a week. Lydiard's rationalization was simple — the more blood vessels your muscles contain, the more oxygen they will get during aerobic or anaerobic stress. Full of such capillaries, Peter Snell won two Olympic gold medals in the 800 meters and one in the 1500. Snell also once held world records in the 880 (1:45.1) and mile (3:54.2).

Of the other two hard training days, one includes a stiffly-paced run of one hour, and the other includes a 30-minute fast run followed by 30 minutes of fast-slow intervals.

Q   **Why the variation in pace? I thought all of the runs were to be done at a comfortable pace.**

A   You should run at whatever pace you desire, but I suggest adding faster paces for a number of reasons, all of which will help your further development as a runner.

The one hour of hard running teaches you precisely where your edge of comfort is. It also teaches you at what pace you *have* control of your running, and at what pace you *lose* it. The idea of this run is to push back the edge while maintaining control.

The pace at which you will run during this hour is quite similar to your racing pace during a marathon. It has been calculated that this pace is 95 percent aerobic and five percent anaerobic — this means you will slightly exceed your aerobic limit during the run. Breathing becomes a tad more difficult — you can't talk in full sentences — but is still under your control. You could go faster if you had to.

Q   **The other hard run includes 30 minutes of fast running, and 30 minutes of fast-slow intervals. How will this help my running, and at what pace should I do these?**

A   This workout adds a touch of anaerobic running to your training program. The purpose is to teach your body how to perform without a complete supply of oxygen, as it will have to perform in races.

Short and fast runs can also teach you concentration, which might indeed be the one ability, more than physical gifts, that separates top-class runners from the rest of us.

The pace at which you run the "fast" 30 minutes should be a spontaneous decision based upon how you feel at the end of the first 30 minutes.

If you happen to feel sluggish at the end of the first 30 minutes, then continue to run comfortably. Your body probably isn't ready for the additional stress of a hot pace.

But if you feel good, then pull out the stops, release the brakes, and go! And don't second-guess yourself — in fact, don't think at all, except to ·concentrate on rhythm and form and breathing, rhythm and form and breathing. Block everything else from your mind, because here is where you either establish the habit of concentration or else take your first step toward becoming a running scatterbrain.

Q   **If I decide to run fast, what is it going to feel like?**

A   I hesitate to tell you because, frankly, it will hurt. But if your decision to run fast was truly spontaneous, the hurt can be overcome by concentration, and near the end of the run, *will* be overcome by the exhilaration of knowing your body and mind are together, and performing at their best.

Q   **How often should I run this fast?**

A   During one workout a week, you should consider the possibility of running fast. The trick is making the decision truly spontaneous, which means that you *will not* necessarily be running fast every week, nor even every month. Worrying about the last time you ran fast can ruin the spontaneity. Just let it happen. And when it does, go to it!

Q   **The fast-slow intervals — what do they accomplish?**

A   Fast-slow interval training accomplishes two things.

For one, fast-slow intervals simulate the anaerobic intensity of shorter races, and when done in a correct balance, add to your general fitness and ability to run well at all distances.

The second thing interval training does is teach your body to move fast, by forcing you to coordinate a quicker than usual rhythm with a longer than usual stride.

A quick rhythm and a long and powerful stride are the two essential ingredients of speed. Although both are more inherent than endurance is, both can be improved by regular exercise, like a series of fast one-minute bursts.

Arthur Lydiard takes the idea of speed development a step further. For six weeks prior to each competitive season, Lydiard moves his training camp to the hills. There his athletes run, in bounding fashion, up steep hills to increase their leg strength (Lydiard's runners all have the thickest and strongest thighs of any comparably sized athletes), and then sprint down the hills to increase their rhythm.

As an alternative to fast-slow intervals, you might consider hill training. Find any 200-300-yard hill of medium steepness, and run up and down it ten times, or for 30 minutes. Contrary to Lydiard's teaching, I recommend running up the hill in a natural, and not bounding, manner. I would also recommend that you do your sprinting in the flatlands. Sprinting down hills is quite jarring, and an open invitation to injury.

Q   **Should the interval training follow the fast 30-minute run?**

A   Here you should be flexible and use common sense. If you ran the 30 minutes fast and hard, allow yourself 10 minutes or so of recovery before starting the intervals. If you don't recover adequately during those 10 minutes — if you still have difficulty breathing — skip the intervals. Your body is telling you that you've already had enough anaerobic stress for the day.

If you chose not to run fast for 30 minutes, but instead ran comfortably for an hour, then by all means try the intervals. The only excuse for not doing them now is if you are grossly fatigued or have sore legs which prohibit fast running.

Q **How quickly should I run the fast part of the intervals?**

A This will take some experimentation, because the correct pace to run intervals is, on one hand, as fast as you can, but on the other, slow enough to complete the entire workout without exhausting yourself.

The first time you approach interval training, do it cautiously. Concentrate on a quick rhythm, long stride, and staying relaxed. Don't expect breathing to be easy, but neither should you be gasping for air. If you are so tired that you must stop and bend over after each one-minute burst, you are doing them too fast. The idea is to keep moving for the entire 30 minutes.

If all this sounds rather complicated or vague, it is. It took me no less than four years of constant trial and error to learn the correct way of running intervals.

Q **And that is?**

A With controlled abandon, and though tired at the end, feeling as if you could run one or two more if you had to.

Q **How should I run the slow part of the interval?**

A Run as slowly as you wish (I fight the temptation to use the word jog), but keep moving. If you are so tired at the end of each fast run that you must stop or walk, then you are running too quickly.

Q **Why do you suggest running fast-slow intervals in a one:two ratio?**

A   This just seems to work best for most runners. A two-minute recovery interval prevents the one-minute hard interval from being either too fast or too slow. If you run the fast-slow intervals in a one:one ratio, the recovery time is too short, and soon the fast becomes indistinguishable from the slow. And if the recovery time is too long, say three or four minutes, the steady level of anaerobic intensity is broken. The purpose of this workout is then defeated.

Q   **Why do you include 30 minutes of interval training per week, instead of, say, 15 minutes or one hour?**

A   That's a very good question.

       The success or failure of interval training depends upon doing the right amount, and balancing it with the rest of your volume training.

       This correct balance will vary from race to race, and from season to season. When your aim is to build general endurance, as it is in this chapter, you need to do some, but little interval training. When you start to point toward a specific race, the percentage of interval training you do will depend upon the length of the race.

       In the next chapter I will show you the percentage of interval vs. volume training required to race optimally at each racing distance, so that you may balance your schedule accordingly.

       But to answer your question, I include 30 minutes of interval training in this chapter because that represents 10 percent of your weekly running. As you will see in the next chapter, a training program with 10 percent interval training best prepares you for a 10-mile race, which is roughly between the two distance racing extremes — the mile and the marathon. When you decide to point for any race between a mile and a marathon, the training you now do will put you within easy reach of optimum performance. You can move up to the marathon (increase volume, lessen intervals) or down to the mile (increase intervals, lessen volume) or anywhere in between with confidence and ease.

                              *   *   *

Q   **Why does your proposed schedule include five days a week? In**

previous chapters you suggested running only three days a week.

A   Relative to the harder workouts, the two 30-minute days are almost like taking a day off. They add something to your fitness without adding to your stress.

Q   **Then why not run every day of the week?**

A   Five days of running a week — two easy and three hard — happens to give me the best balance of stress and adaptation. For you, it may be only three or four days, or perhaps six.

I am a strong disbeliever in running seven days a week, despite the fact most world-class runners do. I think *every* runner needs to take one day off to let the body adapt to the week of stress. The great miler, Herb Elliott, trained punishingly, yet always rested for one day of the week.

For good measure, and because I hate to be sick or injured, I rest for *two* days of the week. I'm in this game first, to have fun, second, to have good health, and third, to become the best runner I can, but only when I can maintain fun and good health. When I run for more than five days a week, my interest in the sport drops as sharply as the risk of injury or ill health rises.

Q   **What stress-related problems can occur when training at an advanced level?**

A   At this point, you should keep a hundred dollars stashed in an old pair of Adidas in case you need to visit the podiatrist.

Seriously, if you aren't properly aligned, balanced and flexible, there is a better than even chance you'll suffer some kind of overuse injury while training at an advanced level. Therefore, you must increase your stretching and muscle balancing exercises proportionately to the increased volume of running. And if you are among the majority with less-than-perfect feet, you should buy some kind of shoe insert, as described in Chapter 13. If you can stay aligned, balanced and flexible, your chances of injury are minimal.

The other potential hazard of training at an advanced level is general overstress — I hope by now you have read Chapter 12 so that you are familiar with the warning signs. Overstress is both easily detectable and reversible, but only if you know what to look for.

The best argument in favor of running hard for only three days a week, and running at all for only five, is that this virtually wipes out the possibility of overstress. Weary athletes, take heed!

Q   **Getting back to the seven-step method to advanced training — have you softened your position? Are you going to give it to me?**

A   There is an overused maxim that seems appropriate here. It goes: Give a man fish, and you've fed him for one night. But teach him *how* to fish, and you've succeeded in feeding him for a lifetime.

That is to say I refuse to give you a seven-step method to advanced training. But I will leave you with seven principles of training which you can apply at any level:

Seven Principles of Training

1. Run hard only three days of the week, and allow yourself at least one full day of rest each week.

2. Know the signs of overstress.

3. Stretch for at least five minutes before and after each run.

4. Always run gently for 30 minutes before increasing the pace.

5. Learn to distinguish between pain and fatigue.

6. Volume Running: When you add it to your training, add no more than 30 minutes every two weeks.

7. Interval Training:

   a) Don't add it to your training until you can run comfortably for an hour.

b) Don't let the time set aside for interval training exceed 10 percent during general endurance training.

c) Run hard, but don't exhaust yourself.

d) Never try it with sore or injured legs.

Dr. Duncan McDonald, leading, and Mark Schilling are two of America's top racers.

CHAPTER NINETEEN

Racing

Part One: What Is It Like?

Q   **I've never raced before — how does it differ from everyday running?**

A   If running is having a crush on a girl, racing is calling her for a date.

If running is fishing, racing is when the line suddenly jerks.

If running is an amusement park, racing is the giant roller coaster.

If running is Las Vegas, racing is the casino.

If running is buying Christmas gifts, and then hiding, wrapping, and placing them under the tree, racing is watching your loved ones tear open the packages.

If running is memories of your father, racing was the time he placed you on a bicycle and pushed you down the hill.

If running is memories of your mother, racing was when she dressed you for your first day of school.

If running was junior high, racing was that first Friday night dance.

If running was high school, racing was when your basketball team made it to the state finals.

If running was college, racing was when you finally chose your major, what you wanted to be, and how you wanted to define your existence.

*   *   *

Q   **What is it like to wake up for the day of a race?**

A   The day of a race is:

Not needing a cup of coffee to wake up.

Wondering if two rolls of toilet paper are enough.

Driving hundreds of miles, and worrying about the effect this might have on your sciatica.

Stopping at a cafe full of people, ordering porridge, toast and honey.

Driving the race course backward, and thinking it all seems downhill.

Seeing your dream of a trophy fade away when a tall, thin stranger wearing USA Track arrives.

Tension when the race officials can't find your name on the registrant list. A sigh of relief when they finally do.

Pinning the competitor's number to your shirt, and when pulling the shirt on, discovering you pinned the front to the back.

Talking with other runners, and telling them how rotten you feel. And then wondering if you really do feel that badly.

Thinking about the last month of training. Wondering if it has been good enough.

Butterflies.

Slipping away from the crowd to warm up by yourself, and then feeling much too alone.

More butterflies. And lots of yawning.

Another bowel movement urge — is that possible?

Hearing the last call for your race while sitting in the gas station toilet.

Wanting to go home. Questioning the purpose of this nonsense.

Going back to your car, and switching to your racing flats. Tying them in double knots.

Removing your warmup suit, and feeling the cool breeze touch your warm thighs.

A few quick stride-ups, and amazement at how light and bouncy you feel. Renewed confidence.

More fast stride-ups to impress the competition.

Taking deep breaths to suppress the yawning. Telling yourself that now is the time.

Walking to the starting line with fellow runners, but not exchanging words.

Positioning yourself in the pack, as far up as possible without arousing suspicion.

Listening to the starter shout instructions, and responding with nervous laughter when he cracks a joke.

Feeling suspended in time as you await the gun, and the test of things to come.

Q **And after that?**

A It is your script to write.

*   *   *

Part Two: Training for Racing
Section One: Training to Finish Your First Race

Q **If I have never raced before, what is a good distance to choose for my first race?**

A If you have never raced before, or are returning to racing after a long layoff, your prime consideration should be choosing a race which you know you can finish — in which the distance itself is not prohibitive.

Q **You mean, if I've never run 10 miles in practice I should avoid entering a 10-mile race?**

A You have the right idea, but it isn't quite as restrictive as you think. The drama and adrenaline of a race will carry you to paces and distances you wouldn't have thought possible based upon your training. A lot of marathoners, including Frank Shorter, never run 26 miles in practice, yet not only finish, but finish well. In the same way, you might do quite well in a 10-mile race despite never having run that far in practice.

A far better indication of your ability to perform and finish a race is your average weekly mileage in the three months preceding the race. You have an excellent chance of finishing strongly any race if a) your average weekly mileage for the preceding three months is *at least double* the racing distance, and b) once a week you take a practice run of *at least 75%* of the racing distance.

So, if you want reasonable assurance of finishing (without walking or slowing drastically) a 10-mile race, your minimal preparation must be three months of 20-mile weeks, with one long run of 7-8 miles each week.

Below are standard long distance races, and the minimal weekly/three-month training needed to finish them.

○ *6 miles/10 kilometers* Three weekly runs: 4 miles, 3 miles, 5 miles

○ *15 kilometers/10 miles* Four weekly runs: 5 miles, 4 miles, 8 miles, 3 miles

○ *20 kilometers/15 miles/25 kilometers* Four weekly runs: 8 miles, 6 miles, 11 miles, 4 miles

○ *30 kilometers/20 miles* Five weekly runs: 10 miles, 5 miles, 15 miles, 4 miles, 7 miles

○ *The Marathon* Five weekly runs of 12 miles, 5 miles, 20 miles, 5 miles, 10 miles

Q   **Your suggested minimums seem quite high to me, especially for the longer races. I have a friend who finished a marathon on about half of the weekly mileage you suggest.**

A   I suppose I could be accused of being conservative in my suggested minimums if finishing the race, however slowly, was the only criterion. What I'm trying to do with my suggestions is save you the pain and embarrassment of having to walk, hobble or hitchhike during the last stages of the race. I would like to see you finish respectably, which means at nearly the same pace at which you started.

I am frankly quite weary of the hordes of ill-prepared pedestrians who turn marathons into six-hour farces just for the sake of finishing. Such clowns are not only burdensome to the race officials, who must sit it out in the heat, rain or cold while getting paid nothing, but also to the entire sport, which is seen not as legitimate, but as a carnival, a fad.

Section Two: Advanced Race Training

Q **How will this section differ from the previous?**

A This section will show you how to train specifically for any racing distance between a mile and a marathon (note: for this to have meaning, it must be assumed that you are capable of training on an advanced level as described in Chapter 18).

To race well at any given distance, you must a) increase the minimum weekly volume of section one, and b) find the right aerobic vs. anaerobic training balance.

○ *Minimum Weekly Volume* In the previous section we discussed the weekly mileage you needed to run to be assured of finishing races. In this section the concern is finding the weekly minimum needed to race *competitively* at any distance.

Consider the following table:

Weekly Mileages For Optimal Racing Results

Racing Distance	Minimum	Preferred	World Class Example Low	World Class Example High
			Kip Keino	John Walker
1500m/Mile	30-40	50+	(3:34.2m) 40-60	(3:49.4) 70-100
			Duncan McDonald	Marty Liquori
3 Mile/5000m	40-50	60+	(13:19.4m) 60-70	(13:15.1m) 80-120
			Ron Clarke	Lasse Viren
6 Mile/10,000m	50-60	70+	(27:39.4m) 70-80	(27:38.4m) 110-130
			Jack Foster	Bill Rodgers
6 Miles - Marathon	60-70	80+	(2:11:18) 60-80	(2:09:55) 120-160

○ *Correct Aerobic vs. Anaerobic Training Balance* Every racing distance, from the 100-yard dash to the 100-mile run, requires the maximum use of oxygen, either from sources already within the body (anaerobic fitness) or from supplemental breathing (aerobic fitness) or from a combination of both.

The 100-yard dash is run exclusively on your anaerobic fitness, your capacity to work without the presence of breathed oxygen. Instead you run the hundred powered by oxygen already present within your body — you could, if you had to, run the entire distance without taking a single breath. But as with all anaerobic activity, the tired muscles will demand later restoration of the life-giving oxygen. You fulfill this oxygen debt by continuing to breathe hard after the race is finished.

At the other extreme are ultra-marathons, such as the London-to-Brighton 52-miler and the Lake Tahoe 72-miler. Since finishing an ultra-marathon is the most difficult part, muscle fatigue must be kept as low as possible. To minimize fatigue, you must avoid incurring an oxygen debt. Instead, you must get all of your oxygen from breathing. The trick to racing an ultra-marathon is running at the edge of your aerobic limit — as fast as you can without building an oxygen debt.

Racing events between the shortest sprints and the longest ultra-marathons call for both aerobic and anaerobic fitness. For many years the mile has been called the perfect race because, said its supporters, the mile requires equal amounts of speed and endurance to excel. As evidence were the great milers of history, who could perform well at a range of distances, from cross country (4-6 miles) to the sprints (Jim Ryun once ran a 46.9 quarter mile on the University of Kansas mile relay team).

Now the laboratory has proven that the mile is indeed the perfect test of running. Virtually all tests show that during an all-out mile race, breathing supplies only about half of the oxygen needed. The other half is supplied from within the body, borrowed from every cell. When the race is over, the' debt is slowly repaid. Your breathing takes several minutes to return to normal after a guts-out mile race.

Below is a table of racing distances and their corresponding aerobic vs. anaerobic demands:

Racing Distance	Aerobic %	Anaerobic %
100 yards	0	100

220 yards	8	92
440 yards	17	83
880 yards	33	67
Mile	50	50
2 mile	67	33
3 mile	75	25
6 mile	86	14
10 mile	90	10
Marathon	95	5
50 miles	98	2

The purpose of knowing these percentages is not so that you can win barroom trivia contests, but so that you can point for important races by adjusting your training to the same aerobic vs. anaerobic balance.

That is to say, if you wish to point for a mile race you would, for six weeks preceding the race, spend half of your training time running aerobically — long, slowish runs — and the other half anaerobically — repetitions, hills, intervals, windsprints, etc.

Or if you wish to point for a marathon you would, for six weeks preceding the race, spend nearly all of your training time running aerobically, with only five percent of your time spent running the shorter, faster stuff.

Q **Why do you suggest a six-week point?**

A That's how long it takes for the body to completely turn over a new batch of cells, and thus theoretically adapt to any particular cardiovascular stress.

The first coach to practice this theory was (as usual) Arthur Lydiard who prescribes six weeks of anaerobic hill training as a transition between the aerobic base training period and the competitive track season.

Q **If you are going to paraphrase Arthur Lydiard, why don't you print his complete training schedules?**

A While I fully acknowledge Arthur Lydiard as the world's top distance running coach, I don't feel his intricate training schedules are appropriate in this book. A Lydiard schedule is designed to both point and peak a runner for a narrow range of racing distances within a narrow time period. In other words, a Lydiard schedule is designed to bring to the Peter Snells and Lasse Virens Olympic gold medals and world records in certain events. How the Snells or Virens perform in off-season races or in distances outside their range is of no concern to Lydiard.

My suggestions are admittedly for the real amateurs, for you and me, who may want to perform equally well in the Boston Marathon in April, a one-mile race in June, and a 10,000-meter through the streets of the old hometown in July.

What we need is a plan that strikes the best compromise between Arthur Lydiard and our amateur flexibility. Such is the plan of general base conditioning throughout the year (done in a 9:1 aerobic vs. anaerobic ratio) with six weeks of adjusted training before important races.

Q   **Can you tell me more about the types of anaerobic training we should do?**

A   When not training for a particular race, keep the intervals simple. Do them in a 1:2 ratio — run fast for 1-3 minutes, run slowly for 2-6 minutes, or better yet, run hills, taking two minutes of recovery time for each minute on the hill.

During the race season, I suggest dividing the intervals into three different types:

1. Moderately paced interval runs (or hills) in the same 1:2 ratio of the general conditioning period. Example: 75 second 440s with a 2½ minute recovery run between each.

2. Intensively paced intervals (or hills) in a 1:4 ratio. Example: 65 second 440s with a 4-5 minute recovery run.

3. Windsprints in a 1:1 ratio. Example: Lydiard 50-50s, in which you sprint for 50 yards, run slowly for 50 yards, etc., for 1-2 miles. This is an often neglected, but quite valuable sharpening tool.

Q   **How often should I do these?**

A   I suggest doing each workout once a week, as dessert at the end of your aerobic running. For example, when training for the marathon, I might add 4-5 minutes of intervals at the end of a 90 minute run. Or when training for the mile, I might add 30 minutes of intervals at the end of a 30 minute run. I much prefer this method to devoting an entire workout just to intervals.

Q **How hard should I run the fast part of the intervals?**

A As we mentioned in the previous chapter, you should run intervals, on one hand, as hard and fast as you can, but on the other, slowly enough to keep moving for the duration of the workout. Honest effort builds the body and soul while sustained movement keeps you from overdoing it.

Q **How should I point my training if I want to compete in a variety of distances?**

A If you understand the principles of pointing for specific distances, you can easily make the adjustments in your training to prepare adequately for a wide variety of races.

For example, if you have a month with three races — a one-mile, a two-mile and a six-mile — and you wish to perform equally well in all three, simply average the racing distances and train accordingly. In this example, you would train as a three-miler in preparation for that month.

But if only the six-mile is important to you, train as a six-miler and run the two shorter races as best you can.

In Section Four I will present a model training schedule for a racing season which begins in February and ends in July, and includes races from the mile to the marathon.

Section Three: Peaking

Q **What is peaking?**

A Peaking is cutting your training in order to let your energy reserves build up before a race. In this section we will consider two types — a minor peak for the majority of races, and a major peak for the one or two seasonal races you regard as more important than the rest.

○ *Minor Peak* Here you would reduce your regular training for only three days before competition. Below is an example of a minor peak:

Sunday — full-workout
Monday — full-workout
Tuesday — full-workout

Wednesday — half-workout
Thursday — quarter-workout
Friday — rest or quarter-workout

Saturday — The Race

○ *Major Peak* This takes two weeks, and includes two set-up runs and a gradual reduction in training.

Two weeks from the date of the big event, take a practice run of 75 percent of the race distance (50 percent if the actual race is more than 10 miles), but at the same pace you hope to maintain in the race itself. That is, if you hope (within reason) to race a mile in five minutes, make your practice run 1320 yards, and do it in 3:45. Or if you hope to race a marathon in three hours, make your practice run 13.1 miles, and do it in 90 minutes.

Treat this practice run seriously. Warm up as you would for the actual race, and wear your racing shoes. Measure the distance precisely and con someone into timing you with a stopwatch. Stick to your intended pace for the entire run, but don't be discouraged if the effort was harder than expected. In two weeks you'll be so rested, peaked and pysched that the same effort will carry you much farther.

For the Sunday and Monday following the Saturday set-up run (so-named because it "sets up" your body and mind for the real thing), train at 50 percent of your normal levels. On Tuesday take a full-workout, and for Wednesday, Thursday and Friday, again take only half-workouts.

This brings you to Saturday, one week before the race, and time for another set-up run. This one should be 50 percent of the race distance (25 percent if the race is more than 10 miles), and the pace should be divided into two distinct parts. The first 3/4 of the set-up run should be done at race pace, but the last fourth should be run as fast as you can, flat-out.

For example, if you are hoping to race a five-minute mile, your second set-up run would be 880 yards. For the first 660, you would run at your intended mile race pace, in this case 1:52.5. But for the last 220, you would sprint, using every drop of energy you had. Or if you were hoping to race a three hour marathon, your set-up run would be 6.6 miles. The first five miles would be run at your intended race pace, in 34:20. The last 1.6 would be run as hard as you could.

For the Sunday and Monday following the second set-up run, train at only 25 percent of your normal levels. On Tuesday take a full-workout, and for the rest of the week, again take only quarter-workouts.

Thus you end up with a two-week schedule that looks like this:

Saturday — 1st set-up run. 75% of race distance (50% if race is longer than 10 miles) at intended race pace.

Sunday — half-workout
Monday — half-workout
Tuesday — full-workout
Wednesday — half-workout
Thursday — half-workout
Friday — half-workout

Saturday — 2nd set-up run. 50% of race distance (25% if race is longer than 10 miles). First 3/4 of set-up run at intended race pace. Last 1/4 as fast as you can.

Sunday — quarter-workout
Monday — quarter-workout
Tuesday — full-workout
Wednesday — quarter-workout
Thursday — quarter-workout
Friday — rest or quarter-workout

Saturday — The Race

Section Four: Putting It All Together

Q   **A couple of sections ago, you said you would present a model training schedule for an entire racing season. Are we ready to see it?**

A   Well, since we've already discussed training, pointing and peaking, I guess it's time to put it all together.

The model training schedule I propose belongs to a hypothetical runner whom, because he seeks to race well at every distance, I will name Carter. Carter lives in the Upper Midwest, and for most of the year runs 60 miles a week in a 9:1 aerobic vs. anaerobic ratio. Carter's proposed racing schedule for the first half of the year is this:

February 4 — mile on indoor track
February 11 — 2-mile on indoor track
February 25 — 2-mile on indoor track

April 17 — Boston Marathon

May 6 — 20-kilometer road race

June 10 — mile on outdoor track
June 17 — 15-kilometer road race
June 24 — 5000-meter on outdoor track

July 4 — 10-kilometer road race

As we said, Carter wants to do well in every race, but would especially like to perform well in the Boston Marathon and the July 4th 10-kilometer which happens to go through the streets of his hometown.

Carter's first race is an indoor mile on February 4, which is followed by a pair of indoor two-miles on the 11th and the 25th. When planning his training schedule, Carter must decide how importantly he wishes to treat these indoor races. If they are as important to him as the Boston Marathon is, then he should point for them by training as a two-miler for the six weeks preceding the first race.

But since Carter regards the Boston Marathon as more important, a compromise between pointing for the indoor races and preparing for Boston should be sought. So on December 20, six weeks before the first indoor race, Carter might begin training as a three-miler (to sharpen for the track races), but also include in each training week two runs of more than 20 miles (to prepare for the marathon).

Such a schedule, at 60-70 miles a week, and in a 3:1 aerobic vs. anaerobic balance, might look like this:

Sunday — 25 miles slow
Monday — rest

Tuesday — 5 miles slow, 5 miles fast, 30 minutes of intensively run hills
Wednesday — 5 miles slow, 2 miles of Lydiard 50-50s
Thursday — 10 miles slow, 5 miles fast, 5 miles of 1:2 intervals
Friday — rest or 5 miles slow
Saturday — 5 miles slow, 2 miles of Lydiard 50-50s

This is the schedule Carter would follow through Tuesday, January 31. On Wednesday, February 1, Carter would begin a minor peak for the indoor mile on February 4. The minor peak might look like this:

Wednesday — 4 miles slow, 1 mile of Lydiard 50-50s
Thursday — 4 miles slow, 1 mile fast, 1 mile of 1:2 intervals
Friday — rest or 2-3 miles slow
Saturday — The Race

The week of February 5-11 would be the same as the previous, with full training for the first half, and reduced training for the second half.

After the two-mile race on February 11, Carter has two weeks before his next race on the 25th. For the week of February 12-18 he should resume full training. And for the week following that, he should again train fully until Tuesday, and then start a minor peak on Wednesday.

So, from December 20 to February 25, Carter's training schedule remains basically the same, with the only deviation being the three-day minor peaks before each race.

The day following the last indoor two-mile, on February 25, Carter should begin pointing exclusively for the Boston Marathon on April 17. The two changes he needs to make in his training are a) increasing the weekly mileage, and b) balancing the aerobic:anaerobic ratio. Carter, who normally trains 60-70 miles a week, should, for the next five weeks, increase that to 80-90, and do it in a 20:1 aerobic vs. anaerobic balance.

From February 26 to April 1, Carter's weekly training schedule might look like this:

Sunday — 25-30 miles slow
Monday — rest
Tuesday — 5 miles slow, 8 miles fast, 15 minutes of hills
Wednesday — 5 miles slow, 1 mile of Lydiard 50-50s

Thursday — 20-25 miles slow
Friday — rest or 5 miles
Saturday — 5 miles slow, 9 miles fast, 1 mile of 1:2 intervals

On Sunday, April 2, Carter would rest. On Monday, April 3, Carter would begin a major peak by taking his first set-up run of 13.1 miles at his intended marathon race pace (he does this on a Monday because the Boston Marathon is always held on the third Monday of April, Patriot's Day).

For the week of April 3-9, Carter's training schedule would look like this:

Monday — race warmup of 2-3 miles, set-up run of 13.1 miles at intended Boston Marathon pace
Tuesday — 10-15 miles slow
Wednesday — rest
Thursday — 5 miles slow, 8 miles fast, 15 minutes of hills
Friday — 5 miles slow, 1 mile of Lydiard 50-50s
Saturday — 10 miles slow
Sunday — rest or 5 miles slow

On Monday, April 10, exactly one week from the date of the Boston Marathon, Carter should take his second set-up run of 6.6 miles — the first five miles at race pace, and the last 1.6 as fast as he can.

From April 10-16, Carter's schedule would look like this:

Monday — race warmup of 2-3 miles, set-up run of 6.6 miles — first 5 at race pace, and last 1.6 at flat-out
Tuesday — 5 miles slow
Wednesday — rest
Thursday — 5 miles slow, 8 miles fast, 15 minutes of hills
Friday — 2-3 miles slow
Saturday — 2-3 miles slow
Sunday — rest or 2-3 miles slow

On Monday, April 17, Carter will be at his physical and mental peak for the Boston Marathon.

Let's pause here for a moment, and examine our man Carter. We know he has trained rather intensively for at least four months, and has just completed a fast, but body-beating marathon. Unless Carter has the recovery powers of a Frank Shorter or Bill Rodgers, he probably needs a rest, if not total, at least a great reduction in his weekly mileage. From April 18-May 6 Carter's weekly schedule might look like this:

Sunday — 10 miles slow
Monday — rest
Tuesday — rest
Wednesday — 5 miles slow
Thursday — rest
Friday — 5 miles slow, interspersed with easy striding
Saturday — rest

Q **If Carter is going to take it easy for three weeks, how will he be ready for the 20-kilometer race on May 6?**

A He won't be ready, and if he's smart, he will drop the 20-kilometer race from his schedule. It was foolish to plan for the 20 in the first place.

A well-run marathon actually destroys muscle cells, especially in men, and so it takes at least six weeks to properly recover, since that is the time it takes for a complete turnover of body cells. Marathoners have always known it takes at least that long to feel good again after a hard race. When the United States Olympic Committee originally scheduled the 1976 Olympic Marathon Trials, they placed it with the track and field trials in late June, one month before the Games. The marathoners screamed, and so the USOC moved the marathon trials back to late May. Even that was thought to allow barely enough time. Bill Rodgers said at the time:

"Two months is nothing between marathons."

For Carter, the three weeks of light training following the Boston Marathon should in turn be followed by another two weeks of moderate training, in which the high intensity race pointing is gradually reestablished. This moderate period might consist of 50-mile weeks, done in a standard 9:1 aerobic vs. anaerobic balance. From May 7-20 the weekly schedule would look like this:

Sunday — 20 miles slow
Monday — rest

Tuesday — 5 miles slow, 2 miles fast, 20 minutes of intensively run
      hills
Wednesday — rest or 5 miles slow
Thursday — 15 miles slow
Friday — rest or 5 miles slow
Saturday — 5 miles slow, 2 miles of 1:2 intervals

By May 21, Carter should be at full strength, and ready to start pointing for the next wave of races, beginning with a one-mile on June 3 and concluding with a 10-kilometer on July 4. Since Carter considers the 10-kilometer as most important, he should train basically as a six-miler, but perhaps add a bit more speedwork to accommodate the shorter track races and a longish hard run to prepare for the 15-kilometer.

From May 21 to June 3, Carter should run about 70-80 miles a week in a 4:1 aerobic vs. anaerobic ratio. The schedule could look like this:

Sunday — 20-25 miles slow
Monday — rest
Tuesday — 5 miles slow, 5 miles fast, 30 minutes of intensively run
      hills
Wednesday — 5 miles slow, 2 miles of Lydiard 50-50s
Thursday — 5 miles slow, 15 miles fast
Friday — rest or 5 miles slow
Saturday — 5 miles slow, 5 miles of 1:2 intervals

On the 10th, 17th, and 24th of June, Carter will race at distances from one mile to 15 kilometers. For each of these, Carter should take a minor peak, but otherwise not change his training. From June 4-24 his weekly schedule might look like this:

Sunday — 20-25 miles.
Monday — rest.
Tuesday — 5 miles slow, 5 miles fast, 30 minutes of intensively run
      hills.
Wednesday — 5 miles slow, 2 miles of Lydiard 50-50s.
Thursday — 5 miles slow, 2 miles fast.
Friday — rest or 2-3 miles slow.
Saturday — The Race.

Right after the 5000-meter race on June 24, Carter will begin a major peak for the 10-kilometer road race on July 4. Here is an example of the importance of knowing how to peak, rather than blindly following an exact two-week plan. In this case, Carter does not have two weeks to peak. He has only 10 days, from June 25 to July 4. Adjustments must be made.

The first adjustment Carter should make is using the 5000-meter race on June 24 as the first set-up run. Then from June 25-28 he should train lightly, as follows:

Sunday — 15 miles slow.
Monday — rest.
Tuesday — 5 miles slow, 2 miles of Lydiard 50-50s.
Wednesday — 5 miles slow.

On Thursday, June 29, five days before the July 4, 10-kilometer race, Carter should take another set-up run. But instead of half the race distance, this one should be only two miles, since the recovery period from it is not seven days, but only five. The first 1½ mile of the set-up run should be done at race pace, and the last 880 yards should be run as fast as possible. From June 29 to July 4, Carter's training schedule would look like this.

Thursday — 2-3 miles warmup, 2-mile set-up run — first 1½ miles at
                   10k race pace, last half-mile at flat-out.
Friday — 5-10 miles slow.
Saturday — 5 miles slow, 1 mile of Lydiard 50-50s.
Sunday — 2-3 miles slow
Monday — rest or 2-3 miles slow.
Tuesday — The Race.

Q   **What about after the 4th of July race?**

A   After the 4th of July race, Carter should take another three-week rest, during which he either abstains totally from running (not a bad idea after a strenuous racing season) or trains very lightly, no more than 20 miles a week. After that he should train according to his desire and/or autumn racing schedule.

                              *   *   *

Part Three: Entering

Q   **What sort of races are available for the average runner, no longer in school?**

A   Road races, from five miles to the marathon, offer the out-of-school runner the largest pick of competition. Other types of races include cross country, track meets, ultra-marathons, relays, club runs, and Fun-Runs.

Q   **How do I enter these races?**

A   That depends upon the type of race and who is organizing it.

O   *Road Races* The two main organizational bodies for American road races are the Amateur Athletic Union and the Road Runners Club of America. The AAU or the RRCA (or both) either directly or indirectly sponsor almost every road race in the country, including the Boston, New York City and Honolulu Marathons.

So, in order to officially enter most road races, one must belong to either or both the AAU and RRCA. The yearly membership cost for each is three dollars — their addresses are found in Chapter 21.

On top of the required AAU or RRCA membership, most road races charge an entry fee of 50 cents to three dollars, which pays for trophies, competitors' numbers, result sheets, officials, and the necessary police control. Fees of more than three dollars usually go for such frills as pre-race spaghetti dinners with occasional guest speakers (Cooper, Sheehan, Henderson, *et al*), tee shirts, and post-race beer and bandaids.

Many road races encourage advanced registration by discounting the fee if you enter before the day of competition. A few races, notably some national championships and the Boston Marathon, restrict the number of entrants by imposing qualifying times — in the case of Boston, three hours for all men under age 40, and 3½ hours for all women and for all men over 40. The New York City Marathon stops accepting entrants after the first 5000.

The sizes of road races (the number of entrants) vary even more than the distances and quality of competition. I have raced with 15,000 in the

Top: The informality of a Fun-Run.

Bottom: The swarm of Bay-to-Breakers.

nation's largest race, San Francisco's Bay-to-Breakers, and with 15 in one of its smallest, the Bristol, South Dakota, 15-kilometer. Crowds of more than a thousand are common these days — in metropolitan areas they are the rule.

I used to think beginning racers were smart to avoid big crowds, but lately I've revised my opinion. At Stanford I knew several men and women who began running seriously *after* being hooked by the excitement of their first Bay-to-Breakers.

O *Cross Country Races* Although cross country is the major autumn sport for runners still in high school or college, the racing opportunities for out-of-school runners are thin unless you live in a cross country hotbed like the Northeast, or where your district AAU or RRCA is especially active. Most runners who live elsewhere will be lucky to find one or two races a season, and that often means begging the local high school or college coach for a chance to run unattached (starting well behind the others).

Cross country races in America are usually run on golf courses or in parks, and at distances from 2-3 miles in high school meets to 4-6 miles in college, AAU, RRCA, and United States Track and Field Federation meets.

Runners in Europe believe in a more literal definition of cross country — races in England and the Continent are 10-20 kilometers of mud, rocks, farmers' fields, fences, shallow rivers — a shoe salesman's dream! The Oregon Track Club recently sponsored a "European" cross country race, and the response was encouraging. I hope in the future more clubs do the same.

Among experienced runners, cross country is often the favorite way of racing. Everything attractive about running — the variety and simplicity, the harshness and beauty, the struggle and peace — is brought into a clear light when you are racing up a dirt trail or down the 18th fairway. It is then you might forever stop asking: why do I run?

O *Track Meets* Those out-of-school runners wishing to run in track meets face the same dilemma as cross country runners — limited opportunities. Here again, the opportunities depend largely upon the active concern of local track clubs and the district AAU or USTFF. In other words, if you live on either coast, you're in luck, but if you live in Utah or Alabama, you'll have to travel long distances to get your fill of track races.

In most AAU, USTFF, or club-sponsored track meets, an entry fee of 50 cents to one dollar per event is charged. The usual outdoor lineup of track distance races are the mile (1500 meters), three-mile (5000 meters), six-mile (10,000 meters), and 3000-meter steeplechase. The usual indoor menu consists of the mile and two-mile, with an occasional three-mile or steeplechase.

Because of the small, but fast and experienced racing fields, a track meet is a bad place to make a racing debut.

○ *Ultra-Marathons* These include all races longer than 26 miles, 385 yards. Some of the standard track distances (yes, Phidippides, they do it *on the track*) are 50 and 100 kilometers and 50 and 100 miles. Nearly all of the ultra-marathon track races are sponsored directly by the AAU or RRCA.

Other ultra-marathons not held on a track are the Levi Tie and Ride, a 24-hour survival race over the rocks and trails of the High Sierras, in which humans race horses, and the once-around Lake Tahoe 72-miler.

○ *Relays* The type of relays available to the out-of-school distance runner are not standard track relays, but road and 24-hour relays.

Road relays are most common in England, where they are often a substitute for cross country races. In America, road relays are rare, but much fun because of the team camaraderie. A typical road relay might be 25 miles — five legs of five miles each. Road relays are almost always sponsored by track clubs, and are apart from any official sanction.

A bizarre event which saw its height of popularity in the early 1970s is the 24-hour relay, in which 2-10 runners alternate one-mile legs on the track for 24 hours. No substitutions are allowed — if a team member quits, the team is forced to go with one less member.

I have run in two 24-hour relays — the first time we traveled 242 miles (slightly faster than a six-minute mile average), and for the second we improved to 264 miles (exactly 5:30 per mile). I can say unequivocally that the second 24-hour relay (run in daytime temperatures exceeding 100 degrees) was the toughest physical task I've ever done. Others who have run in 24-hour relays know what I'm talking about.

○ *Club Runs* Many of the larger running and track clubs regularly sponsor their own road and cross country races. These are separate from the AAU or RRCA and are mainly held to stimulate interest in running and the club. The atmosphere of a club run is generally more relaxed than an AAU or RRCA road race. The distances tend to be shorter — thus a club run is an excellent place to make a racing debut.

The best example of regular club runs are those weekly races sponsored by the Dolphin South End Club of San Francisco. No doubt the DSE is partly responsible for the vast number of runners in the Bay Area.

○ *Fun-Runs* Perhaps the best place to run your first race is in a *Runner's World* magazine sponsored Fun-Run. Fun-Runs are the brainchild of publisher Bob Anderson, who sought to provide a network of racing opportunities and *RW* advertising at no cost.

Presently there are more than 200 Fun-Run sites throughout the country and overseas. Depending on the site, they are held weekly, bi-weekly, or monthly.

The original Fun-Run site, at Foothill College in Los Altos, California, meets every Sunday morning regardless of weather or other conflicts — the largest Fun-Run crowd I've seen was on an Easter Sunday. And on each Sunday there are three different races — two shorter distances such as a half-mile and a mile, and one longer, from three to six miles.

A Fun-Run costs nothing to enter, no times are recorded (although someone stands at the finish line and calls out times from a running watch), and nearly everyone has, as the name implies, fun. By writing to Bob Anderson at *Runner's World,* you can find the site closest to you. If there are no sites within an hour's drive, you might want to start your own. Anderson will send you the necessary information.

Q **How can I find the dates and locations of the above races?**

A In this age of running popularity, finding upcoming races in your locale is rather easy. A good number of sources are: your district AAU and

RRCA offices, *Runner's World* magazine (in Coming Events and Fun-Run Update), regional running publications (such as *Nor-Cal Running Review* and *Yankee Runner*), local newsletters, YMCAs, and local running clubs. A list of appropriate addresses are found in Chapter 21.

*   *   *

Part Four: Dressing for the Race

Q   **Is there any difference between dressing for a training run and dressing for a race?**

A   Yes. In training the apparel you wear is for comfort and protection. Lightness is secondary.

But in a race, you must dress in the best combination of comfort and lightness. Protection is secondary.

In training you wear whatever feels best. In a race you wear as little as you can get away with.

Nowhere is the difference more pronounced than in shoes. Training shoes, like those described in Chapter Seven, are built for comfort and injury prevention, with little regard to weight.

But racing shoes are built primarily for comfort and lightness. Injury preventatives (stiff shank, etc.) are included only if they add nothing to the weight.

Q   **I don't recall that you mentioned racing shoes in Chapter Seven. Why not?**

A   You're right — I didn't mention racing shoes in Chapter Seven. For the new runner, nothing is more initially confusing than the variety and selection of shoes. There is enough complexity among training shoes without dragging racing shoes into the picture.

So, I saved the discussion of racing shoes for this chapter.

Basically, there are three types of racing shoes — flats, spikes, and a mutant of the two, waffle racers.

The differences among shoes. From top to bottom: training flats, racing flats, and spikes.

○ *Racing Flats* To the untrained eye racing flats look the same as training flats. The big difference, though, is in weight and thickness of the outer sole. In a typical training flat the outer sole is 30 millimeters thick in the heel and 15 millimeters in the forefoot. The outer sole thickness in a racing flat is only 2/3 of that—20 millimeters in the heel and 10 millimeters in the forefoot.

Similarly, a racing flat weighs only about 2/3 as much as a training shoe. An average pair of racing flats, size nine, might weigh 450 grams, whereas the training counterparts would be closer to 700 grams.

Q   **Who makes good racing flats?**

A   For the most part, the companies which make the best training flats also make the best racing flats.

In my opinion, the five best racing flats available today are:

Nike Elites This popular racing flat has been the top choice of the *Runner's World* survey for the past two years, and deservedly so. Although the blue waffle-soled shoe resembles a training flat, at 450 grams a pair it is one of the lightest on the market. The cost, 34 dollars, is low considering the quality.

Tiger Jayhawks This shoe has been around longer than even the Nike Elite. At 25 dollars a pair, the Jayhawk is the best bargain among top racing flats. This gold and blue shoe weighs 472 grams a pair.

Tiger Ohboris This blue and gold Tiger is the favorite shoe of America's two best marathoners, as well as many other top runners. Unique among racing flats, the Ohbori is shaped like a track shoe — it props the runner on his toes — which is why the faster runners like it so much. For the same reason, though, slower runners should avoid the Ohbori. Running highly on the toes is very fatiguing at a slower pace. The Ohbori weighs 450 grams a pair, and costs 32 dollars.

Converse Marathoners The Marathoner marks Converse's entry into the racing shoe market, and is the only shoe among my top five which comes in more than one width: narrow, medium and wide. If the Marathoner has any fault, it is *too* light, which is to say, too thinly padded. For small runners and those light on their feet, though, it is an excellent shoe. This 32 dollar shoe is available in blue and white, and weighs 414 grams a pair.

E.B. Bostons This finely crafted shoe is my favorite, but is mostly popular among the Europeans. E.B. are the initials of Eugen Brüt-ting, a renowned West German cobbler, but the real influence of E.B. shoes belongs to none other than Arthur Lydiard, who is Brütting's track shoe consultant. Although of feathery weight, the Boston is still well-padded. This blue and white shoe weighs 428 grams a pair and costs 30 dollars.

Five other good, but heavier racing flats are:

Nike Stings This shoe is colored, believe it or not, orange, green and white. Stings cost 36 dollars and weigh 478 grams a pair.

Nike New Bostons This yellow and green shoe is similar in looks and design to its younger brother, the Sting. New Bostons are slightly heavier (488 a pair), but less costly at 27 dollars.

Brooks Floridians More than any other brand, Brooks designs their racing flats to look like training flats, with only a few modifications to cut weight. The result is a shoe that is orthopedically safe, but slightly heavy. The blue and white Floridian comes in narrow, medium and wide, weighs 512 grams a pair, and costs only 20 dollars.

Brooks Texans Except for a slightly different color and sole pattern, the blue and red Texan is indistinguishable from the Floridian. The Texan weighs 518 grams a pair, and costs 25 dollars.

New Balance Super Comps Looking thoroughly New Balance, the yellow and white Super Comp also comes in variable widths, from AA to EEE. Super Comps weigh 530 grams a pair and cost 30 dollars.

Finally, some of the lighter training shoes can be used as racing flats, especially by heavier or less experienced runners. Five of the lightest training flats available today are:

New Balance 320s Joe Henderson, the longtime editor of *Runner's World* and author of *Jog, Run, Race,* prefers to wear these comfort-able trainers in long races such as the marathon. Available in widths AA to EEE, these blue and white shoes weigh 582 grams a pair and cost 28 dollars.

New Balance 220s These yellow and white training shoes are nearly as light as the Super Comp. They are cheaper, too, costing 23 dollars. The pair weighs 536 grams.

Converse World Class Trainers Except for a thicker sole, these training shoes are identical to the Converse Marathoner. Blue and white, they cost 28 dollars and weigh 578 grams.

Nike Waffle Trainers If you want to buy one shoe that best serves all purposes — training, cross country running, racing — you could not do better than the Waffle Trainer. The venerable red and white Waffle Trainer is among the best training shoes, yet weighs only 566 grams a pair. It's inexpensive, too — 28 dollars.

E.B. Lydiard Road Runners, Blue The color distinction is important here because the tan Road Runners are quite a bit heavier. The blue Road Runners weigh 584 grams a pair and cost 39 dollars.

Curiously, Adidas, the foremost maker of running shoes, does not presently have a good racing flat — their *Marathon* is too heavy (610 grams a pair) to be taken seriously. Yet athletes wearing Adidas racing flats have won the last three Olympic marathons, so I suspect it won't be long before Adidas returns to near the top of the racing flat market.

Q **Among the racing flats you listed, there was a weight difference of 170 grams between the lightest and heaviest pair. Shouldn't we always try to wear the lightest?**

A Not always. The lightest racing flats should be reserved for shorter distances and more experienced runners. Light racing flats are very thinly padded, and many runners, especially the newer and heavier, can't tolerate the rather direct impact of foot and pavement.

Someone like Frank Shorter, who weighs only 130 pounds and runs with a feathery stride, can wear the lightest shoes at any distance, including the marathon. Most of us, though, weigh more, train less, and strike the ground more jarringly than Shorter. Possibly we can wear the lightest racing flats in short road races (up to 10 miles), but after that the accumulative jarring becomes more fatiguing than carrying the extra weight of a well-padded, heavier racing flat would be.

As mentioned earlier, the best racing apparel is the least you can get away with. For marathon races, Frank Shorter can get away with taking a light shoe, the Tiger Ohbori, and further shaving its sole to save weight. On the other hand, Joe Henderson feels the least he can get away with in a marathon is a pair of well-worn New Balance 320s.

Following the discussion of spikes and waffle racers, I will present a suggested shoe-wearing chart, matching the range of racing distances with the range of experience and ability.

○ *Spikes* Most out-of-school runners will never find the need to own a pair of spikes. Most won't run in track races often enough to justify their rather expensive price.

Yet, even if you wear them infrequently, there is something magical about owning a pair of spikes. Since I prefer the shorter track and cross country races (in which spikes are worn) to the longer road races, I need only to look at the pair of spikes in my closet to feel excitement, to think back to all those races in high school and college when changing from training flats to spikes meant the moment of truth was near. Even today, when befallen by the flu, I need only to wear my spikes around the house to instantly feel better.

Spikes are constructed to feel much different than either training or racing flats. They should cling snugly to your feet in all places, and prop you to the ball of your foot. The spike uppers are made of either nylon or thin leather. The sole is made of rubber with a plastic spike plate underneath the ball of the foot.

The metal spikes themselves number from four to seven, and can be screwed in and out with the provided spike wrench. For cross country and cinder tracks, metal spikes of ½-inch are used (¾-inch if the surface is muddy; ⅜-inch if the surface is extremely hard). For artificial tracks, use ¼-inch spikes or studs. Most running shops have a full assortment of metal spikes and wrenches for your shoes.

Among the top racing spikes available today are:

All Adidas The crown jewels of the Adidas sports line are racing spikes. Here is where the West German company began and built its reputation. Here is where it continues to dominate the field.

I find Adidas superior to all other racing spikes because of the arch support system. The three-stripe identifying mark of Adidas does more than spice the appearance — on the inside of the shoe it acts as an arch, keeping the foot ever propped into a fast running position.

Three of the better Adidas racing spikes are:

Adistar 2000s, Leather This is the single best distance racing spike in the world. It is expensive, though, at 58 dollars a pair. This blue and white shoe weighs 316 grams a pair.

Spiders This green and black shoe is a slightly heavier, slightly sturdier version of the Adistar 2000. A pair costs 48 dollars, and weighs 372 grams a pair.

Jets This blue and white shoe is a hot bargain for high school runners and others on a budget. It costs 28 dollars and weighs 366 grams a pair.

Other good racing spikes are:

Tiger Spartan Bs This flashy gold and black nylon shoe is a favorite among many, including Lasse Viren, who proudly displayed them to the Montreal crowd after each of his 1976 Olympic track wins. Spartan Bs cost 44 dollars and weigh 346 grams a pair.

Puma Tornadoes This red and white shoe is a raging bargain at 17 dollars. A pair weighs 362 grams.

Puma Kralle 130s If you like the stylish Pumas and want to get the best pair, this is your shoe. Made of leather, this red and white shoe costs 40 dollars and weighs 330 grams.

Nike Vainqueurs If you like a substantial heel lift with your spikes, this is your shoe. Shaped more like a racing flat than a spike, this green, yellow and white nylon racer costs 40 dollars and weighs 368 grams a pair.

Saucony Speedsters At 18 dollars, this blue and white nylon shoe competes with the Puma Tornado as the best bargain among top spikes. It weighs 332 grams a pair.

Saucony Scats A women's version of the Speedster, this one both costs and weighs less — 16 dollars and 318 grams a pair.

○ *Waffle Racers* The last category of racing shoes, waffle racers, are a combination of spikes and racing flats — built like a spiked shoe with an outer sole of a waffled racing flat. Waffle racers are perfectly suited for cross country races run on a variety of surfaces — grass, dirt, pavement — but are also good for short road races.

Presently, there are only two waffle racers on the market:

Nike Waffle Racers This yellow and green nylon shoe is the original waffle racer. On top, it looks like a spiked shoe, the Nike Vainqueur. On the bottom it looks like the Nike Elite. At 30 dollars and 398 grams a pair, it is a must for serious cross country runners.

Adidas Arrows On top, this nylon waffle racer looks like a yellow and gold Adidas Jet, a spiked shoe. On the bottom, it looks like the Adidas TRX, a waffled training shoe. The Arrow weighs 422 grams a pair and costs 20 dollars.

*   *   *

Q   **You mentioned all of these shoes for clarification, yet I'm only confused more. In any given race, what are the best shoes to wear?**

A   You'll discover the best shoes to wear for each race as you become more experienced. But for starters, the following chart can help you to avoid costly mistakes.

Suggested Shoe Types for Each Race

Race Distance	Beginner	Intermediate	Advanced
1-6 miles, track	A-E	A-C	A-B
1-6 miles, cross country	B-E	A-C	A-B
1-6 miles, road	C-E	B-C	B-C
6-15 miles, track	D-E	B-D	A-C
6-15 miles, cross country	D-E	C-D	B-C
6-15 miles, road	D-E	C-D	B-C
15 miles - Marathon, track	E	E-D	C-D
15 miles - Marathon, road	E	E-D	C-D
Ultra-marathon, track	E	E	D
Ultra-marathon, road	E	E	D

A   Spikes (Adidas Adistar 2000)
B   Waffle Racers (Nike Waffle Racer)
C   Light Racing Flats (Converse Marathoner)
D   Heavy Racing Flats (Brooks Texan)
E   Light Training Flats (New Balance 320)

*   *   *

Q   **What are the clothing differences in training and racing?**

A   In warm weather the differences are slight — in fact, the same cotton tee shirt and nylon shorts you wear in training are fine for racing.

More official looking, though, is a sleeveless top, made of cotton, nylon, or nylon mesh. The least expensive can be purchased for three or four dollars in underwear departments. This is what I wear (I own six differently colored tops, from black to psychedelic, which I bought for 20 dollars), and at races runners ask me where I get my fashionable uniforms!

The flashiest racing uniform available today is a two-piece nylon tricot/ nylon mesh sleeveless top with matching nylon tricot shorts. Frank Shorter Sports, Marty Liquori Sportswear (distributued through Athletic Attic), and Starting Line Sports sell this uniform. The cost, though, is quite steep — 10 dollars for the shorts and 15 dollars for the top.

Of course if you belong to a track or running club, you have the option of wearing the club uniform in races. The two most distinctive club uniforms I've seen lately belong to the Buffalo Chip Track Club of Sacramento, California, and the Prairie Dog Track Club of Dickinson, North Dakota.

The rule in colder weather is: Wear as little as you can get away with. And if you must add clothing, start with the extremities.

On the matter of cold weather race-dressing, experience is the best teacher. Below is a suggested clothing list based upon my experience of racing in temperatures of zero to 100 degrees.

Above 60 degrees   Sleeveless top and shorts.

40 to 60 degrees   Tee shirt and shorts.

20 to 40 degrees	Tee shirt and shorts, turtleneck and light mittens (add cut-off longjohns and stocking hat if windy).
0 to 20 degrees	Tee shirt and shorts, turtleneck and light mittens, full-length longjohns and stocking hat (add windbreaker jacket if windy).

As you can see, the suggested clothing for racing in cold weather is significantly less than similar cold weather training apparel. However, the list isn't as scant as it looks. The fast pace, and adrenaline of a race will keep you warmer than you think.

Q **What should we wear before and after the race?**

A That will be discussed in the next part of the chapter.

*   *   *

Part Five: The Hours Before

Q **What should I eat as my last meal before a race?**

A General diet and pre-race meals, including the carbohydrate loading controversy, are discussed exhaustively in Chapter Eight.

There are three points to remember when selecting your last meal before a race:

1. Eat mostly of complex carbohydrates (cereals, breads, salads, etc.), and avoid, as much as possible, meats and fats.

2. Eat lightly — stop the moment you feel slightly filled. As Arthur Lydiard says, no runner is going to starve during a race, yet many chow down as if that were a possibility. Don't you.

3. Eat several hours before the race. If the pre-race meal is light, allow four hours. If the meal is heavier, allow five or more.

Q **How soon before the race should I arrive at the site?**

A   For the smallest and simplest races, arrive at least an hour before.

For larger races, arrive early enough to take care of parking, entry registration, etc., so that you still have an hour to yourself before the starter fires the gun.

Q   **Why do I need an hour to myself before the race starts?**

A   You don't *need* an hour, but I strongly believe that a few minutes of collecting your thoughts followed by a thorough warmup will greatly enhance your race performance.

Q   **Collecting my thoughts before the race sounds like serious business. You're not getting heavy on me, are you?**

A   I think part of the fun of racing *is* taking it seriously — waking up excited, letting the excitement build during the day, and for a few quiet moments before the race, harnessing that excitement to a goal: racing to the best of your ability.

To me, that is heavy business, much more so than the everyday sobrieties of finishing homework or reporting to the boss.

*   *   *

Q   **What do you mean by a thorough warmup?**

A   Having done a thorough warmup before the race means you arrive at the starting line feeling at the peak of your mental and physical powers, ready to uncork the energy and excitement you've kept bottled for this occasion.

To do this, of course, you must dispense with the usual preliminary blahs by first running gently for 20-30 minutes. As you read in Chapter 17, it takes this long for the body to become oxygenated and for the muscles to loosen.

And to the 20-30 minutes of gentle running I would add 5-10 minutes of stretching and a few stride-ups of 100-200 yards, done at least as fast as race pace.

Thus my idea of a thorough race warmup takes 30-45 minutes, and is broken into parts like this:

1. 5 minutes of stretching.
2. 20-30 minutes of easy running.
3. 5 minutes of more stretching.
4. 1-2 minutes of changing into racing shoes.
5. 5 minutes of stride-ups.
6. Wait for the race. The ideal time between the last stride-up and the start of the race is 5-10 minutes, so plan your warmup accordingly. During the wait you must stay warm and relaxed. Walking or gentle running is advised.

Q **Your suggested warmup is certainly complete, but might not it also be too much? Isn't there a possibility of tiring yourself with a long warmup?**

A Admittedly, the suggested warmup is for advanced runners racing in shorter distances. For less experienced runners and everyone racing long distances (more than six miles/10 kilometers), the warmup must be abbreviated so that enough energy remains to finish the race.

When I am training 70-80 miles a week I consider myself an advanced runner (while writing this book I'm doing 30-40 a week, a good inter-mediate level). As an advanced runner, I would use the full warmup for races less than 10 kilometers. For races 10 kilometers to 15 miles, I would cut my warmup to 20-30 minutes. For races more than 15 miles, I would cut the warmup even more, to 10-20 minutes, and then take the first two miles of the race slowly. In other words, I would use common sense, based upon the race distance and my level of fitness.

Below is a table of suggested warmup times, based upon the race distance and runner's level of fitness:

Suggested Pre-Race Warmup Times (in minutes)

Race Distance	Beginning Racer	Intermediate Racer	Advanced Racer
1-3 miles	20-30	30-45	30-45
3-6 miles	10-20	20-30	30-45
6-15 miles	5-10	10-20	20-30
above 15 miles	shouldn't race	5-10	10-20

Q **What should we wear during the warmup?**

A   In the hours before the race, including the warmup, you should wear enough clothing to keep your body amply warm, even if you do nothing but sit on the ground. The importance of keeping your muscles warm and loose before the race can't be understated. Just like the baseball pitcher who wears a jacket between innings, even on a balmy night, runners must also wear sufficient clothing during the warmup, even when it appears we could wear less.

In training I refuse to wear a warmup suit until the temperature drops below 50 degrees. In racing I won't wear one unless I absolutely have to. But when warming up for a race, I will wear a full suit in any temperature below 70 degrees. This might seem extreme, but I place high value on being loose before the race. The only exception I would make is for the longest races (more than 15 miles), in which one needs to start the race with as much body fluid as he can hold. In that case, a warmup suit should not be worn above 60 degrees.

Here is a suggested list of warmup clothing (for races more than 15 miles, lower the temperatures by 10 degrees):

> *Above 70 degrees* No warmup suit necessary.
> *50-70 degrees* One layer of warmup clothing.
> *40-50 degrees* Two layers of warmup clothing.
> *Below 40 degrees* Two layers of warmup clothing, plus gloves or mittens, a stocking hat, and a jacket heavy enough to keep you warm even as you lie on the ground and stretch.

Q   **When should I remove my warmup clothes?**

A   That question reminds me of the unique command given by the starter in cold weather states, like North Dakota. The first command is not "on your marks" or "get set," but: "Runners, remove your warmup clothes."

That is to say, don't shed your warmup clothing until you have to. To lose your carefully stored body heat moments before the race is to negate the value of your warmup.

For races with large crowds, I suggest you wear a nondescript grey sweatsuit as warmup clothing. That way, you won't worry about theft as you toss the sweats to the sidelines moments before the race.

Q **How soon should I arrive at the actual starting line?**

A First let me say that you should do your warmup reasonably close to the starting line in case either your timing or the race schedule is fouled up.

The worst fate that can befall a runner is missing the start of a race, and if not that, being caught unprepared for the start. Would anyone want to live with the memories carved in the minds of the two US sprinters who missed their race calls at the 1972 Olympics?

So, stay within seeing and hearing distance of the starting line during your warmup. When finished, remove your warmup clothes (if the temperature is comfortably warm; otherwise leave them on until the last moment), saunter over to the starting line, and listen for instructions.

*   *   *

Part Six: The Race

Q **Where should I take my place in the race field — toward the front, middle, or back?**

A Regardless of where, a smart runner takes his place in the field as late as possible.

In large events like Bay-to-Breakers, the race officials begin herding the runners to the starting line up to a half-hour before the race starts. Runners foolish enough to join the pack who follow orders will completely ruin their chances for a good warmup, and will become cold and stiff from standing obediently among the herd.

My suggestion is to ignore the officials and remain on the sidelines, where you can stay warm and loose, until the last possible moment.

Q **But if everyone did that . . .**

A I know. But do it anyway. Besides, not everyone will ignore the officials — most will attentively jump into line the moment the starter blows his whistle. In case you haven't discovered, there is a universal maxim, if not law, working here. It says: For every smart person there are nine stupid people.

Let the other 90 percent stand and squeeze and squish against each other. You just stay warm and relaxed, on the sidelines, ready to jump in at the last moment.

Q **That brings me back to my first question. Where should I jump in — front, middle or back?**

A Jump in where you think you belong. But don't cheat — don't take your place too far to the front, where it is obvious the runners are faster than you.

I say this not as a call for fairness, but for your own protection. If you initially get caught in a pace faster than your ability, you'll blow your race in the first few hundred yards.

Of course, in smaller races you won't have to waste your time plotting such strategy. Just go to the starting line when called, and the race will begin shortly.

Q **What are the usual starting commands?**

A For track races, the usual command is: "On your marks (two second pause), get set," and then the fire of the gun.

For cross country and road races, the command is only: "Runners to your marks," followed by the gun. In many club runs and most fun-runs, there won't be any gun — the starting command is followed by a simple: "Go!"

In larger races you won't even hear the gun unless you are standing near the front. If that is the case, be alert for movement ahead.

Q **And after the start?**

A After the start, you must immediately try to find running room, and then quickly find the correct pace.

○ *Finding Running Room* Ten years ago no one dreamed this would ever be a problem, except, perhaps, in the Boston Marathon. But now, crowded fields of more than a thousand are commonplace.

Where you will find running room immediately after the start of a large race is like predicting weather in Iowa, or the flow of traffic on the Massachusetts Turnpike. Assume anything, especially regularity, and you're likely to be wrong.

Instead, you must pay attention, and react accordingly. The second worst disaster, after missing the race, is tripping at the start. Only this could be perilous, and frankly I'm quite surprised (and relieved) that a trampling hasn't yet occurred in one of the larger races. I'm not sure that runners at the start of the New York City Marathon are much more orderly than are soccer fans in Argentina.

Even in track races, the shoving and pushing can be a problem. The most physically brutal races I've run in were indoor two-miles with 20 others, all eager to be in the top five at the end of the first 160-yard lap. The solution there was a mad dash of 30-40 yards, enough to find room and good positioning without inflicting exhaustion.

In a road race, though, the equivalent mad dash would last much longer, and would put you deeply into oxygen debt from the start. Being overly aggressive will also cost energy you'll need later.

So the solution to finding running room at the start of a crowded race takes nothing less than patience, alertness, opportunism, and luck. When you do find it, shift your concentration to the next item.

○ *Finding The Right Pace* Here, the temptation is to match strides with the faster runners and the fools chasing them. Do that, and you'll end up a very tired fool.

The best race plan — I'll say it again — the best race plan starts with finding your own correct pace, and not being influenced by others.

Your opponents are not others, but yourself and the watch. Racing against others is only for those with a good chance of winning or placing, or for the end of the race, with the finish line in sight and an old rival looming ahead.

But for 99 percent of all runners, and for 90 percent of the distance, the race is with yourself and against the watch. And the way to win is with careful and prudent pacing.

Q   **How should we pace ourselves?**

A   Ideally, you should spread your energy equally over the entire distance, and finish the race with nothing left.

The best way to do this is to first calculate the fastest time you are capable of running given the situation —weather, terrain, your fitness, etc. — and then set the pace accordingly.

Thus if you think a five-minute mile is the fastest you can run, set a pace of 75-second 440s. If a three-hour marathon is the highest you can reach, set a pace of 6:50 miles.

Q   **Even though my training and fitness indicate I am capable of running a three-hour marathon, the very idea of running 26 consecutive miles in 6:50 seems staggering.**

A   That's quite normal — the thought of running the entire distance at race pace *is* staggering. Frank Shorter, who has run several marathons at a sub-5:00 pace, says he can't conceive of that kind of effort when he's training for 15 miles at a six-minute pace. Ron Hill, a 2:09 marathoner, refuses to think about racing the entire distance while he's waiting at the starting line.

What Shorter, Hill, and most experienced racers have learned to do is divide the race into segments, and take each segment as a rung on a ladder — one at a time.

At the start, you must think only of the start — finding running room, positioning, etc.

That accomplished, you must think only of finding the right pace.

And once you've found the right pace, you must think of nothing but maintaining it — around each turn, past each telephone pole, from one mile to the next — or of adjusting it to the terrain or your fatigue, while keeping the same effort and intensity — up and down each hill, during the last quarter of the race, after the glycogen is depleted.

In other words, you must think of the present and nothing else, certainly not the entire distance yet to be run.

Q   **That must take a lot of concentration.**

A   I'm glad you said that. Because concentration is one of the two secrets to racing.

One proven difference between top-class runners and the rest is presence of mind, the ability to concentrate on nothing but running. In 1975 Dr. Michael Pollock of the Institute of Aerobics Research studied a group of top American distance runners, Frank Shorter and Steve Prefontaine among them, for maximum oxygen uptake, bodyfat, etc., and found results quite predictable of world class runners — Prefontaine had the highest oxygen uptake ever tested, Shorter produced almost no lactic acid, and so on.

But the most surprising and revealing results of Pollock's tests came from the answers to the question: what do you think about during a race? To a man, the runners said they thought about pace, rhythm, breathing, fatigue; in short, everything connected with running and racing.

By comparison, the answers given to Dr. Pollock by runners of lesser experience and ability — the four-hour marathoner types — indicated thoughts dissociated from running. Some passively dissociated: ''I guess my mind sort of wanders.'' But many actually tried to take their mind off running: ''I play my favorite albums in my head,'' or ''I imagine building a house, brick by brick.''

According to Dr. Pollock, the differences in concentrative ability between top runners and the rest could possibly be greater than the differences in physical ability.

I am convinced the secret of the Shorters and Marty Liquoris lies not only in their heart and lungs. Watch world class runners and you sense the intensity, the monomania. Shorter says he concentrates so hard during a marathon that the more than two hours of running seem compressed into 45 minutes.

Q   **Can you give me an example of mentally dividing a race into segments?**

A   My favorite racing distance is the mile on an outdoor track, and for that I

The race concentration of Marty Liquori.

will mentally divide the race into turns and straightaways. At the beginning of each turn or straightaway, I will concentrate on my rhythm, stride, pace, relaxation, and tactics against others if needed. I will try to maintain the intensity of thought for the length of the turn or straightaway, but at the end of each I will take a mental pause of a half-second or so, enough for refreshment, but not enough to break my concentration.

For a longer race, such as the marathon, my segments will be longer, my concentration not as intense — I will pace my mind as well as my body. My segments might be landmarks from a mile to three or four miles apart, between which I will concentrate on stride, rhythm, pace, relaxation, and equally important, how I feel: if the pace is too fast, if I need water, or how I can save precious steps by cutting corners and running tangents.

Not only does this present-mind intensity help me draw the most from my running tank; it also relieves me from worrying about the distance yet to be raced.

Q **If concentration is one secret of racing, what is the other?**

A The other secret is dealing effectively with the inevitable moment of truth, which usually occurs somewhere between the first and third quarters of a race — between the first and third laps in a mile; between six and 20 miles in a marathon.

As Ron Clarke once said, the moment is intangible and fleeting, but sure. You don't know exactly when it will come, but it will, and if you fail to deal with it decisively and immediately, you could very well blow your race.

Q **This moment of truth — is it the pain?**

A Not entirely — I think the moment of truth is instead the question that immediately follows the first hint of pain: Am I ready to go through with it?

The real pain of a race is not the actual physical hurt, but the nibbling temptation of knowing you can stop the hurt whenever you wish. It is not the pain of a wounded soldier, but of a prisoner of war having to choose between torture and confession, between winning and losing, as it were.

To win, you must make the right choice, and make it swiftly. To postpone the moment of truth until after the pain has started is to allow temptation to get the upper hand, making the decision that much tougher.

Q **If the moment of truth is so fleeting and intangible, why wait for it? Why not decide beforehand how to deal with it?**

A Deciding beforehand how you will react to the moment of truth is academic. That is not to say you shouldn't get psyched up for a race, but only to warn you that every race is filled with psyched-up runners who are shot down by the sudden moment of truth.

Q **How should I answer the moment of truth?**

A When the moment arrives, simply accept the fact you will have to finish the race with pain. Then forget about it — your pain is greatly minimized once you've made a firm decision to plunge ahead — and resume concentrating on the race.

Having fun is not always taking yourself seriously.

CHAPTER TWENTY

Why Running Is Fun For Some And Boring For Others

Q   What makes running a boring activity for many people?

A   Running becomes a bore when we kill its joy, spontaneity and fun. We do this by overplanning, expecting too much from ourselves, running for the wrong reasons, and sacrificing other enjoyable activities for running.

I recommend the following ways to ruin the fun in your running:

Never run without timing yourself. A wristwatch is good; a stopwatch held in the hand is better. It's important to know the final time of every run in tenths of a second. It's also important to make each run faster than the previous, for this is how you improve. The external pressure of the watch, that unforgiving minute, keeps you from slacking.

Measure each of your running courses to the tenth of a mile. A car odometer isn't accurate enough. You really need a measuring wheel, or better yet, a tape.

Plan each day's run to the smallest detail. Predetermine how fast you should be running at each checkpoint along the course. Memorize in advance the corners you can cut to save time. If your shoelace unties, ignore it. Stopping to tie it might cost thirty seconds.

Count your mileage, to the nearest tenth. Keep accurate records of how far you've run each day, week, month and year. Never miss an opportunity to tell your friends the total.

Hold yourself responsible for a certain number of miles run a week, and prorate this on an hourly scale. That way, if you've run only 24 miles by 11 p.m. on Saturday, you'll still have an hour to run the other mile.

Keep meticulous count of the number of days you've run consecutively. You never know who might be keeping records. For inspiration, think of Lou Gehrig's 2130 consecutive games. Again, tell your friends as often as possible. They'll love you for it.

To keep the streak going, force yourself to run despite injuries and illnesses. In fact, you might give yourself bonus points based on severity of debilitation, say, one point for the common cold and strained muscles, two for the flu and tendinitis, up to five for pneumonia and broken bones.

Hurry your runs as much as possible. Running is only leisure, so you dare not spend too much time doing it.

Here is a time-saving hint: Start all runs without previously stretching or warming up.

On your everyday runs, set a fast pace from the start, and try to maintain the rest of the way. Bring pain upon yourself quickly. You get more out of it that way.

Remember the athlete's creed: Pain Equals Gain.

Once you've begun the day's run, don't stop until you've finished. To do so would ruin the effects of the run.

If you can talk or breathe comfortably, you are running too slowly. The run is worthless if you don't raise your pulse to 140 beats a minute.

Gravitate to runners who like to compete in practice. Especially good are those who try to stay one step ahead during the whole run. If your partner's pace is too fast, speed ahead of him. Call his bluff. Above all, never be intimidated or show weakness in training runs.

Set the highest goals for each run, and for your career. After you've run a mile in six minutes, think about one in four. Then, when you fail, you will get angry. Remember, an angry runner is a tough runner.

Run the same routes every day. A 440 yard track is best.

Never listen to other runners, unless they give you advice. Other people are the best judges of you as a runner.

Don't drink any fluids on the run. That parch in your throat is natural. Learn not to give in to bodily wants.

If you are stranded on a road and unable to continue, refuse all ride offers. Limp home, if you must.

Learn to despise runners not as good as yourself. Don't listen to them. Avoid understanding them.

Worship runners better than yourself. Promise yourself to one day beat them all.

Learn to hate yourself for bad efforts. Punish yourself for bad days. Skip dessert or sex. This is a useful motivational tool.

Consider everything you do in terms of how it will affect your running. Never eat anything you like if it won't improve your times. Never try sex that way — God forbid, you might pull a muscle.

Sacrifice all of life's fun for running. Go to bed early. Anyone can stay up late, drink wine and talk with friends. Anyone can attend a symphony or water ski. It takes a person of indomitable character, like you, to say, "No, I must go run."

Q **I understand your point. It's funny, but in high school I was actually told to believe much of that nonsense.**

A Nonsense still lives in certain places. It's unfortunate that men spend their energies teaching others how to be miserable. I was taught the same things in high school.

Here is how to keep the fun in your running:

For your everyday runs, either choose to run for a certain amount of time, say, 30 minutes, or for a certain distance, say, four miles. Avoid setting a goal of four miles in 30 minutes, and never feel each run has to be faster than the previous. Self-inflicted, needless pressure is the last thing you need for a leisure activity. Even the best runners in the world rarely time themselves in training runs.

Measuring your courses isn't necessarily bad, but a rough estimate of distance is all you really need. Who cares if a training run is 10 miles or 10.5? You are not timing yourself, remember?

Plan each day's run for weather, amount of time you want to spend running, etc., but be flexible. You might feel tired and want to go slowly. Or you might feel fresh and want to, as the British runners say, bash it. Let your body choose the pace and distance of the day.

If you count your mileage, preface your total with "about." Don't say anything more precise than "about 25 miles a week." Mileage totals aren't important. Quality of enjoyment is.

Neither should you hold yourself to a certain number of miles a week. Never say, "I have to run 25 miles this week." If you end up running 25, fine. If you run 24, that's fine, too. Is there really much of a difference?

Don't count the number of days you've run consecutively. Once you build a streak, you'll want to protect it at all costs. "Damn this pneumonia," you'll say. "I must run, anyway." How much better to say you *try* to run every day.

Run if you want to, run if you can. Some colds and injuries are mild enough to try running. Some aren't. Use your head. I once ran the San Francisco Bay-to-Breakers race while nursing a bad cold. Two days later I had strep throat, and a week later, mononucleosis. Think of it this way: When sick or injured, you have far more to lose than gain by running.

Don't hurry your runs. Running is leisure; luxuriate in it. If you can spare only 20 minutes, that's too little for a run. Do yoga or take a sauna instead.

Always spend at least five minutes stretching before you run. Stretching is an effective injury preventative, and its meditational qualities will relax you and put you in the proper mood for running.

Begin your runs slowly, spending the first ten minutes walking, jogging and stretching. Check out your body — it may be tired today. There is plenty of time to run faster. You get the most out of running when moving at your aerobic limit, which is as fast as you can run comfortably, and without breathing hard. Nobody in the world runs fast and comfortably at the outset, when the muscles are tight and the blood hasn't flowed. This takes a few minutes, and is not to be rushed.

Pain by itself does not equal gain. Gain results from general consistency and occasional hard effort. Seeking pain for its own sake is not only needless, but destructive.

Don't be afraid to stop. Stopping ruins nothing. On the other hand running when dehydrated or injured can ruin just about anything.

Any pace faster than sedentary is beneficial. The only worthless runs are those you don't enjoy.

Avoid runners who like to compete in practice (unless, of course, you feel like competing that day). If someone escalates the pace, and you don't feel like following, don't.

Always be open for suggestion, but take lightly the advice of others. Try everything yourself. Never believe that some other knows you better than you do.

Set the vaguest goals for each run — "I want to run seven miles and have fun" — and let your career unveil itself. For those of you who choose to compete, avoid setting time goals. Set only the goal of improving the body, and making it one with the mind. Your results and times can only be a function of this.

Experiment with different routes, keeping those you enjoy, and dropping those you don't. Choosing to run by time rather than distance will encourage you to seek different routes. Get to know where you live via your running.

Indulge your body, and heed its wants. If you are thirsty, drink. If you are tired, slow down. If you are exhausted, stop. Work with your body, not against it.

If you find yourself stranded on a road and unable to continue, take the first offered ride. When you get home, reward yourself for using common sense.

Runners are neither good nor bad; they are only fast or slow. Feel affinity with all of them; you have something in common. Lend encouragement to slower runners; you were once as slow as they. Respect, but never worship faster runners. Be your own hero.

Efforts are neither good nor bad. All are good, and some are merely better than others. Learn to love yourself for all efforts. You have only one body and mind — work with them lovingly. Reward yourself whenever you want to.

Sacrifice nothing for running. If running conflicts with other activities, make a choice of positives. Go to bed when you want to, based on a positive choice. Staying up late to drink wine and talk with friends is fun, sometimes more fun than running, sometimes not. You choose. It takes a person of character and good mental health to choose what he wants.

*   *   *

Q   **Aren't there times when sacrifice and self-denial are needed to improve as a runner?**

A   Hard work is necessary, but sacrifice and self-denial are never justified.

If hard work, which can be exhilarating and joyful at the proper times, isn't done out of a positive choice, it shouldn't be done at all. Running is leisure, running is fun. Sacrifice nothing for it.

To illustrate a point, last year I decided to become a health food aficionado. I would shop only at health food stores, drink Hindu yak milk and grow my own sunflower seeds.

After a few weeks of this, I realized my decision to be a health food nut came not from a positive choice, but from a sense of duty and obligation; it was the right thing to do; if you loved your body you would never drink homogenized milk again. I was subscribing to some unwritten law that said runners must eat health foods. Yet I knew that given the choice between salted peanuts and raw sunflower seeds, I'd secretly choose the former.

Still I persisted. My payoff was not better health, but righteousness, the same payoff sought by prohibitionists and virgins. I both hated and envied hamburger eaters.

After a few more weeks of this self-imposed torture, I grew bitter, as sacrifice and self-denial will always make one bitter. Then one day I read (while eating my usual breakfast of stone-ground flour and raisins) an article on Frank Shorter, in which Shorter said he ate for energy, beer and Hostess cupcakes. Whether Shorter was facetious or not, I didn't care. That was it! I flushed my bee pollen and brown rice down the disposal, ran to McDonalds, and now happily await the judgment of my body and health food nuts everywhere.

Similarly, if you are running from a sense of duty or obligation or just because it is good for you, then you are sacrificing. Quit before you become bitter, as you will.

Learn to distinguish between sacrifice and choice.

Q   **I don't fully understand the difference between sacrifice and choice. I mean, let's say you are at a party, and . . .**

A   Well, say you are faced with the choice of staying late at a party where you are having fun, or leaving early to go to bed, so you can get up early the following morning and run. If running early in the morning gives you more pleasure and satisfaction than partying, then leaving early is no sacrifice. It is a choice between positives.

Or, if you leave the party early not because you would rather run the next morning, but instead feel you must run the following morning if you want to race well in the Boston Marathon the following week, then leaving the party is no sacrifice. You realize a good performance at Boston will bring you more pleasure and satisfaction than the party. You've made a choice between positives.

But, if you leave the party simply out of duty or obligation, which you can't explain other than you "just know" running is more wholesome than partying, you are sacrificing and denying yourself. In the end you will be a worse runner for it, because, sooner or later, if you have any mental health, you'll realize you're choosing bad times over good times for no rational reason. The realization will make you angry and bitter, and you'll blame running instead of yourself.

The person who leaves the party early because he wants to run is not sacrificing. He is choosing.

The person who leaves early because tomorrow's run will help his Boston Marathon is not sacrificing. He is choosing.

But the person who runs out of a mysterious sense of duty is sacrificing. He is not making a choice of positives. He is not making a choice at all.

He is a slave, and he won't last long in running, because slavery is no fun.

Q **You said hard effort is sometimes necessary. When? Somehow this seems to contradict the idea of fun.**

A Hard effort, at certain times, is fun, exhilarating, and quite necessary if one is to ever experience the peak of running, and of life. To deny hard effort when the body feels ready and the mind is called is to asphyxiate the spirit. At such times, you must do it, or die.

For some runners, the urge to run hard happens several times a week. For others, it happens once a year. The frequency doesn't matter.

What happens is this: You are out on a six mile run, taking the first two miles slowly, letting the body warm up. During the next two miles you slip into your customary pace, your aerobic limit. But today you feel amazingly light and fresh. Your normal pace feels ridiculously easy.

Suddenly, with two miles left, you feel the urge to release the brakes, step on the gas and gun it home. Go to it! Your pace increases, you feel pushed from behind. Your head cautions you to slow down. Don't! To slow down now is to miss that rare and wonderful opportunity to taste life at its peak, teetering on its edge.

Now this is becoming the fastest two miles you have ever run — you are almost sprinting. With a mile to go, the joyous pain of honest effort creeps into every cell. Your reason begs you to stop. But no. The reason is no longer in control; the body has taken over, and together with the mind, it is one. Tremendous. You mustn't deny yourself this incredible look at yourself. Never will you see yourself in such harmony. Never will you see so clearly your strengths and fears. You are daring to achieve your ultimate, and here, right here, you will either succeed or fail.

Yes, it hurts, plenty. But is this pain a sacrifice? No, to deny yourself this pinnacle of living is the ultimate sacrifice. You are denying what you can be.

Tomorrow you can rest, take it slowly, recuperate. And, if you need it, the day after that and the week after that. For if you feel this superlative joy and exuberance only once a year, you have still won the highest payoff for any runner.

At times like this, and only then, is hard effort desirable and necessary. (The trick to racing is making these moments happen in the race.) To deny these moments is to smother, and possibly kill, a vital part of yourself.

*   *   *

Q **I sometimes get bored with running the same courses, but there don't seem to be any interesting places to run where I live. Have you any suggestions?**

A Never allow yourself to be bored, with running or anything you do. The places to run are limited only by your imagination.

You can start by learning as you run about your town or city. Have you ever run through its poorest section? Its wealthiest section? Its business districts? Its industrial parks?

Have you explored all of its parks? Run alongside its railroad tracks? Crossed each of its bridges?

Have you yet run through its college campuses? On its high school tracks? On all of its playgrounds?

Have you ever run through its airport? Any of its shopping centers? Through its busiest department store? Up the steps of its tallest building?

What is within an hour's drive of your city? Have you run on all of the surrounding country roads? Have you ever run across a farmer's field, with the farmer chasing you on his tractor? Have you ever been chased by a bull? Have you ever chased a jackrabbit?

Are there any lakes close to your area? If so, have you run around them? Are there any wooded forests with horse trails? Are there any mountains or large hills worth climbing? Beaches? Rivers? Do the rivers have sandbars? Have you ever sprinted barefoot across a sandbar on the Mississippi River?

What are the most interesting places in your state? Have you run by each of them? If you take vacation trips, do you run then? Have you ever run the rim of the Grand Canyon? Across the Golden Gate Bridge? Past the

When was the last time you were silly?

hot springs and geysers in Yellowstone? Up Mt. Washington? Along the main strip of Las Vegas at midnight? Across Death Valley in the summer? Up the steps of the World Trade Center?

Have you been to France and run underneath L'Arc de Triomphe with the gendarme chasing, mistaking you for a purse snatcher? Have you run alongside the Thames River and watched the Oxford crew? In the Bavarian Forest when you're hopelessly and pleasantly lost? Across the Kremlin without your visa? From the Plains of Marathon to Athens and dreamed you were Phidippides?

When do you run? Have you ever run eastward at dawn to watch the sunrise? Or westward at dusk to watch the sunset? Have you ever skipped work or class to run in the middle of the afternoon? Have you ever run in rush hour traffic and waved at the motorists? Down the middle of the busiest street in your town at three in the morning?

Have you ever run during a warm summer rain, and worn old shoes to purposely splash in every mud puddle you could find? Have you ever run in a blizzard and had three pair of sweatsuits and no visibility? Have you ever run on a November morning and left the first snow tracks of the year?

Have you ever run in the early morning hours along the beach and become lost in the fog? Have you ever sprinted homeward, looking over your shoulder, and tried to beat the first raindrops of a midwestern thunderstorm?

What do you see when you run? Do you see life? Have you ever run past a hospital as parents were taking their firstborn home? Past a zoo where grade schoolers are learning the difference between African and Indian elephants? Have you recently seen classes adjourning on Friday afternoon at the local high school? Have you yet run by a church as the newlyweds were getting into the car? Have you ever run by a retirement home and been encouraged to run faster by the crowd playing croquet?

What do you hear as you run? Have you ever listened to the chatter of playground basketball players? The sound of ambulance sirens? Fallen leaves rustling in a sudden gust of wind? Ocean waves breaking?

What do you smell on your runs? A newly tarred street? A diesel engined

When was the last time you were lacivious?

Have you ever raced a San Francisco cable car?

truck? Freshly cut grass? Grilled steaks on a warm summer evening? The chlorine, sweat and sun lotion of a public swimming pool? The smell of spring thaw?

Finally, with whom do you run? Have you ever run with the local high school cross country team? Its fastest runner? Have you ever run with a world class runner? With an overweight beginner who might greatly benefit from your encouragement? Have you ever run with a blind person, and let them touch your arm for contact and assurance? With a newcomer, whom you proudly showed your town's sights? With someone who spoke no English?

Have you ever run with your children or parents? Your brother or sister? Your best friend? Your dog? Have you ever run with your wife or husband, or someone with whom you share the rest of your life?

Running puts you on stage with life's greatest shows. Don't miss any of them.

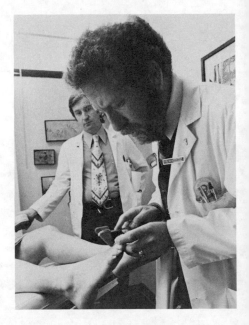

Find the addresses for shoe companies, doctors, and book sellers in this chapter.

CHAPTER TWENTY-ONE

Contacts

Q   **Where can I find the right contacts for races, medical information, etc.?**

A   As I promised you elsewhere in the book, you can find the appropriate names and addresses in this chapter.

○ *Races* The best way to find races in your locale is to know of the organizational bodies, mostly which include your district AAU or RRCA, *Runner's World* magazine (for Fun-Runs), and local track and running clubs.

— *AAU* To find your district address, write to the national AAU office: Amateur Athletic Union, 3400 West 86th Street, Indianapolis, Indiana 46268.

— *RRCA* Write to the national office for your district office: Road Runners Club of America, 2737 Devonshire Place N.W., Washington, D.C. 20008.

— *Fun-Runs* For a list of Fun-Run sites around the country (there are more than 200 of them), write to *Runner's World* publisher, Bob Anderson, at: Box 366, Mountain View, California 94042.

— *Club Runs* The best way to find the names and addresses of your local track and running clubs is through your district AAU or RRCA newsletter. Write to the national AAU and RRCA.

○ *Books* From *Aerobics* to *Zen Running,* World Sports Library has the most complete list of running, health, and diet books. Currently more than 2000 titles available. World Sports Library, Box 7251, Mountain View, California 94042.

○ *Magazines* National publications include:

— *Runner's World,* Box 366, Mountain View, California 94042. Monthly; $9.50 a year, $18.00 for two years. With a circulation of 300,000, *RW* is the most popular running magazine today.

— *The Runner,* One Park Avenue, New York, New York 10016. Monthly; $12.00 a year, $1.50 each issue. A sister of *New Times* magazine, this Hirsch publication promises to give *Runner's World* a good run for the money. Expected publication date: August, 1978. First run issue of 100,000 copies.

— *Runner and Jogger,* 2943 Cataldi, San Jose, California 95132. Monthly; $9.00 a year. Edited by the world's foremost student of running and jogging, Dave Prokop. Late 1978 publication date.

— *Running Times,* 1816 Lamont Street N.W., Washington, D.C. 20010. Monthly; $10.00 a year. Until recently, *Running Times* was a tabloid, but now it is printed in slick magazine form. Major coverage of Eastern U.S. running.

— *Track & Field News,* Box 296, Los Altos, California 94022. Monthly; $11.00 a year. *T&FN* deserves its nickname, "the bible of the sport." A must for any serious racer and fan.

As well, many fine regional publications and newsletters are now available. These are often associated with track and running clubs, and so to find the addresses you must contact the clubs through your district AAU and RRCA.

○ *Medical Research and Information* Some of the country's best running and health research information is available from the following:

— *Institute of Aerobics Research,* 11811 Preston Road, Dallas, Texas 75230. This is the center founded by Dr. Kenneth Cooper.

— *Human Performance Laboratory,* Ball State University, Muncie, Indiana 47306. This center is run by Dr. David Costill, an early pioneer in measuring human performance.

— *Institute of Environmental Stress,* University of California, Santa Barbara, California 93105. As mentioned in Chapter 16, the best research on the effect of running upon women is conducted here.

— *American Medical Joggers Association,* Box 4704, North Hollywood, California 91607. The AMJA can put you in touch with physicians used to treating runners.

— *Medical Advice, Dr. George Sheehan* For answers to your running-related medical problems, write to Dr. Sheehan, *Runner's World,* Box 366, Mountain View, California 94042.

— *Cardio-Gram* magazine, La Crosse Cardiac Rehabilitation Program, University of Wisconsin, La Crosse, Wisconsin 54601. Bimonthly; $5.00 a year. Of chief interest to cardiac patients and those with family history of cardiac disease.

Information on running related injuries can be obtained from the following:

— *Medical Advice, Dr. George Sheehan* For answers to your injury questions, write to Dr. George Sheehan, *Runner's World,* Box 366, Mountain View, California 94042.

— *World Sports Library* This large mail order house also has the most complete selection of running injury books, including Dr. Steven Subotnick's *The Running Foot Doctor* and *The Fifteen Most Common Running Injuries,* and Dr. Sheehan's *Medical Advice To Runners.* Ask for the complete catalogue of books. Box 7251, Mountain View, California 94042.

— *The Physician and Sportsmedicine* magazine 4530 West 77th Street, Minneapolis, Minnesota 55435. Monthly; $24.00 a year. This is the magazine for orthopedists, podiatrists, and athletic trainers. Not an easy read for laymen, but nonetheless a must for those wanting to become their own best physician.

— *American Academy of Podiatric Sportsmedicine* 19682 Hesperian Boulevard, Hayward, California 94541. Write to this address to find your nearest sports podiatrist, or answers to your injury questions.

— *Langer Laboratory, Inc.* 21 East Industry Court, Deer Park, New York 11729. This is the maker of Sporthotics, the orthotic especially designed for runners. If you can't find a runner's podiatrist, instead visit your local podiatrist and have him send your foot casts to Langer Laboratory, Inc.

○ *Shoe Companies* If you have difficulties with your shoes, write to the manufacturer for information.

— *Adidas* Adidas USA, Inc., Box 4137, 2382 Townsgate Road, Westlake Village, California 91359.

— *Brooks* Brooks Shoe Manufacturing Company, Factory Street, Hanover, Pennsylvania 17331.

— *Converse* Converse Rubber Company, 55 Fordham Road, Wilmington, Massachusetts 01887.

— *Eaton* Charles A. Eaton Company, 147 Centre Street, Brockton, Massachusetts 02403.

— *E.B. Sport (Lydiards)* E.B. International, Box 27, Bernardsville, New Jersey 07924.

— *New Balance* New Balance, 38-42 Everett Street, Boston, Massachusetts 02134.

— *Nike* Blue Ribbon Sports, 6175 112th Street, Beaverton, Oregon 97005.

— *Pony* Pony Sports and Leisure, Inc., 251 Park Avenue South, New York, New York 10010.

— *Puma* Beconta, Inc., 50 Executive Boulevard, Elmsford, New York 10523.

— *Saucony* Saucony Shoe Manufacturing Company, 12 Peach Street, Kutztown, Pennsylvania 19530.

— *Tiger* Onitsuka Company, Limited, 13512 Newhope Street, Garden Grove, California 92543.

○ *Shoe Repair* If you can't find someone to replace the soles and make other repairs on your running shoes, write to the following:

— *Fleet Feet Company* 612 Emery, Longmont, Colorado 80501. $8.00 a pair includes resoling, repair of minor tears, laces, and return postage.

— *Fresh Tracks* 27 West Rayburn Road, Millington, New Jersey 07946. $11.95 per pair includes resoling, repair of tears, replacement of missing eyelets, new insoles and arches, and return postage.

— *Power-Soler* 1065 West Broad Street, Falls Church, Virginia 22046, or 4330 West Desert Inn Road, Las Vegas, Nevada 89102. $11.50 per pair for resoling.

— *Tred 2* 2510 Channing Avenue, San Jose, California 95131. $13.45 per pair for new soles, repair of tears, reinforcement of weak or worn stitching, new laces, and return postage.

○ *Mail Order Running Equipment* If you live in a small town, or can't find what you want in your city, write to the following:

— *Athletic Attic* Box 14503, Gainesville, Florida 32604. Distributors of Marty Liquori Sportswear.

— *Athletic Department* Box 743, Beaverton, Oregon 97005.

— *Athlete's Foot* Main Office, 725 Liberty Avenue, Pittsburgh, Pennsylvania 15222. More than 140 Athlete's Foot stores nationwide.

— *Phidippides* 1544 Piedmont Road, N.E., Atlanta, Georgia 30324.

— *Starting Line Sports* Box 8, Mountain View, California 94042.

— *Sub 4* 17972 Sky Park Circle, Suite K, Irvine, California 92714.

Index

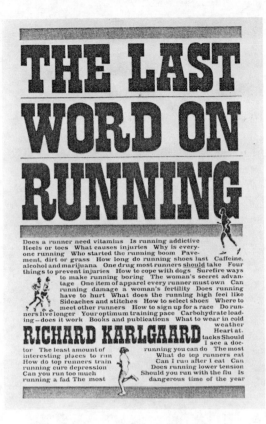

THE LAST WORD ON RUNNING is available at most bookstores. If not available at your bookstore, please use the coupon below.

Caroline House Publishers/TDS
P. O. Box 978
Edison, New Jersey 08817

Please send me _____ copies of THE LAST WORD ON RUNNING at $7.95 per copy. I enclose my check/money order for $ _____ (please include 75¢ per order for postage and handling).

Name

Address

City   State   Zipcode

For the Professional...
For the Intermediate...
For the Beginner...

HE VAN DER MEER TENNIS BIBLE

the first time, the world-famous "teacher
he pros" has put all his knowledge of
is instruction into a book for all tennis
ers, from beginner to teaching profes-
al.

dreds of illustrations and photos comple-
t the step-by-step approach to learning
game from the beginning, as Dennis
hes the pros in his ten-day TennisUniver-
(for $495).

book is the most advanced tennis in-
ction manual ever published.

're invited to examine THE DENNIS
N DER MEER TENNIS BIBLE for 10
s on an absolute no strings attached
ey-back guarantee. If you decide the
k is not an invaluable investment, just
rn it within 10 days and we'll refund
r payment in full, no questions asked.

ers such subjects as:

he Fundamental Strokes.
classical form and development of the
is stroke is analyzed, showing a com-
e picture of the ideal stroke and its use.

he Physical Movements.
nents of the stroke are isolated and ana-
d to provide a basic understanding of
physical movements which comprise the
ke.

he Progressions.
full stroke is then assembled into a pro-
sive pattern, which allows the tennis
er to self-teach and self-correct each
ke.

● **Drills and Play Situations.**
Specific drills and play situations are revealed, which can be used to improve the
player's strokes and instill confidence.

● **Corrective Techniques.**
Special techniques that expand a player's
ability to notice and correct flaws are given.

● **Tactics and Strategy.**
The basic fundamentals of playing the game
to win are outlined, including adjusting for
weakness in your own, or your opponent's
game.

● **Myths in Tennis.**
Here Van der Meer explodes scores of tennis
myths, many still used by teaching professionals not familiar with recent develop-
ments in tennis instruction!

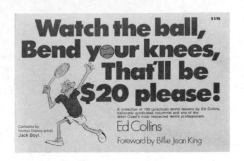

A comprehensive and competent instructional book for players all levels. I also recommend it as a supplementary handbook r teaching pros." —Cliff Drysdale

LLIE JEAN KING SAYS

have no qualms about the contribution Collins' book will make to the tennis ustry. Since the day Ed and his wife Judy pped by our tennis camp in Lake Tahoe, vada, seven years ago, I have followed ir careers with interest. Ed spent two years ching with the best tennis professional in world, Dennis Van der Meer. Judy rked on layouts and graphics for our blications.

ince then, Ed has learned and implemented best in modern tennis teaching techques. The Ed Collins Tennis College in Diego is widely known as one of the st successful programs in the country, d his newspaper column and magazine ticles regularly instruct thousands of ten- buffs.

is innovative methods will make it easier you to learn tennis or improve particular gments of your game. As Ed lectures, the y is to learn tennis in a logical progres- n. By following the guidelines Ed sets t in this book, I guarantee you will have re success and more fun."

Not everyone can go to California and take lesson from Ed Collins. The next best ing is to read this book."

Ron Bookman, Editor
World Tennis Magazine

ED COLLINS is one of the most respected tennis teaching professionals on the West Coast. Over the past four years his programs in San Diego have attracted more than 10,000 students from all over the country. Five hundred tennis teachers and coaches have attended Ed's professional workshops through the University of California. In addition, his innovative teaching philosophies and methods have been published in books, magazines and his nationally syndicated tennis column, "First One In," is read coast to coast.

★ ★ ★

"Represents some of the soundest teaching of any book on tennis."

Dennis Van der Meer

Caroline House Books are distributed to the book trade by Stein and Day Publishers.

■ Caroline House Publishers/TDS
■ Box 978, Edison, NJ 08817

■ Please send me_____copies of
■ WATCH THE BALL, BEND YOUR
■ KNEES, THAT'LL BE $20 PLEASE! I
■ enclose $5.95 plus 75¢ postage and hand-
■ ling for each order of books.

■ Total amount enclosed $_____
■ Charge to ☐ Masthercharge
■   ☐ BankAmericard/Visa

■ Card No._____Expiration date_____

■ Name_____

■ Address_____

■ City_____State_____Zip_____